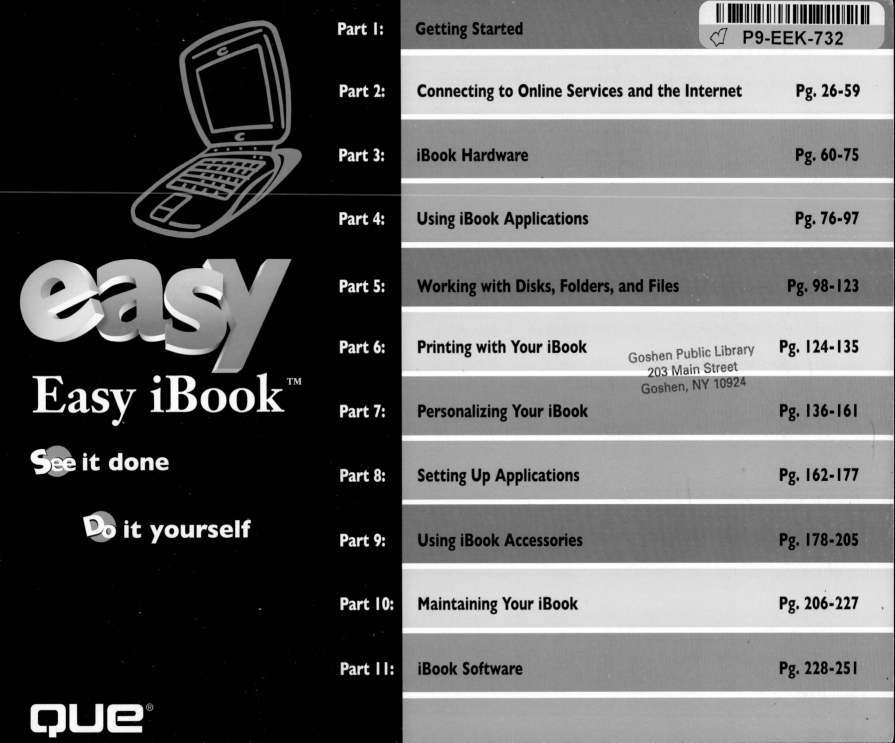

easy
Easy iBook™

See it done

Do it yourself

que®

Part 1:	Getting Started	
Part 2:	Connecting to Online Services and the Internet	Pg. 26-59
Part 3:	iBook Hardware	Pg. 60-75
Part 4:	Using iBook Applications	Pg. 76-97
Part 5:	Working with Disks, Folders, and Files	Pg. 98-123
Part 6:	Printing with Your iBook	Pg. 124-135
Part 7:	Personalizing Your iBook	Pg. 136-161
Part 8:	Setting Up Applications	Pg. 162-177
Part 9:	Using iBook Accessories	Pg. 178-205
Part 10:	Maintaining Your iBook	Pg. 206-227
Part 11:	iBook Software	Pg. 228-251

Part 1: Getting Started

1 — Setting Up Your iBook
2 — Starting Up Your iBook
3 — Using Mac OS Setup Assistant
4 — Opening and Closing a Window
5 — Collapsing and Expanding a Window
6 — Moving a Window
7 — Resizing a Window
8 — Scrolling a Window
9 — Navigating Menus
10 — Using Context Menus
11 — Arranging Windows on the Desktop
12 — Using a Dialog Box or Control Panel
13 — Looking Up Help Topics with Mac OS Help
14 — Looking Up a Help Topic with Sherlock 2
15 — Getting Context-Sensitive Help
16 — Shutting Down Your iBook

Part 2: Connecting to Online Services and the Internet

1 — Setting Up for the Internet
2 — Using EarthLink's TotalAccess
3 — Connecting to AOL
4 — Starting Internet Explorer
5 — Connecting to Apple's Web Site
6 — Typing an Address
7 — Browsing with Links and Toolbar Buttons
8 — Adding a Site to Your Favorites List
9 — Going to a Site in Your Favorites List
10 — Organizing Your Favorites
11 — Working with Page Holder
12 — Searching the Internet with Sherlock 2

13 — Using the History List
14 — Quitting Internet Explorer
15 — Starting Outlook Express
16 — Reading Mail
17 — Responding to Mail
18 — Creating and Sending New Mail
19 — Subscribing to Newsgroups
20 — Reading Newsgroup Messages
21 — Posting New Messages
22 — Replying to a Newsgroup Message
23 — Quitting Outlook Express

Part 3: iBook Hardware

1 — Adding a USB Device
2 — Connecting a Printer
3 — Replacing the Battery
4 — Charging the Battery
5 — Connecting to a Network
6 — Networking with AirPort
7 — Connecting Your Palm Device
8 — Adding Memory
9 — Checking iBook Memory
10 — Troubleshooting iBook Hardware

Part 4: Using iBook Applications

1 — Starting an Application from the Apple Menu
2 — Starting an Application from an Alias
3 — Starting an Application and Opening a Document
4 — Switching Between Applications

5 — Switching Between Open Documents
6 — Saving a Document
7 — Opening a Document
8 — Creating a New Document
9 — Selecting Text
10 — Copying Text
11 — Moving Text
12 — Copying Data Between Documents
13 — Closing a Document
14 — Quitting an Application

Part ▶ **6: Printing with Your iBook**

1 — Selecting a Printer
2 — Setting the Default Printer
3 — Printing a Document
4 — Viewing the Print Queue
5 — Pausing and Restarting a Print Job
6 — Canceling a Print Job
7 — Changing Printer Settings
8 — Adding a Desktop Printer
9 — Deleting a Desktop Printer

Part ▶ **5: Working with Disks, Folders, and Files**

1 — Navigating Your Hard Disk with the Trackpad
2 — Opening and Closing Folders
3 — Changing the View for a Folder
4 — Sorting Window Contents
5 — Changing View Options
6 — Finding Files and Folders with Sherlock 2
7 — Using Sherlock 2 to Search File Contents
8 — Selecting Folders or Files
9 — Selecting All Folders and Files
10 — Creating a Folder
11 — Copying Folders and Files
12 — Moving Folders and Files
13 — Renaming Folders and Files
14 — Creating a Pop-up Folder Window
15 — Creating an Alias to a File or Folder
16 — Changing a Folder or File Label
17 — Synchronizing Folders and Files with Your Desktop
18 — Deleting Folders and Files
19 — Emptying the Trash

Part ▶ **7: Personalizing Your iBook**

1 — Showing and Hiding Applications
2 — Moving the Applications Menu
3 — Choosing a Desktop Picture
4 — Choosing a Desktop Pattern
5 — Choosing a Theme
6 — Changing Highlight Colors on Your iBook
7 — Synchronizing Colors on Your iBook
8 — Using Energy Saver
9 — Tweaking Your Monitor
10 — Using the Control Strip
11 — Changing How Your Sound Works
12 — Recording an Alert Sound
13 — Changing the System Alert Sound
14 — Changing How Your Trackpad Works
15 — Changing the System Date and Time
16 — Using Location Manager
17 — Customizing Your Keyboard Controls

Part 8: Setting Up Applications

1 — Adding Aliases
2 — Renaming an Alias
3 — Deleting Aliases
4 — Adding Applications to the Apple Menu
5 — Deleting Applications from the Apple Menu
6 — Adding Folders to the Apple Menu
7 — Rearranging the Apple Menu
8 — Starting an Application When You Start Mac OS
9 — Installing Applications
10 — Uninstalling Applications
11 — Using AppleScript
12 — Using File Sharing

Part 9: Using iBook Accessories

1 — Creating Multiple User Accounts
2 — Using Stickies
3 — Typing Text in Stickies
4 — Creating Text Documents with SimpleText
5 — Viewing Fonts with Key Caps
6 — Viewing an Image with SimpleText
7 — Formatting Text in SimpleText
8 — Using Scrapbook
9 — Using Sherlock 2
10 — Playing an Audio CD
11 — Changing the Volume
12 — Playing a Media File
13 — Editing Audio and Video with QuickTime Player
14 — Editing a QuickTime Movie Using QuickTime Player
15 — Using Calculator and Graphing Calculator
16 — Selecting Network Devices with Chooser
17 — Surfing the Net with Network Browser
18 — Using Keychain Access

Part 10: Maintaining Your iBook

1 — Displaying Disk Information
2 — Viewing a Battery's Life
3 — Scanning Your Disk for Errors
4 — Using the Reset Button
5 — Defragmenting a Disk
6 — Backing Up Files on Your iBook
7 — Restoring Backup Files
8 — Restoring Your iBook's Software
9 — Using Apple System Profiler
10 — Maintaining Your iBook Hardware
11 — Rebuilding Your Desktop
12 — Increasing Application Memory
13 — Displaying System Information
14 — Using Extensions Manager
15 — Performing a Clean Install of Mac OS
16 — Getting a Software Update

Part 11: iBook Software

1 — Viewing Files with Adobe Acrobat
2 — Starting AppleWorks's Word Processor
3 — Formatting Your Word Processing Document
4 — Creating a Spreadsheet with AppleWorks
5 — Drawing and Painting with AppleWorks
6 — Creating a Database with AppleWorks
7 — Sending a Fax
8 — Synchronizing Data with Your Palm Device
9 — Managing Data with Your Palm Device
10 — Finding Facts in the World Book Encyclopedia
11 — Playing Nanosaur
12 — Playing Bugdom

Copyright© 2000 by Que® Corporation

International Standard Book Number: 0-7897-2272-0

Library of Congress Catalog Card Number: 99-65966

Printed in the United States of America

First Printing: December 1999

02 01 00 99   4 3 2 1

About the Author

Lisa Lee has written *Easy iMac, Easy Linux, Upgrading and Repairing Your Mac, Guide to Mac OS 7.6 Update*, and co-authored *Sams Teach Yourself Mac OS 8.5 in 24 Hours*. She was also a contributing author for *The Macintosh Bible 6th Edition* and *Zen and the Art of Resource Editing* (Second Edition). She has helped develop Macintosh hardware and software products for over 10 years. She has been a forum leader on America Online (AFCLisa@aol.com) for many years, helping others use their Macs. In her spare time, she uses her Macs to create art and music, and write stories to put on her Web site (http://www.flatfishfactory.com).

Acknowledgments

This book is dedicated to Mike Neil.

Thanks to Chris Will, who asked me to write this book. I share the credit for this book with the team at Macmillan who helped develop, edit, design, and lay out every page of this book.

This book would also not be possible without Apple's iCEO, Steve Jobs, and the Mac OS and iBook teams who have brought another super, cool product to the world.

Special thanks to my friends who supported my iBook efforts: Paul Rybicki, Yun Shin, Robert Stones, Terry Rawlings, Dave Falkenburg, Jorg Brown, Nia Fuller, Andy Bates, Christiane Petite, Joel Black, Rob Moore, Chris Berarducci, Eric Murakami, Michael Emery, Sandy Williamson, and Marta Justak. Finally, thanks to my family for all their support: Laura, Jackie, Julie, Jason, Ron and Jeanette Lee, and Gary and Beverly Neil.

Associate Publisher
Greg Wiegand

Acquisitions Editor
Stephanie J. McComb

Development Editor
Nicholas J. Goetz

Technical Editor
Terry Rawlings

Managing Editor
Thomas F. Hayes

Project Editor
Lori A. Lyons

Copy Editor
Kay Hoskin

Proofreader
Jeanne Clark

Indexer
Kevin Kent

Team Coordinator
Sharry Lee Gregory

Production Designer
Trina Wurst

Layout Technicians
Cheryl Lynch
Jeannette McKay

Illustrator
Laura Robbins

Cover Designers
Anne Jones
Karen Ruggles

Copy Writer
Eric Borgert

How to Use This Book

It's as Easy as 1-2-3

Each part of this book is made up of a series of short, instructional lessons, designed to help you understand basic information that you need to get the most out of your computer hardware and software.

 Each step is fully illustrated to show you how it looks onscreen.

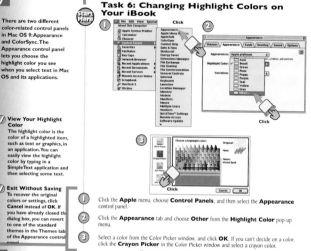

 Click: Click the trackpad once.

 Double-click: Click the trackpad twice in rapid succession.

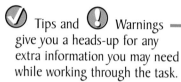 **Tips and Warnings** give you a heads-up for any extra information you may need while working through the task.

Pointer Arrow: Highlights an item on the screen you need to point to or focus on in the step or task.

 Each task includes a series of quick, easy steps designed to guide you through the procedure.

 Selection: Highlights the area onscreen discussed in the step or task.

 Items that you select or click in menus, dialog boxes, tabs, and windows are shown in bold. Information you type is in a `special font`.

 Drag

 Next Step: If you see this symbol, it means the task you're working on continues on the next page.

 Click & Type: Click once where indicated and begin typing to enter your text or data.

 Drop

How to Drag: Point to the starting place or object. Hold down the trackpad button, move the mouse to the new location, then release.

 End Task: Task is complete.

Introduction to the iBook

Here's to the mobile ones. Those who love to compute wherever they go, while they are on the go. Whether a modem, Ethernet, or AirPort is used to connect it to the Internet, the iBook is no doubt the most exciting portable Macintosh Apple has ever made. After you charge it, it's ready to go. However, even though it's very easy to use, there's so much you can learn to do with it, too.

Easy iBook provides step-by-step, concise, full-color visual instructions explaining how to use everything on your iBook. Don't furrow your brow by reading through paragraphs of explanations to learn some of the best, basic features of your iBook. Even if you already have a Macintosh computer, you can learn all about the coolest features in Mac OS 9, including how to customize Mac OS, use the accessory applications installed with Mac OS, and maintain your Macintosh system. If you have never used a computer before, this book shows you what's possible on an iBook.

Easy iBook does not cover advanced computing topics or the technical inner workings of your iBook. When you are ready to learn more complex topics about Mac OS, read *Sams Teach Yourself Mac OS 8.5 in 24 Hours*. If you have a question about something that is not covered in this book, please send me email at `lisalee@spies.com`. I will reply to any reader email you send me (except spam or mean-spirited ones).

You can read this book cover to cover, use it as a reference to figure out how to do a particular task with your iBook, read it while your iBook recharges, or share it with a friend as a conversation piece. Anywhere you go, *Easy iBook* lets you see it done and do it yourself.

Getting Started

iBook is the newest Macintosh from Apple; it's an iMac to go. It is on its way to being the most popular Macintosh portable ever made. iBook includes the latest version of Mac OS, the Macintosh operating system. It is also missing many of the things previous Macs had, such as serial, SCSI, and ADB ports. Instead, iBook has one USB port in addition to a few other ports, such as Ethernet, modem, and stereo sound output. Plus, you can add an AirPort card to your iBook to enable wireless networking.

Tasks

Task #		Page #
1	Setting Up Your iBook	4
2	Starting Up Your iBook	5
3	Using Mac OS Setup Assistant	6
4	Opening and Closing a Window	10
5	Collapsing and Expanding a Window	11
6	Moving a Window	12
7	Resizing a Window	13
8	Scrolling a Window	14
9	Navigating Menus	15
10	Using Context Menus	16
11	Arranging Windows on the Desktop	17
12	Using a Dialog Box or Control Panel	18
13	Looking Up Help Topics with Mac OS Help	20
14	Looking Up a Help Topic with Sherlock 2	22
15	Getting Context-Sensitive Help	24
16	Shutting Down Your iBook	25

Task I: Setting Up Your iBook

Before you can take your iBook on the road, you need to charge its battery. Apple includes a helpful picture guide to walk you through the steps to set up your iBook. This task summarizes your out-of-box experience with your iBook: how to set up its hardware features, recharge it, and use it when you're on the go.

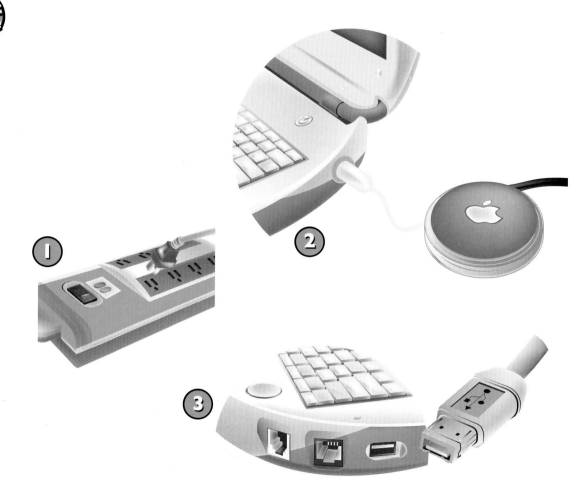

✓ **Keeping It Clean**
Try to keep your iBook out of direct sunlight and away from moisture or dust.

I Take the power cable from your iBook's power adapter and plug it into a wall power source.

2 Connect the other end of the power adapter cable to your iBook. The ring surrounding the power cable connection turns orange if your iBook battery is charging or green if the battery is completely charged.

3 Connect any external devices, such as external speakers, an external USB keyboard, or a mouse.

Task 2: Starting Up Your iBook

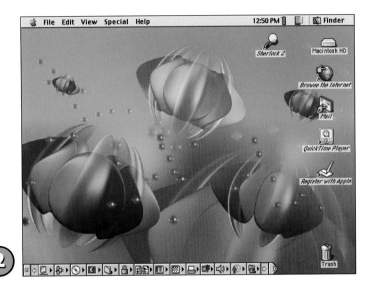

Open your iBook, and then press the **Power** button.

The iBook starts, ultimately displaying the desktop.

Starting up your iBook involves starting up both the hardware and the software. When you press the **Power** button, it turns the iBook hardware on, as well as the software: Mac OS.
Several things happen after you press the **Power** button. The first thing you will see is that the monitor turns on. Listen for the iBook chime, then look for the happy Mac icon on your monitor. As Mac OS loads, it will show some of the software loading onscreen until it loads the desktop. The desktop consists of the menu bar and icons.

Not Starting Up?
If your iBook does not power up, the battery might not have charged successfully, or your power adapter might not be completely connected to the wall power source or your iBook. Also, try turning up the monitor brightness levels by pressing the **F2** key.

Task 3: Using Mac OS Setup Assistant

The first time you turn on your iBook, Apple's Mac OS Setup Assistant application will automatically start. Mac OS Setup Assistant configures several settings in Mac OS, such as the date and time, as well as printer and network settings. Many of the settings in Mac OS Setup Assistant are also covered in other tasks in this book.

✓ **Change Your Settings At Any Time**
You can start Mac OS Setup Assistant to change your Mac OS settings at any time. The application is located in the Assistants folder on your hard disk. To start Mac OS Setup Assistant, double-click the **Macintosh HD** icon, and then double-click the **Assistants** folder. Finally, double-click the **Mac OS Setup Assistant** icon.

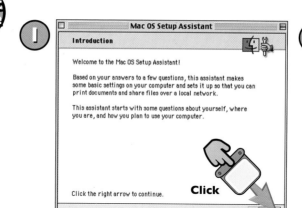

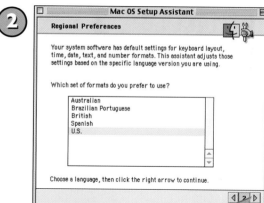

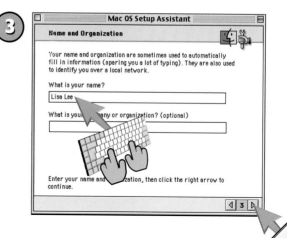

1 Read the Introduction page, and then click the right-arrow button.

2 Select a Regional Preference (U.S. is chosen as the default), and then click the right-arrow button.

3 Type your name, and then click the right-arrow button.

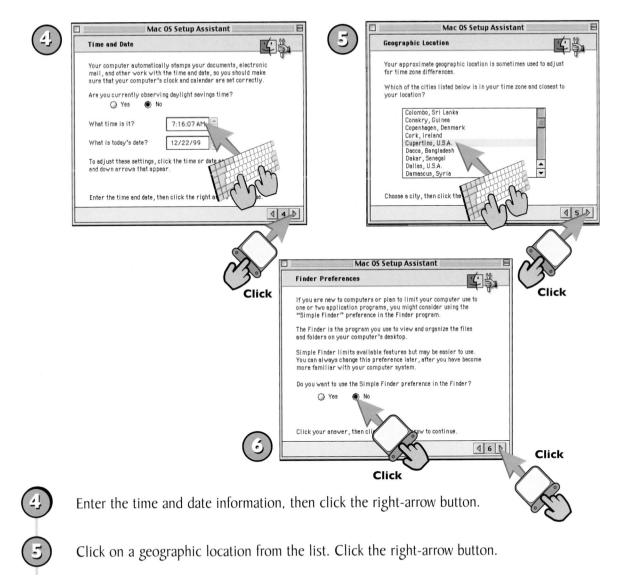

panel, see Part 7, Task 15,
"Changing the System

**You Lose Your
Settings if You Quit**
You can quit Mac OS Setup
Assistant at anytime.
However, none of the data
you entered will be saved if
you quit before you click
the **Go Ahead** button in
step 11 of this task.

**Change Settings
Before Clicking Go
Ahead**
If you want to change any
of the settings you
previously entered while
you were in Mac OS Setup
Assistant, click the left-
arrow button to move to a
previous page and the
right-arrow button to
move to the next page in
the Setup Assistant.

**Set Date and Time
Manually**
Date and time settings can
be set in the Date and
Time control panel. For
more information about
the Date and Time control
panel, see Part 7, Task 15,
"Changing the System
Date and Time."

4 Enter the time and date information, then click the right-arrow button.

5 Click on a geographic location from the list. Click the right-arrow button.

6 Choose a Finder Preferences setting (the default setting is No). Click the right-arrow
button.

PART I

✓ What Is Simple Finder?
Simple Finder provides a subset of regular Finder features in Mac OS. For example, Simple Finder contains fewer menu items and no command-key shortcuts.

✓ Finder Setting Options Available
There are several Finder setting options you can change at any time. To turn Simple Finder on or off, click **Edit** and choose **Preferences**; then click the **General** tab.

✓ No Password?
If you do not type a password in step 7, Mac OS Setup Assistant will not let you complete the setup process. Use a password that is relatively easy to remember. Having a password will help keep the data on your iBook safe, especially while you're connected to the Internet.

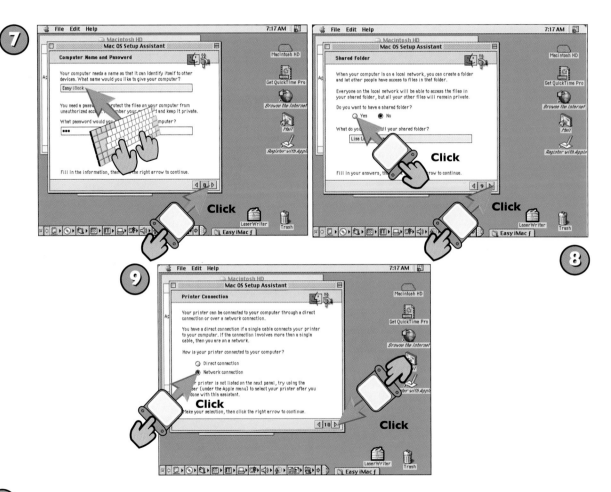

⑦ Type a computer name and password for your iBook. Click the right-arrow button to continue to the next page.

⑧ If your iBook is on a network, click **Yes** to share a folder with other computers. Type a name for shared folder, and then click the right-arrow button.

⑨ If you have a printer connected to your USB port, choose **Direct connection.** Choose **Network connection** if you use a printer on the network. Click the right-arrow button.

Next Step

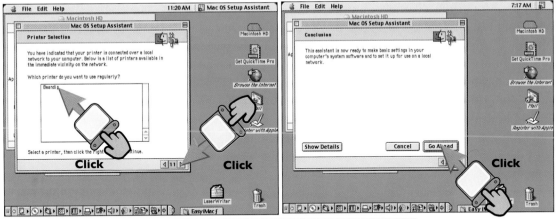

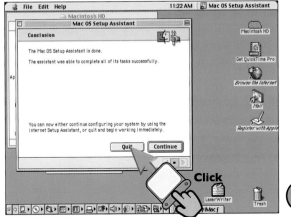

Learn More About How to Share Your Files
For more information about sharing files and folders on a network, see Part 8, Task 12, "Using File Sharing."

See All Your Settings with Show Details
To review all the Mac OS settings you have input, click the **Show Details** button in Step 11.

Configure Your iBook for the Internet
Click **Continue** if you want to configure your Internet setup information. For more information about Internet Setup Assistant, see Part 2, Task 1, "Setting Up for the Internet."

10 Click on a printer name (in this case, **Beandip** is my network printer). Then click the right-arrow button.

11 Click **Go Ahead**. Mac OS Setup Assistant will configure Mac OS. Click **Cancel** to quit and discard changes made by the Mac OS Setup Assistant.

12 Click **Quit** to exit Mac OS Setup Assistant.

Task 4: Opening and Closing a Window

Mac OS displays all its information in onscreen boxes called *windows*. You need to know how to open windows to work with the information on your computer. Windows are represented onscreen by small pictures called *icons*. You can double-click an icon to display the contents of a window, presented by Mac OS with a folder icon. You close a window after you finish working with it and its contents. Too many open windows clutter the desktop as well as the Applications menu.

Practice Your Double-Click

If nothing happens when you double-click an icon with the trackpad or trackpad button, it might be because you did not click quickly enough or because you single-clicked, moved the cursor, and single-clicked again. You have to click twice in rapid succession.

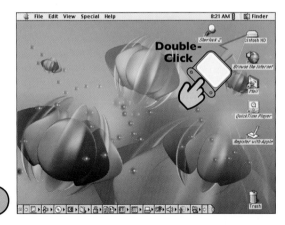

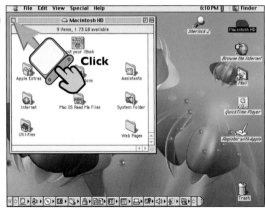

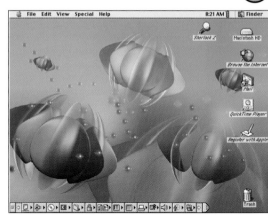

(1) Double-click the **Macintosh HD** icon.

(2) The contents of this icon are displayed in a window.

(3) Click the **Close** button (the empty square in the top-left corner of the window).

(4) The window is closed.

End Task

Task 5: Collapsing and Expanding a Window

Start Here

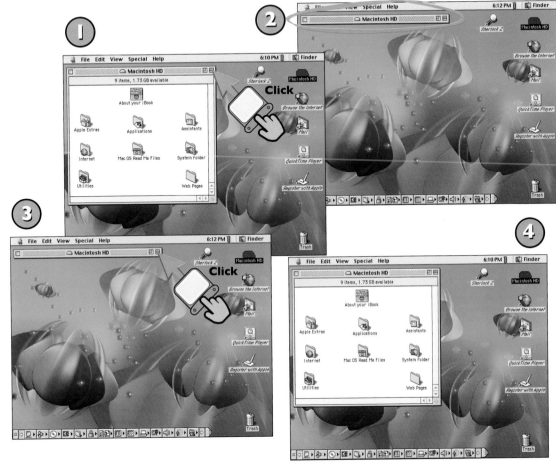

You can reduce (collapse) a window so that it is still available, but not displayed on the desktop. You might want to minimize a window to temporarily move it out of your way, but keep it active for later use. You can enlarge (expand) a window so that it reopens to its original size.

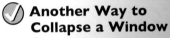

✓ **Another Way to Collapse a Window**
You can also collapse a window by double-clicking the window's title bar. Choose the **Options** tab in the **Appearance** control panel to turn on this feature.

✓ **Option-Collapse or Expand All Windows**
You can collapse or expand all open windows in an application, such as Finder, by holding down the **Option** key while clicking the **Collapse** button in a window.

① Click the **Collapse** button in the window you want to minimize.

② The bottom part of the window disappears, but the window's title bar remains visible.

③ Click the **Collapse** button again to expand the window.

④ The window reappears at its original screen size.

Task 6: Moving a Window

As you add more applications, folders, aliases, and so on to the desktop, you'll need more room to display these elements. You can easily move the windows around so you can view a full screen of window content.

Start Here

Click

Drag

Drop

(!) **Watch Where You Click When Moving a Window**

Be sure to point to the title bar when moving a window. If you point to any other area, you might resize the window instead of moving it.

① To move an open window, point to its title bar. Click and hold down the mouse button.

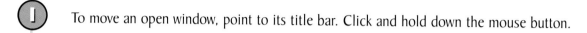

② Drag the window to its new position. You can see the border of the window as you drag. When the desired location is reached, release the mouse button.

③ The window and its contents appear in the new location.

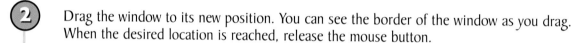

End Task

Task 7: Resizing a Window

Start Here

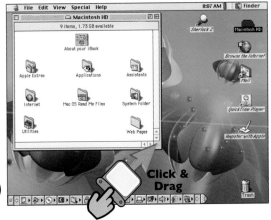

Click & Drag

①

Release

②

④

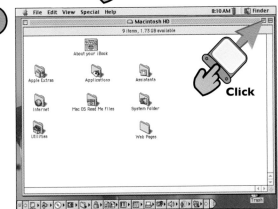

③

Click

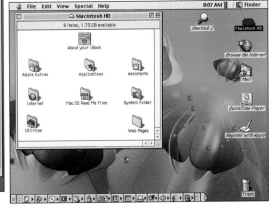

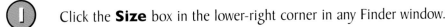

In addition to being able to move a window, you can resize a window to whatever size you want. Resizing a window is helpful if you want to view more than one window at the same time, or if you want to maximize a window to view as much of it as possible. If you maximize a window, you can easily restore it to its original size.

✓ **See More Desktop Items**
Restoring the window to a smaller size lets you view other windows in the background, or gain easy access to items on the desktop.

✓ **Two Zoom Button Modes**
The first time you click the **Zoom** button, it will resize the window to show all window content at the smallest window size.

① Click the **Size** box in the lower-right corner in any Finder window.

② Drag the border to resize the window, and then release the mouse button. The window is resized.

③ Click the **Zoom** button in a maximized window.

④ The window returns to its previous size.

End Task

Task 8: Scrolling a Window

If a window is resized so that it is too small to show all its contents, scrollbars will appear along the bottom or right side of a window. You can use these scrollbars to navigate a window to see the other contents.

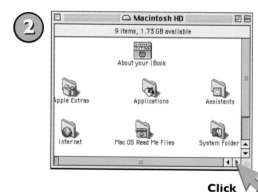

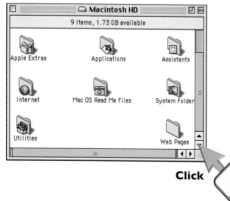

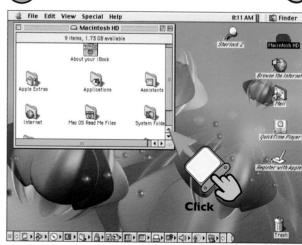

Click

Click

Click

Click

✓ Page Up or Page Down with the Scrollbar

You can click anywhere in the scrollbar to jump in that direction to another part of the window. You can also click the scrollbar to scroll quickly through the window.

(1) Click the left arrow to scroll left through the window.

(2) Click the right arrow to scroll right through the window.

(3) Click the down arrow to scroll down through the window.

(4) Click the up arrow to scroll up through the window.

Task 9: Navigating Menus

Start Here

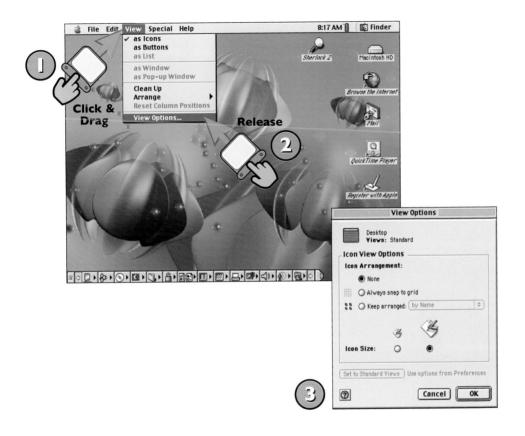

Although you can perform many tasks by clicking the various onscreen objects, you must choose commands to perform the majority of tasks. Commands are organized in menus to make them easy to find. Both the Macintosh Operating System (Mac OS) and its applications have a menu bar; each menu then contains a group of related commands.

The menu bar lets you customize Mac OS settings, get help, and more. The menu bar, located at the top of the screen, contains the **Apple, File, Edit, View, Special,** and **Help** menus. Clicking the **Apple** menu enables you to open any applications, documents, or network servers that you recently had open. You can use the **Apple** menu to access most of the applications installed by Mac OS.

1. In the menu bar, click the menu name (in this case, the menu name is **View**).

2. Click the command you want.

3. The View Options window opens.

Task 10: Using Context Menus

Contextual menus, also called context menus, shortcut menus, quick menus, and pop-up menus, provide common commands related to the selected item. You can, for example, quickly copy and paste, create a new folder, move a file, or rearrange icons using a contextual menu.

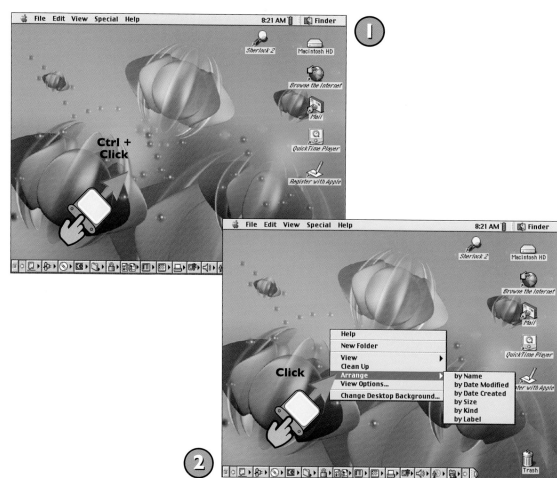

✓ Watch the Cursor Change
When you hold down the **Control** key while clicking, the cursor will change from an arrow to a menu.

✓ Different Menus for Different Windows
Different context menus appear depending on what you're pointing to when you control-click the mouse.

① Hold down the **Ctrl** key and click the item for which you want to display a contextual menu. For instance, **Ctrl**+click any blank part of the desktop.

② Click the command you want in the contextual menu.

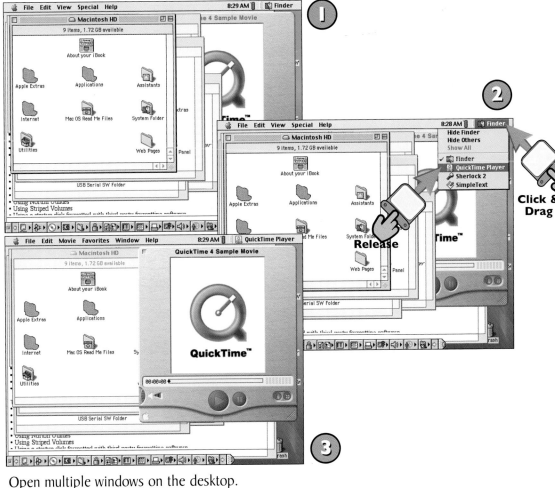

As you work, you will often have several windows open on the desktop at one time. These windows will probably overlap, which can make it difficult to find what you want. To make your work easier and more efficient, Mac OS enables you to arrange the windows on the desktop in several different ways.

① Open multiple windows on the desktop.

② Open the **Applications** menu and select the application you want.

③ The window and the application you selected move to the front of the screen.

✓ **Make a Window Active to Use It**
To work in any one of the open windows, click the desired window to make it active. The active window moves to the front of the screen and its title bar is a different color.

✓ **Click on the Title Bar**
Be sure to use the window's title bar to move a window. If you miss the title bar, you won't be able to move the window.

When you choose certain commands, a dialog box prompts you for additional information about how to carry out the command. Dialog boxes are used throughout Mac OS; luckily all dialog boxes have common elements and all work in a similar way.

Task 12: Using a Dialog Box or Control Panel

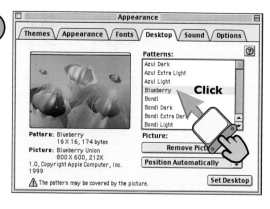

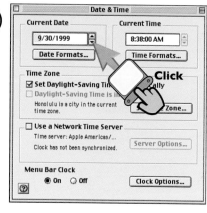

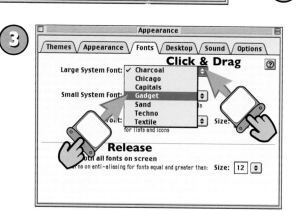

(✓) **Most Dialog Boxes Are Unique**
Different dialog boxes have different options. The figures in this section are meant to show the types of items you might find in a dialog box.

(✓) **Control Panels Are Not Dialog Boxes**
Control panels differ from dialog boxes; settings are saved in control panels when the control panel window is closed.

(1) To view a tab, click it.

(2) To use a list box, scroll through the list and click the item you want to select.

(3) To use a pop-up menu, click the arrow to the side of the box and then select the desired item from the list.

(4) To use a spin box, click the arrows to increment or decrement the value or type a value in the text box.

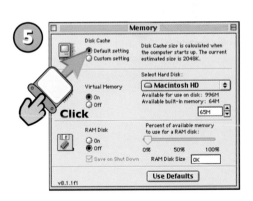

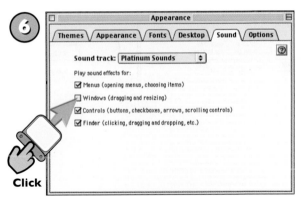

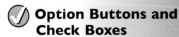

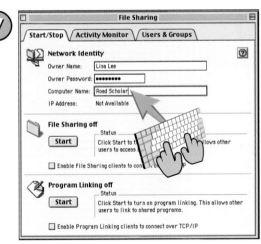

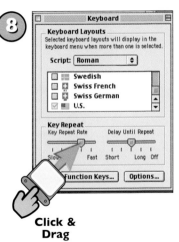

Click

Click

**Click &
Drag**

✅ **Option Buttons and
Check Boxes**
Dialog boxes contain
various types of elements,
including option buttons
and check boxes. You can
choose only one option
button within a group of
option buttons; choosing a
second option deselects
the first. However, you can
select multiple check boxes
within a group of check
boxes.

✅ **Click OK to Close a
Dialog Box**
When a dialog box is open,
you cannot perform any
other action until you
accept any changes by
clicking the **OK** button. To
close the dialog box
without making a
selection, click the **Cancel**
button.

⑤ Click an option button to activate it.

⑥ Click a check box to select it (or to deselect a check box that is already checked).

⑦ Type an entry in a text box.

⑧ Click and drag a slider to change or adjust a particular setting.

End
Task

Task 13: Looking Up Help Topics with Mac OS Help

Use the **Help** menu to locate help for performing specific procedures with your iBook, such as printing a document or playing QuickTime movies.

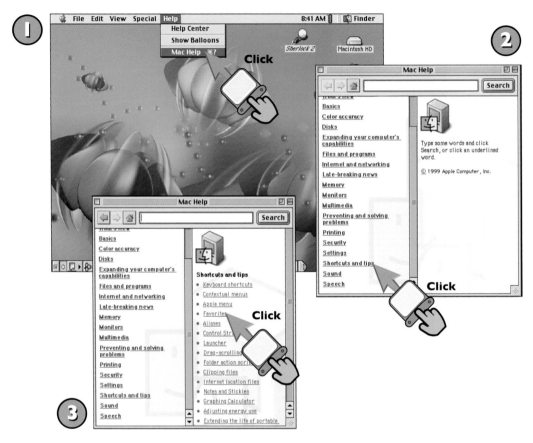

✓ **Print a Help Topic**
Click **File** and choose **Print** to print a help topic.

✓ **View Information with Help Links**
You can click any of the underlined text in the help area to display a definition of that term or to display related help information.

① Open the **Help** menu and select **Mac Help**.

② Select the help category that seems most relevant to your needs (in this case, click **Shortcuts and tips**).

③ Narrow your search by clicking an appropriate help topic (for now, click **Favorites**).

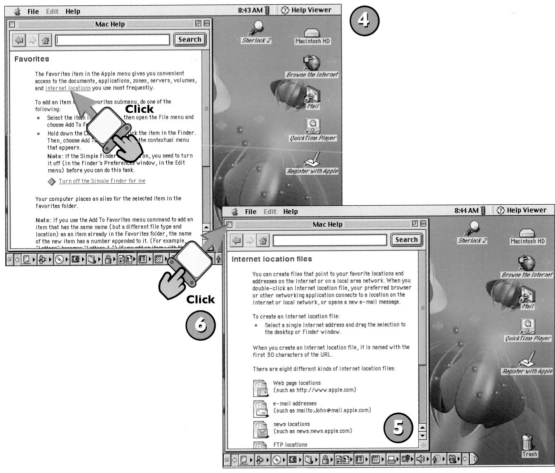

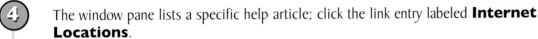

④ The window pane lists a specific help article; click the link entry labeled **Internet Locations**.

⑤ Review the help information.

⑥ Click the **Close** button to close the **Help** window.

✓ **Search for a Help Topic**
Search for a help topic by typing text into the text box at the top of the window. Type a word or two that represents a topic you want to search for.

✓ **Navigate Help Topics**
Click on the left- or right-arrow buttons in the Help window toolbar to navigate through any help topics you view. Click on the **Home** button to return to the main Help window.

Task 14: Looking Up a Help Topic with Sherlock 2

If you want to find help on a topic via the Internet, such as the latest iBook troubleshooting tips, use Sherlock 2 (of course, to use Sherlock 2 to search the Internet, you must be connected to the Internet via a network connection or via an ISP).

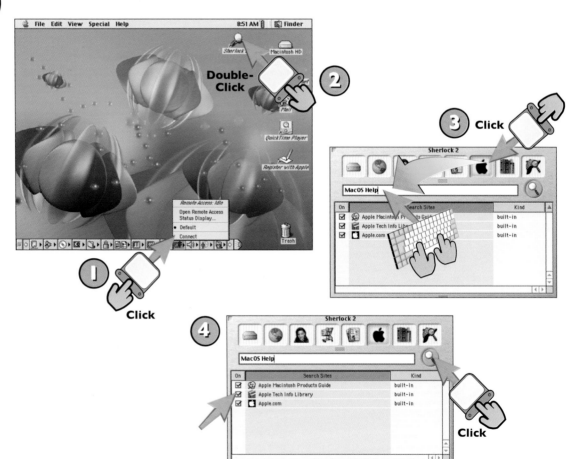

Start Here

Double-Click

Click

Download More Sherlock 2 Plug-Ins
You can extend Sherlock 2's searching capabilities by adding plug-ins available at Apple's Web site (www.apple.com/sherlock).

1. Connect your iBook to the Internet.

2. Double-click the **Sherlock 2** icon on your desktop.

3. Click on the **Apple** button. Then type one or more words that relate to the topic about which you want to find information (in this case, I've typed MacOS Help).

4. If it's not already selected, click the **Apple Tech Info Library** check box. Click the **Search** button.

Next Step

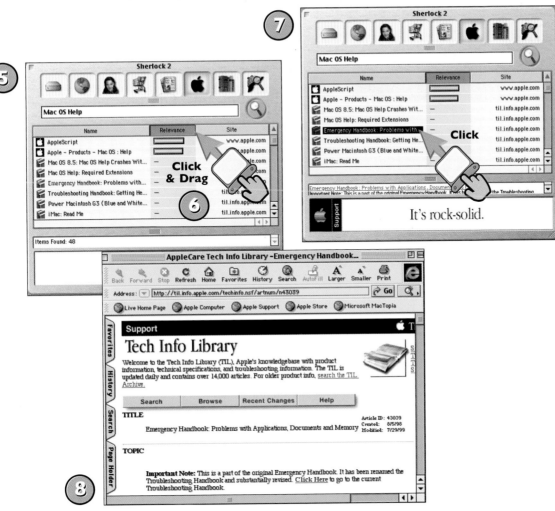

5 Review the results of the search.

6 Resize any column in the results window by dragging the edge of the column heading.

7 Click an entry in the list box (I've clicked **Emergency Handbook: Problems with Applications, Documents and Memory** link), and then click a link in the bottom pane.

8 Review the selected information in Internet Explorer.

Task 15: Getting Context-Sensitive Help

When you open a window or control panel, you might not know what each option does. If you have questions about an option, you can view a description of that option by following the steps in this task.

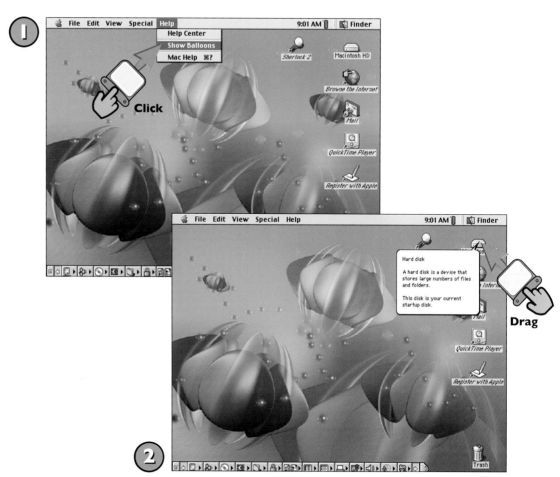

Click

Drag

✓ **Balloon Help Can Slow You Down**
You might want to turn off balloon help if you do not need to use it. Leaving it on can slow down the overall performance of your iBook.

1 Select **Show Balloons** in the **Help** menu.

2 Move the mouse over an icon or window element (in this case, the hard drive icon). Review the information in the help balloon.

Task 16: Shutting Down Your iBook

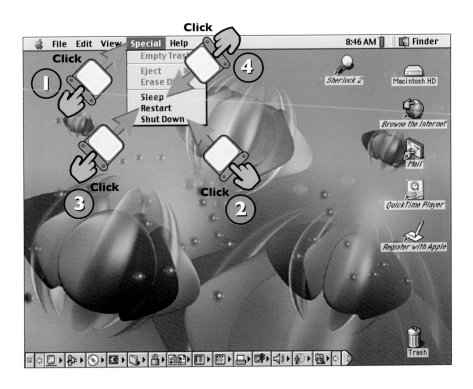

If you turn off the power to your computer before you properly shut the computer down, you could lose valuable data or damage an open file. Mac OS provides a safe shutdown feature that checks for open programs and files, and warns you to save unsaved files. You should always shut down before you turn off the power.

(!) Keep the Battery Charged
Be sure to keep your battery charged. If your iBook runs out of power while you are using it, you could lose some or all of your data. Also, your iBook does not have a backup battery. If your iBook battery loses its charge for several minutes, you will need to reset some of your software settings, such as the date and time.

1 After you've closed down all open programs, click the **Special** menu.

2 Select the **Shut Down** menu command to power off your iBook.

3 If you choose **Restart**, your iBook will power off, and then start back up.

4 If you select **Sleep**, your iBook will go into low-power mode until you open your iBook or press any key to wake it up.

PART 2

Connecting to Online Services and the Internet

If you have an Internet connection and an account with an Internet service provider (ISP), you can venture beyond your iBook to resources available from online services, such as America Online, or from the Internet. Your iBook also provides Internet Explorer 4.5, a Web browser that offers you complete and convenient browsing for the Internet. As with any browser software, you can use Internet Explorer to view World Wide Web pages, to search for specific topics, and to download and upload files. In addition to browsing the Web, you can use Internet Explorer 4.5's mail application, Outlook Express, to exchange email messages with others who are connected to the Internet. You can also use Outlook Express to participate in newsgroups.

Tasks

Task #		Page #
1	Setting Up for the Internet	28
2	Using EarthLink's TotalAccess	32
3	Connecting to AOL	34
4	Starting Internet Explorer	35
5	Connecting to Apple's Web Site	36
6	Typing an Address	37
7	Browsing with Links and Toolbar Buttons	38
8	Adding a Site to Your Favorites List	40
9	Going to a Site in Your Favorites List	41
10	Organizing Your Favorites	42
11	Working with Page Holder	44
12	Searching the Internet with Sherlock 2	46
13	Using the History List	48
14	Quitting Internet Explorer	49
15	Starting Outlook Express	50
16	Reading Mail	51
17	Responding to Mail	52
18	Creating and Sending New Mail	53
19	Subscribing to Newsgroups	54
20	Reading Newsgroup Messages	56
21	Posting New Messages	57
22	Replying to a Newsgroup Message	58
23	Quitting Outlook Express	59

Task 1: Setting Up for the Internet

To explore the Internet, you must have a modem and an Internet connection. You can get this connection through an online provider such as America Online, or you can get an account from an independent Internet service provider (ISP). Before you can take advantage of all the benefits of the Internet, you have to get your Internet connection set up. Mac OS makes it easy to set up by providing the Internet Setup Assistant application to guide you through the steps.

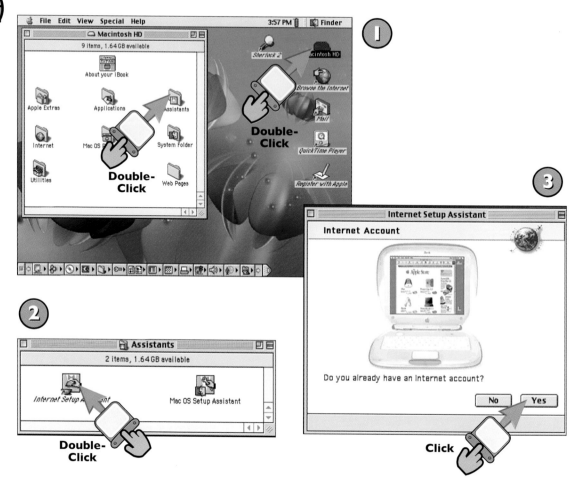

Internet Account Required for This Task
This task assumes that you already have an Internet account from an Internet service provider, such as EarthLink, Netcom, Best, or AT&T.

 Double-click the hard drive icon to open the Macintosh HD window, and then double-click the **Assistants** folder.

 Double-click the **Internet Setup Assistant** icon.

 Click on the **Yes** button on the first and second screens of the Assistant.

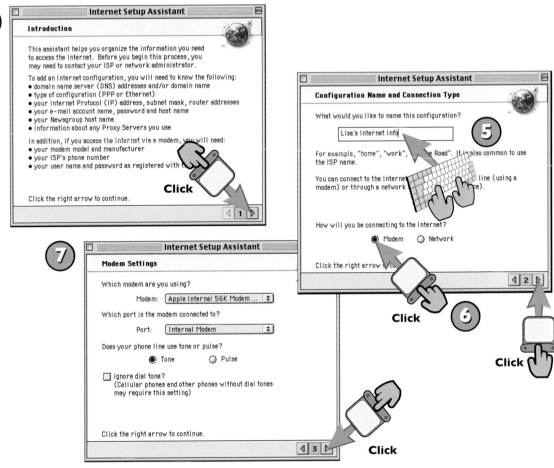

Click

Click

Click

Click

Click

 Can't Find an ISP?
You can find local ISPs in the Yellow Pages. In addition, there are nationwide providers, such as **AT&T WorldNet, Mindspring,** and **EarthLink.** Be sure to compare pricing and services when selecting an ISP.

 ISP Checklist
If you are trying to decide whether to use a particular ISP, consider the following:
- Does it provide local phone number access?
- Does it provide 800 number access?
- Is its software easy to set up?
- Does it provide an email account?
- How reliable is its support?
- Does it provide free space for your own Web site?
- Does it provide any custom content or services on its Web site?
- Does it provide any software extras?

4 Read the introduction page and click the right-arrow button to continue.

5 Type a name for your Internet configuration (it can be anything you like).

6 Click the **Modem** radio button (unless you're connecting via a network), and then click the right-arrow button to continue.

7 Adjust the modem configuration by selecting the appropriate settings from the pop-up menus, and then click the right-arrow button to continue.

Setting Up for the Internet Continued

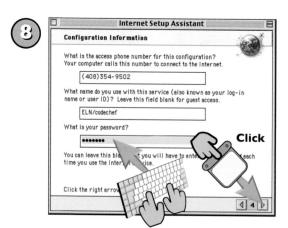

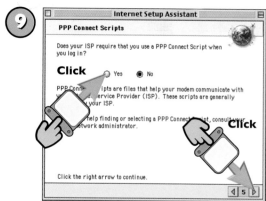

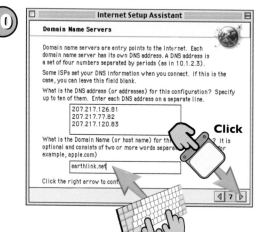

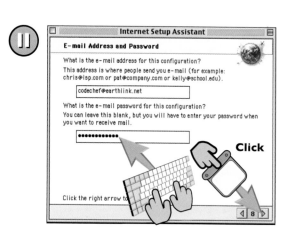

 **Customize Your Dialing Options**

If your phone line requires a prefix (for instance, if you have to dial a 9 to reach an outside line), you add the prefix to the phone number in the **Configuration Information** page of the Internet Setup Assistant.

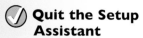 **Quit the Setup Assistant**

You can quit the Internet Setup Assistant at any time. However, none of the data you entered will be saved unless you complete the Assistant. Luckily, you can go through the setup process more than once.

 Type the phone number, username, and password information for your ISP, and then click the right-arrow button to continue.

 If your ISP requires a PPP Connect Script, click **Yes**. Click the right-arrow button. If an IP address has been assigned, click **Yes**. Click the right-arrow button.

 Type at least two DNS addresses and the domain name server name. (Get this information from your ISP.) Click the right-arrow button to continue.

If your ISP has provided you with an email account, type the appropriate information in the text fields. Press the right-arrow button to continue.

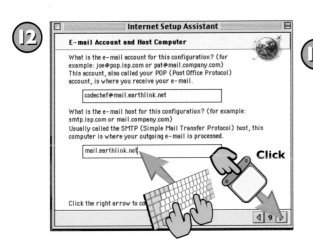

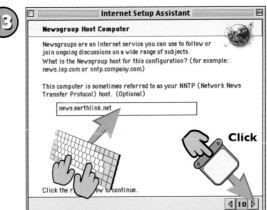

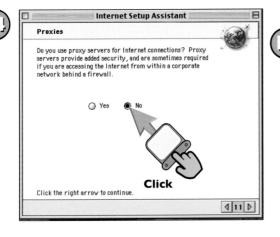

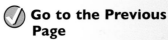

What's PPP?

PPP is an acronym for **Point-to-Point Protocol.** It is a network protocol commonly used to translate data exchanged between computers connected to the Internet.

Go to the Previous Page

You can go back to a previous page at any time by clicking the left-arrow button.

Customize the Behavior

iBook is set to disconnect after 10 minutes if there is no modem activity. You can turn off this feature in the Remote Access control panel. To adjust settings in the Remote Access control panel, click the **Apple** menu, choose **Control Panels,** and then choose **Remote Access.** Click the **Options** button, and then click a tab to view options settings for Remote Access.

12 Type the email host information (in this case, `mail.earthlink.net`). Click the right-arrow button to continue.

13 Type the host name of the news server (or use the default news server), and then click the right-arrow button to continue.

14 If you need to use proxy servers with your Internet connection (you probably don't), click **Yes**, and then type the proxy server information in the next screen.

15 Click the **Go Ahead** button to save the information.

Task 2: Using EarthLink's TotalAccess

An alternative to using Internet Assistant is to use EarthLink's TotalAccess software to connect to the information superhighway. It works similarly to Internet Setup Assistant but can only create an EarthLink Internet account for you.

✓ **Never Heard of EarthLink?**
EarthLink is one of the largest Internet service providers in the United States.

✓ **Where to Find EarthLink**
If the TotalAccess software did not come preinstalled on your iBook, you can download it from EarthLink's Web site at www.earthlink.net.

✓ **Ground Zero**
To get to the Internet Applications folder, double-click the hard drive icon, double-click the **Internet** folder, and then double-click the **Internet Applications** folder.

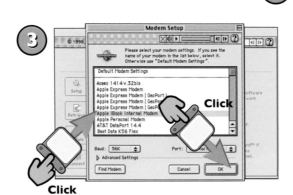

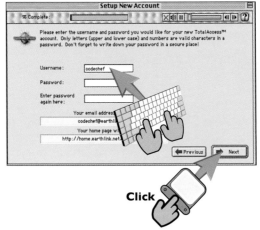

1. From within the Internet Applications folder, double-click the **EarthLink TotalAccess** folder, and then double-click the **Registration & Utilities** icon.

2. Click the **Setup** button.

3. Choose **Apple iBook Internal Modem** in the modem list window and click **OK**.

4. Type in a name and password and click **Next**. Type in your billing information on the following screens to continue your registration.

Next Step

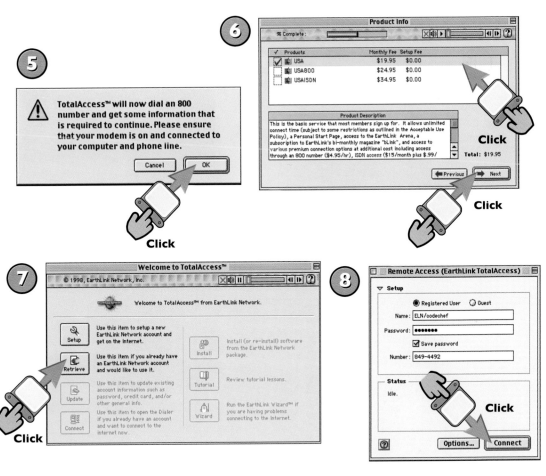

⑤ After your billing information has been entered, TotalAccess dials into the EarthLink network to complete the registration steps. Click **OK** if your modem is connected to a phone line.

⑥ Click on the EarthLink product or monthly fee you want to use and click **Next**. Continue through the remaining screens until you complete your account registration.

⑦ After your account has been created, click the **Retrieve** button if you want TotalAccess to configure your iBook to dial into the EarthLink network.

⑧ You can also add the EarthLink login, password, and dial-in phone number information manually into the Remote Access control panel. Click **Connect** to connect to the Internet.

✓ What's in an Account Name?
If you select a name that is not available, the EarthLink Setup software will let you choose a new name at the end of the account setup process.

End
Task

Task 3: Connecting to AOL

America Online (AOL) is the most popular online service company. AOL provides content, bulletin boards, email, and other services for subscribers. You can also access the Internet through AOL. iBook conveniently enables you to try out America Online; you'll find the AOL installer application on the iBook Software CD-ROM in the CD Extras folder.

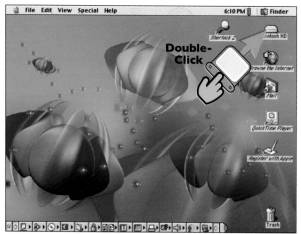

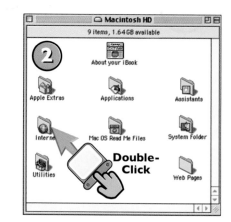

✓ **Click Cancel if You Don't Want to Continue**
You can cancel the setup at any time by clicking the **Cancel** button.

✓ **Trial Subscription Will Expire**
AOL, like most online providers, offers a trial subscription. After that subscription expires, you must pay for the service. Be sure you understand all the fees involved before you sign up.

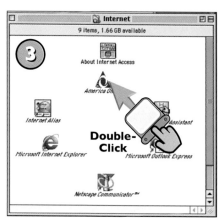

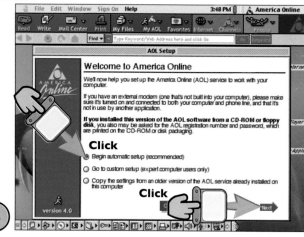

① Double-click the hard drive icon to open the Macintosh HD window.

② Double-click the **Internet** folder icon.

③ Double-click the **America Online** icon.

④ Click on a radio button, and then click on the **Next** arrow. Follow the onscreen instructions to create a new account.

Task 4: Starting Internet Explorer

Start Here

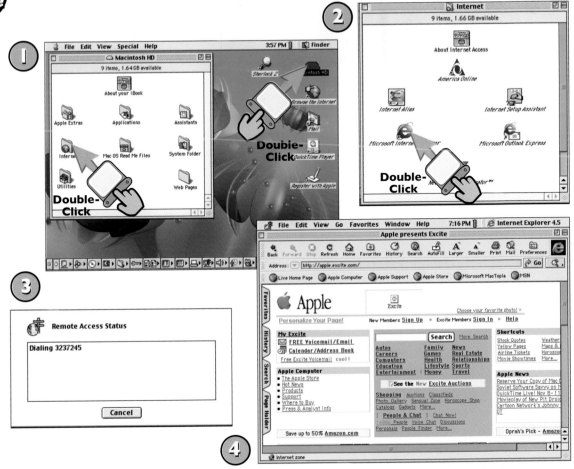

After you have your Internet connection set up, you can start Internet Explorer and browse the Internet.

✓ **Problems Connecting?**
If you have problems connecting—the line is busy, for instance—try again. If you continue to have problems, choose a different local number to dial into, or check with your ISP.

✓ **Autoconnect and Disconnect**
Your iBook is set up to disconnect after 10 minutes if there is no modem activity. If you need to use Outlook Express or Internet Explorer, you will automatically be reconnected when you start either of these applications.

✓ **Use Remote Access to Reconnect**
To manually reconnect to your ISP, click the **Apple** menu, choose **Control Panels**, and then choose **Remote Access**. Click the **Connect** button to reconnect.

① Double-click the hard drive icon to open the Macintosh HD window, and then double-click the **Internet** folder icon.

② Double-click the **Microsoft Internet Explorer** icon. You can also double-click the **Browse the Internet** icon on the desktop.

③ Wait for Remote Access to connect to your ISP.

④ Mac OS connects to your ISP. The Internet Explorer window appears and you see your start page (in this case, `http://apple.excite.com`).

End Task

Task 5: Connecting to Apple's Web Site

As you browse the Internet, you will probably need to visit Apple's Web site for support, new product information, developer information, or to download a software update for your iBook.

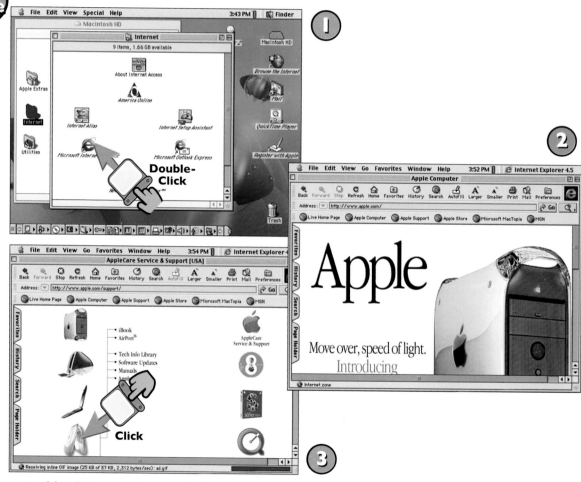

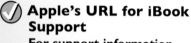

Apple's URL for iBook Support
For support information about iBook, go to www.apple.com/ support/iBook/.

1. Double-click the **Microsoft Internet Explorer** icon in the Internet window (to access the Internet window, see the preceding task).

2. Type **apple** in the **Address** field, and then press **Return**. Apple's Web page will load.

3. After Apple's Web page loads, click the **Support** link.

Task 6: Typing an Address

Start Here

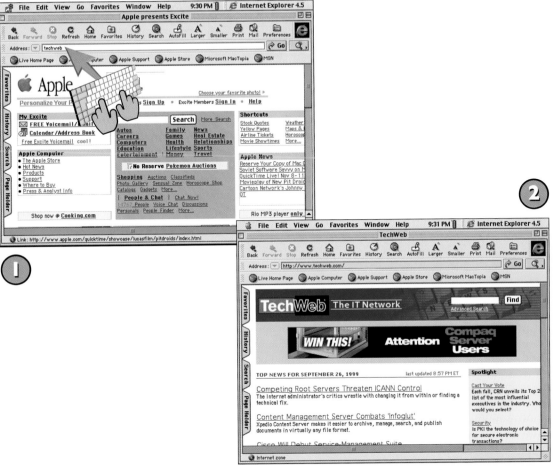

Typing a site's address is the fastest way to get to that site. An address, or *URL* (uniform resource locator), consists of the protocol (usually `http://`) and the domain name (something like `www.nba.com`). The domain name might also include a path (a list of folders) to the document. The extension (usually .com, .net, .gov, .edu, or .mil) indicates the type of site (commercial, network resources, government, educational, or military, respectively).

1 In the **Address** bar of the Internet Explorer window, type the address of the site you want to visit (in this case, `techweb`), and then press **Return**.

2 Internet Explorer displays the page associated with the URL you typed.

✔ **Type in the Exact URL**
Make sure you type the address correctly. You must type the periods, colons, slashes, and other characters in the exact order.

End Task

Task 7: Browsing with Links and Toolbar Buttons

Information on the Internet is easy to browse because documents contain *links* to other pages, documents, and sites. Simply click a link to view the associated page. You can jump from link to link, exploring all types of topics and levels of information. Links are also called *hyperlinks*, and usually appear underlined and sometimes in a different color. You can also use the buttons in the toolbar to navigate from page to page.

Start Here

Click

Click

✓ **No Old Links Here**

If you see an error message when you click a link, it could indicate that the link is no longer valid or that it is inaccurate. If the message indicates that the server is too busy, wait awhile and then try again.

1 From the MSNBC page (`www.msnbc.com/news/default.asp`), click a link (in this case, `msnbcsports.com`).

2 The page for that link appears (in this case, `www.msnbc.com/news/SPT_Front.asp`). Click the **Back** button in the toolbar to go to the previous page you visited.

Click

Click

✓ Try Out Apple's Links
Click any of the buttons in
the Favorites toolbar to
see some sites selected by
Apple. You can select to
view sites in several
categories. The figures in
this task show the links
from the **MSN** sports page.

**✓ Images Can Be Links,
Too**
Images can serve as links.
You can tell whether an
image (or text) is a link by
placing your mouse
pointer on it; if the pointer
changes into a pointing
hand, the image (or text) is
a link.

③ Click the **Forward** button to move forward through the pages you've already visited
(you must click on the **Back** button before you can use the **Forward** button).

④ To return to your start page, click the **Home** button in the toolbar.

Task 8: Adding a Site to Your Favorites List

When you find a site that you especially like, you might want a quick way to return to it without having to browse from link to link or having to remember the address. Fortunately, Internet Explorer enables you to build a list of favorite sites and to access those sites by clicking them in the list.

If You Like a Web Site
You can subscribe to certain sites and set up Internet Explorer to update the sites regularly.

Removing an Item
To remove a site from your Favorites list, choose **Favorites,** and then click **Open Favorites.** Select the site you want to delete, and then press the **Delete** button.

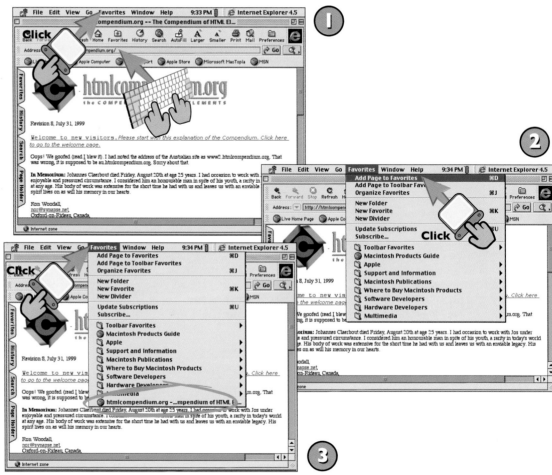

In Internet Explorer, visit a Web site that you want to add to your Favorites list. Then click the **Favorites** menu (do not click the **Favorites** toolbar button).

Click the **Add Page to Favorites** command.

Click the **Favorites** menu. The name of the Web page appears at the bottom of the **Favorites** menu.

Task 9: Going to a Site in Your Favorites List

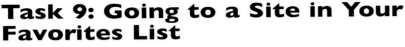

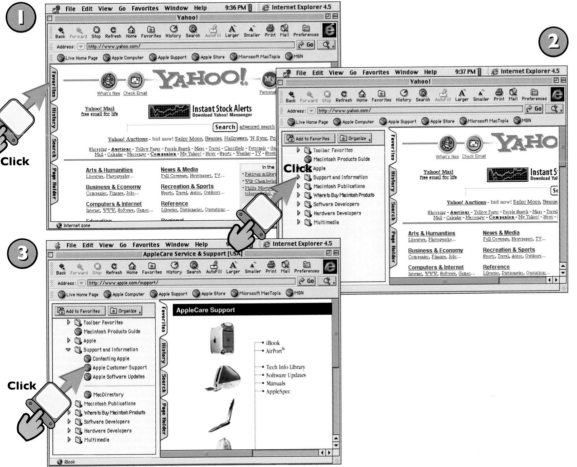

After you have added a site to your Favorites list, you can easily reach that site by displaying the list and selecting the site.

✓ **To Close a Window Pane**
To close the **Favorites** pane, click its tab.

① Click the **Favorites** tab in the Internet Explorer window.

② The pane on the left side of the screen contains your Favorites list; the pane on the right contains the current page. Click on the arrow next to a folder to view Favorites stored in that folder.

③ Click the site you want to visit (in this case, **Apple Customer Support**). Internet Explorer displays the site you selected from the Favorites list.

✓ **Use Folders to Group Your Favorites**
You can set up folders to group sites together. For more information on adding folders, see the next task.

Task 10: Organizing Your Favorites

If you add several sites to your Favorites list, it might become difficult to use. You can organize the list by grouping similar sites together in a folder. You can add new folders and move sites from one folder to another.

Start Here

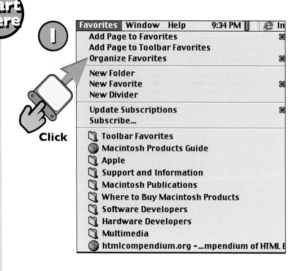

Click

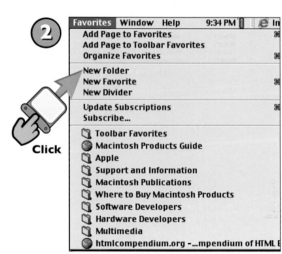

Click

✓ **Drag and Drop to Organize Favorites**
You can drag a site from the list to a folder where you want to place the site.

✓ **Rename Any Favorite**
To rename a site or folder in your Favorites list, click the name of the site or folder and wait about one second. Type a new name, and press **Return**.

① Click the **Favorites** menu in the Internet Explorer window's menu bar, and then choose **Organize Favorites**.

② To create a new folder, click **Favorites** and choose the **New Folder** command.

③ The default name is **untitled folder**. Type the folder name and press **Return**.

Next Step

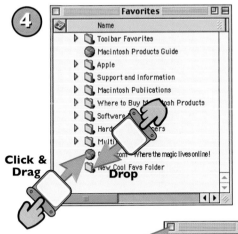

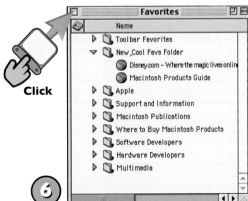

④ To move a site to the new folder (named **New,Cool Favs Folder**), select the site and drag it to the folder you want.

⑤ The site appears under the folder where you placed it.

⑥ When you finish moving all the sites you want to rearrange, click the **Close** box.

Click &
Drag

Drop

Click

✓ **Remove a Favorite Web Site**
To delete a site, select it and press the **Delete** button on the keyboard or drag the site to the **Trash**.

✓ **Add a Favorite Site to Your Apple Menu**
You can also add a favorite URL, file, or folder to the Favorites folder located in the Apple menu. Click on the **Apple** menu and choose **Favorites**. Then click and drag a favorite item to the open Favorites window.

✓ **Reorganize Favorites by Renaming Them**
Favorites are listed in the order they are added to the Favorites menu. To move an item to the top of the menu, add a space to the beginning of the name of the favorite.

End Task

Task 11: Working with Page Holder

If you have been surfing the Web and have grown tired of clicking the **Back** button, a new feature in Internet Explorer 4.5 called **Page Holder** is a great alternative. Page Holder lets you keep a Web page in the pop-up window of Internet Explorer, allowing you to store two Web pages in one Internet Explorer window.

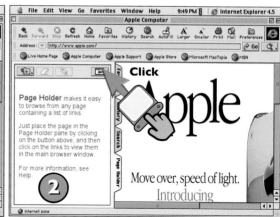

✓ **View Links Only**
If you do not want to view an entire page in Page Holder, click the **Link** button to view only the links on the page stored in the Page Holder window.

✓ **Favorites Button**
You can add a URL in the Page Holder window to your Favorites menu by clicking on the **Favorites** folder icon in the Page Holder toolbar.

(1) Load a Web page, and then click the **Page Holder** tab in the Internet Explorer window.

(2) Click the left arrow icon in the Page Holder window to move the page in the main window into the Page Holder window.

(3) The page from the main window appears in the Page Holder window.

(4) Type a different URL into the same window (in this case, `http://news.cnet.com`). Click **Return**.

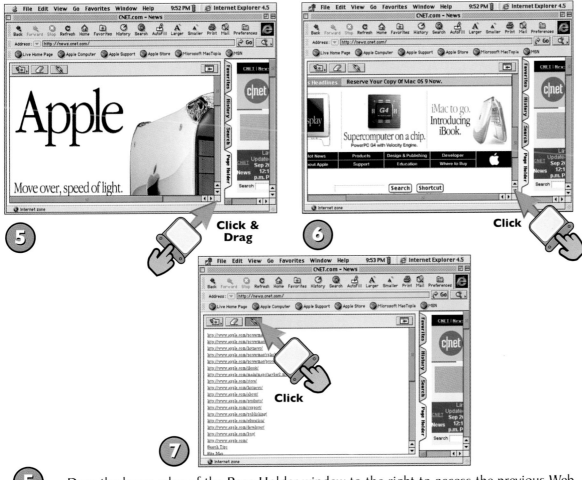

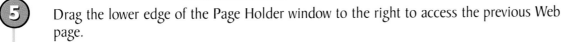

⑤ Drag the lower edge of the Page Holder window to the right to access the previous Web page.

⑥ Click on the scrollbar controls to view or select any links in the Page Holder window.

⑦ Click the **Links** button to only view the links available in the Page Holder window.

✅ **Clear a Page with the Erase Button**
You can clear the Page Holder window by clicking on the **Erase** button in the Page Holder toolbar.

✅ **Hide the Page Holder Window**
By clicking the **Page Holder** tab, you can hide the Page Holder window.

Task 12: Searching the Internet with Sherlock 2

The Internet includes far too many kinds of computers and even more Web sites and Web pages to be counted. Looking for the site you want by browsing can be like looking for a needle in a haystack. Instead, you can search for a topic, and find all sites related to that topic. To search, you can use a search engine on the Internet or one on your iBook. The basic procedure is the same, but the results of the search can vary. Sherlock 2 is the search engine built into Mac OS 9.

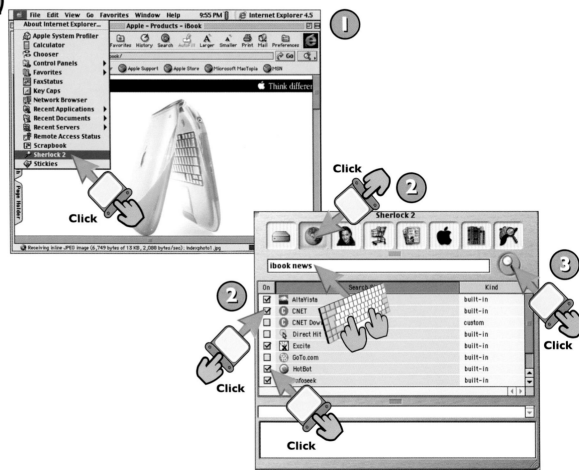

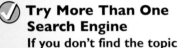 **Try More Than One Search Engine**
If you don't find the topic you want, try a different search engine such as www.dogpile.com. The result may be different.

① Click the **Apple** menu and choose **Sherlock 2**. You can also start Sherlock 2 by double-clicking the **Sherlock 2** icon on the desktop.

② Click on the globe icon on the toolbar. Click on a check box to select the Web sites you want to search. Then type one or two words you want to search for.

③ Click the **Search** button.

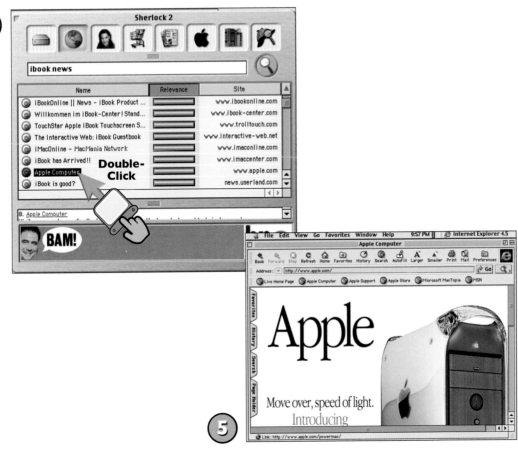

Double-
Click

BAM!

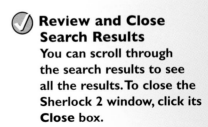

Apple

Move over, speed of light.
Introducing

Review and Close Search Results
You can scroll through the search results to see all the results. To close the Sherlock 2 window, click its **Close** box.

Sherlock 2 Shortcut
You can start Sherlock 2 directly from Internet Explorer. Click on the magnifying glass button in the Address toolbar in Internet Explorer, and then select **Open Apple Sherlock**.

The results of the search are displayed in the Sherlock 2 window. Scroll down until you find the link you want, and then double-click it.

The page you selected appears.

Task 13: Using the History List

As you browse from link to link, you might remember a site that you like, but not remember that site's name or address. You can easily return to sites you have visited by displaying the History list. From this list, you can select the day you want to review, and then the site you want to visit.

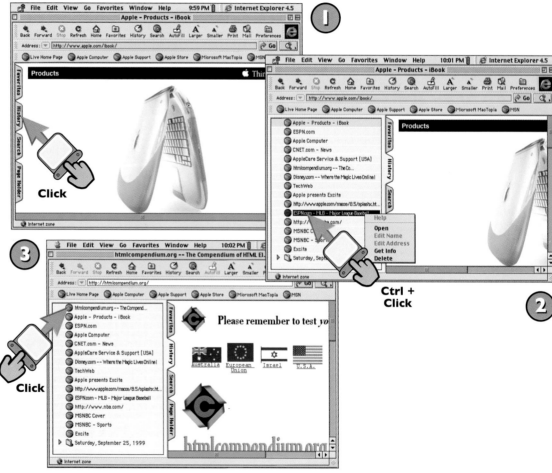

✓ Menu, Please
Hold down the **Control** key and click on any item in the History list to access menu commands for that item.

✓ Organize Your History List
You can select how many days the history is kept, and you can clear the History list. Choose **Go**, click **Open History**, and then select the folder representing the day you want to remove. To clean the history, select all items in the window and move them to the **Trash**.

① Click the **History** tab.

② Internet Explorer displays the History list in a pane on the left side of the window. If necessary, select the day whose list you want to review.

③ Click the site you want to go to. Internet Explorer displays the site you selected.

Task 14: Quitting Internet Explorer

Click

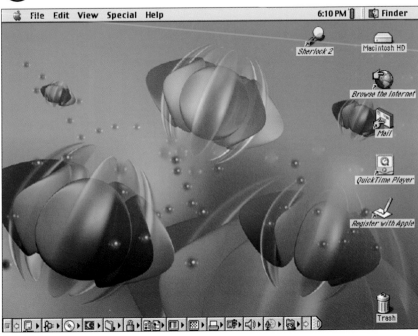

When you finish browsing the Internet, you need to quit Internet Explorer and end your connection to your Internet service provider.

1 To quit Internet Explorer, click the **File** menu and choose the **Quit** command.

2 Mac OS exits Internet Explorer and returns you to the desktop.

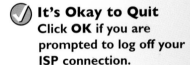

✓ **It's Okay to Quit**
Click **OK** if you are prompted to log off your ISP connection.

You can use Outlook Express to create, send, and receive email over the Internet. You can also send files by attaching them to your messages.

Task 15: Starting Outlook Express

✓ **What You Need**
To use Outlook Express, your iBook must be configured to connect and interact with an email service on the Internet.

✓ **Auto-disconnect Set to 10 Minutes**
iBook is set to disconnect after 10 minutes if there is no modem activity. If you need to use Outlook Express or Internet Explorer, you will automatically be reconnected when you start either of these applications.

✓ **From Internet Explorer**
To start Outlook Express from Internet Explorer 4, click the **Mail** button in the toolbar.

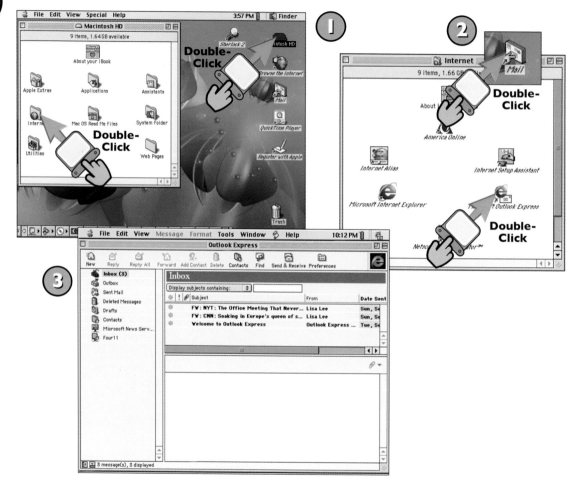

① Double-click the **Macintosh HD** icon, and then double-click the **Internet** folder icon.

② Double-click the **Microsoft Outlook Express** icon. You can also start Outlook Express by double-clicking the **Mail** icon on the desktop.

③ Outlook Express is started.

Task 16: Reading Mail

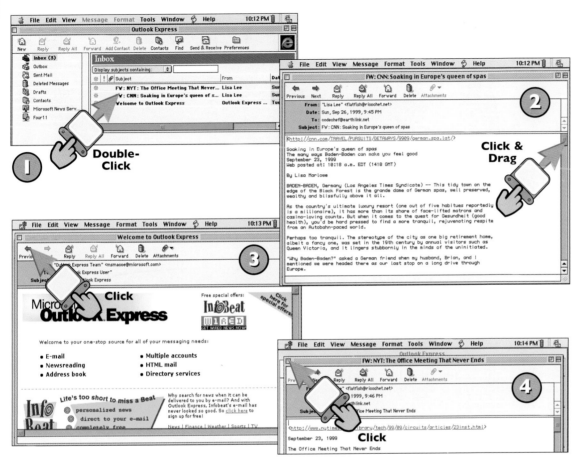

Double-Click

Click & Drag

Click

Click

When you start Outlook Express and get connected to your ISP, the messages are downloaded from your Internet mail server to your iBook. The number of messages in your inbox appears in parentheses next to the Inbox link in the folder list (the pane on the left side of the screen). The message list (the upper-right pane) lists all messages. Messages appearing in bold have not yet been read; you can open and read any message in the message list (whether it's bold or not). For more information about how to set up your email account, refer to Task 1, "Setting Up for the Internet."

✓ **Print Your Email**
To print an open message, choose **File**, select **Print**, and then click **Print** in the Print dialog box. To save an open message, choose **File** and then click **Save As**. Assign the message a filename and location, and then click the **Save** button.

1 In the message list of the Outlook Express window, double-click the message you want to read. You can also click on an email message to view it in the preview window.

2 The message you selected is displayed in its own window. You can scroll through the contents to read the message.

3 To display the next message in the message list, click the **Next** arrow; to display the previous message, click the **Previous** arrow.

4 To close the message, click the **Close** box.

End Task

Task 17: Responding to Mail

You can easily respond to a message you've received. Outlook Express completes the address and subject lines for you; you can then simply type the response.

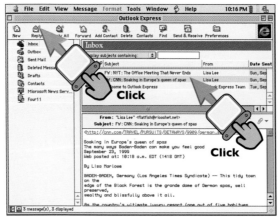

✓ Forward an Email Message

To forward a message, click the **Forward** command in the **Message** menu or click the **Forward** button in the toolbar. Type the address of the recipient, and then click in the message area and type any message you want to include. Finally, click the **Send** button.

✓ Use the Menu Command to Reply

You can also choose the **Reply to Sender** command in the **Message** menu.

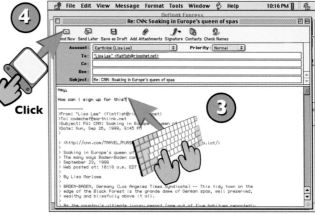

Display the message to which you want to reply, and click the **Reply** button in the toolbar.

The address and subject lines are completed, and the text of the original message is appended to the bottom of the reply message.

Type your message.

Click the **Send Now** button.

Task 18: Creating and Sending New Mail

Start Here

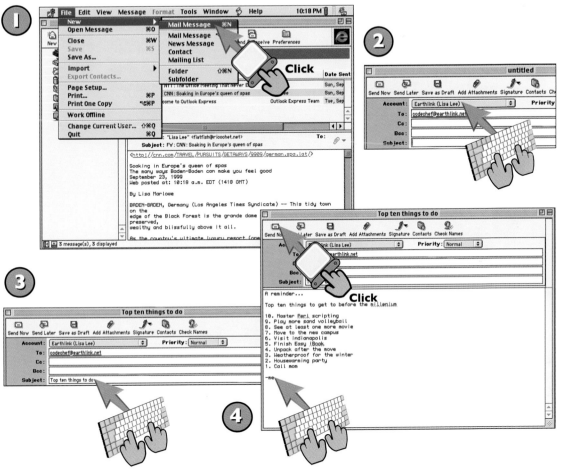

Click

Click

You can send a message to anyone with an Internet email address. Simply type the recipient's email address, a subject, and the message. You can also send carbon copies (**Cc**) and blind carbon copies (**Bcc**) of messages, as well as attach files to your messages.

✓ **Add Attachments to An Email**
To attach a file—such as a spreadsheet or word processing document—to your message, simply drag and drop the file to the open message window in Outlook Express. To add a file to an email, click **Message** and choose **Add Attachments**, or press **Command+E**. In the Add Attachments dialog box, choose the file you want to attach and click the **Add** button.

1 In the Outlook Express window, click **File**, choose **New**, and then click **Mail Message**.

2 Type the recipient's address (as well as any Cc and Bcc addresses). Addresses are in the format **username@domainname.ext** (for example, **afclisa@aol.com**).

3 Type a subject in the **Subject** text box, and then press **Tab**. The Tab key moves the cursor to the next text edit field in Outlook Express.

4 Type your message. When you've completed the message, click the **Send Now** button.

🛈 **AOL and Outlook Express**
If you have an AOL account, you cannot access your AOL email using Outlook Express.

End Task

Task 19: Subscribing to Newsgroups

A *newsgroup* is a collection of messages relating to a particular topic. Anyone can post a message, and anyone who subscribes to the newsgroup can view and respond to posted messages. You can join any of the hundreds of thousands of newsgroups on the Internet to exchange information and learn about hobbies, businesses, pets, computers, people of different walks of life, and more. You use Outlook Express for both email and newsgroups.

✓ Search for a Newsgroup Topic
You can search for a specific word—for example, **chocolate** or **saxophone**—by entering the word in the **Display Newsgroups Which Contain** text box.

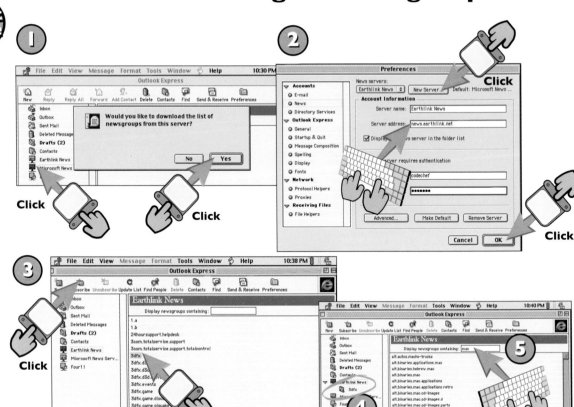

1 In the Outlook Express folder list, click the news server icon (in this case, **Microsoft News Server**). Click the **Yes** button to download the list of newsgroups from the server.

2 Click the **Preferences** button in the toolbar to configure your news server. Click the **New Server** button and type in the news server information for your ISP. Click **OK**.

3 After the list of newsgroups loads, click a newsgroup, and then click the **Subscribe** button in the toolbar.

4 An icon for the newsgroup you subscribed to (in this case, 3dfx) is added to the folder list below the EarthLink News news server entry.

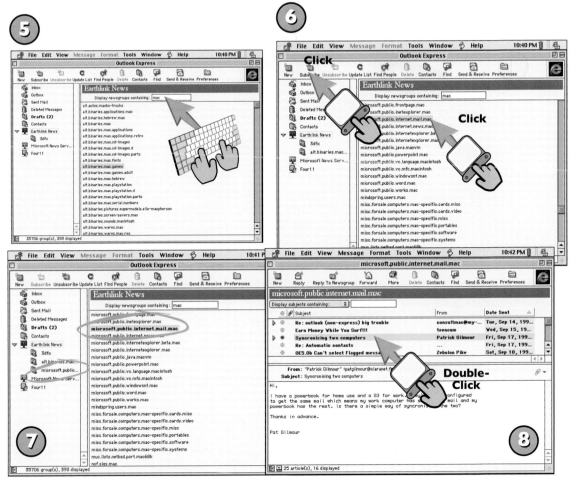

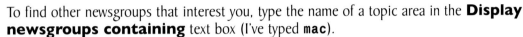

(5) To find other newsgroups that interest you, type the name of a topic area in the **Display newsgroups containing** text box (I've typed **mac**).

(6) Select a newsgroup from the **Newsgroups** list (in this case, **microsoft.public.internet.mail.mac**) and click the **Subscribe** button.

(7) The newsgroup icon is added below the **EarthLink News** news server icon in the Outlook Express folder list. The newsgroup also appears in bold text in the main news server list window.

(8) Click or double-click on a newsgroup icon in the folder list to view the messages for that newsgroup; double-click one of the messages to view it.

✓ **Unsubscribe from a Newsgroup**
To unsubscribe to a newsgroup, click the **Microsoft News Server** icon. Select the newsgroup to which you want to unsubscribe, and then click the **Unsubscribe** button.

✓ **Update Your Newsgroup List**
To update a newsgroup list, select a news server and click the **Update List** button in the toolbar.

Task 20: Reading Newsgroup Messages

After you have subscribed to a newsgroup, you can review any of the messages in that group. When a new message is posted, it starts a *thread*, and all responses are part of this thread. You can review all the current messages in the thread.

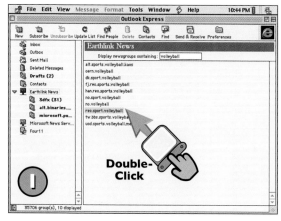

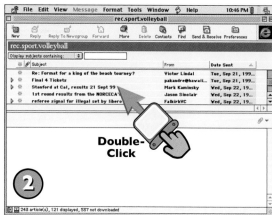

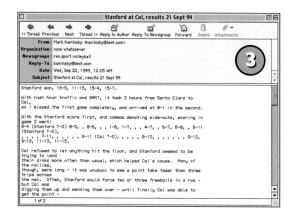

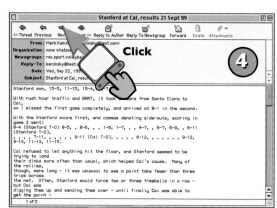

When to Unsubscribe
Keep in mind that newsgroups are not usually monitored. Many who participate in newsgroups have strong differences in opinion, but also agree to disagree while subscribing to the mail list. You might come across messages that you find offensive personally or ethically. If so, it may be best to unsubscribe from that newsgroup.

1 In the folder list of the Outlook Express window, double-click the newsgroup you want to review.

2 A list of that newsgroup's messages appears in the message list. Double-click the message you want to read.

3 The message is displayed in its own window.

4 To display the next message, click the **Next** arrow; to display the previous message, click the **Previous** arrow in the toolbar.

Task 21: Posting New Messages

Start Here

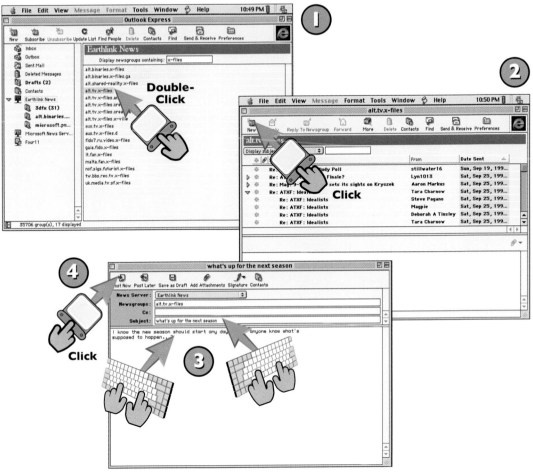

After you review messages, you might want to post your own opinion or ask a new question. One way to do this is to post a new message or start a new thread.

1 In the list of folders, select the newsgroup to which you want to post a new message.

2 Click the **New** button.

3 Enter subject line, review the addressee, and type your message.

4 Click the **Post Now** button on the toolbar.

Cancel If You Don't Want to Post a Message

If you change your mind about posting a message, you can cancel the message if you have not already clicked **Post**. Simply click the message's **Close** button and, when prompted, click the **Don't Save** button to confirm that you don't want to save the message.

End Task

Task 22: Replying to a Newsgroup Message

If you come across a newsgroup message to which you want to respond, you can post a reply to that message.

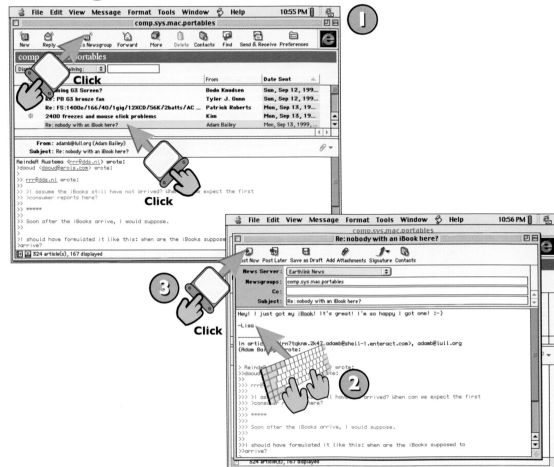

Reply Directly to a Message
You can also reply to messages privately by emailing the author as opposed to the entire group. To send such an email message, click the **Reply to Sender** button. Type your message, and click the **Send Now** button.

1 Display the message to which you want to reply, and then click the **Reply to Newsgroup** button.

2 Type your message.

3 Click the **Post Now** button.

Task 23: Quitting Outlook Express

Start Here

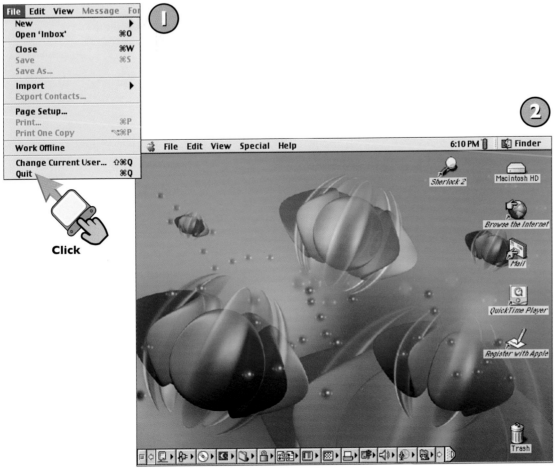

Click

When you have finished reading, writing, and sending email or posting to newsgroups, you can quit Outlook Express. Click the **OK** button if you are prompted to disconnect from your **ISP** when you quit Outlook Express.

① To quit, click the **File** menu and choose the **Quit** command.

② Mac OS exits Outlook Express and returns you to the desktop.

iBook Hardware

The Internet is growing at its fastest pace ever these days. One of the best ways to stay wired is to have a mobile, speedy, easy-to-use computer that lets you get to the Internet with, or without, the wires. iBook hardware consists of: a 12-inch bright, TFT SVGA active matrix, flat-screen display; a 24X CD-ROM drive; a 3.2GB IDE hard disk; a mono speaker; a 2D/3D ATI Rage mobility graphics chip set with 2X AGP; 4MB of SDRAM video memory; one USB port; a 16-bit stereo sound output port; a modem; and a 10/100 Ethernet port—plus, of course, the built-in keyboard and trackpad. Plus, you can use a fully charged battery for up to six hours before recharging it. You also can add an AirPort card in the card slot located below the keyboard.

A floppy drive is not included with an iBook, nor does it have traditional SCSI, serial, or ADB ports for connecting hard drives, keyboards, or a mouse. The best and the worst thing about an iBook is that it has a USB port. The best part is that one USB port can support as many as 127 devices. The worst part is that if you have older Macintosh hard drives or a scanner, you can't use them with your iBook, at least not without an adapter. You can purchase an adapter for ADB, SCSI, or serial devices, to get your Macintosh peripherals to work with the USB port. Plus, Macintosh developers are introducing more and more new USB products as more iBooks and Macintosh computers are taken home. In this part, you learn how to use these cool iBook hardware features.

Tasks

Task #		Page #
1	Adding a USB Device	62
2	Connecting a Printer	64
3	Replacing the Battery	65
4	Charging the Battery	66
5	Connecting to a Network	67
6	Networking with AirPort	68
7	Connecting Your Palm Device	70
8	Adding Memory	72
9	Checking iBook Memory	73
10	Troubleshooting iBook Hardware	74

Task 1: Adding a USB Device

USB (Universal Serial Bus) is new standard hardware port and software technology shipping on today's PCs and Macs. USB technology enables you to connect mice, keyboards, printers, joysticks, hubs, scanners, cameras, palm-computing devices, and hard drives to your iBook. You can swap USB devices without having to power off your iBook, and you can plug several USB devices into hubs to extend the number of devices attached to your iBook. To use most USB devices, you must install software—such as extensions, control panels, and drivers—in order to access the USB hardware. This task will explain how to connect an Iomega USB zip drive to your iBook.

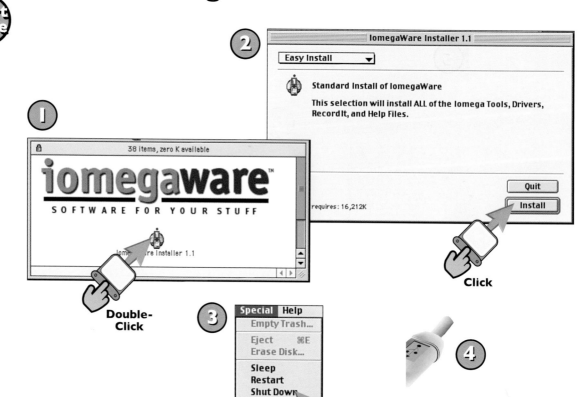

1. Insert the CD-ROM with USB software into your iBook, and double-click the installer icon.

2. Follow the prompts to install the USB software for your USB device.

3. Click the **Special** menu and choose **Shut Down** to power off your iBook.

4. Connect the USB and power cables to the USB device (in this case, a USB Type B connector connects to the zip drive).

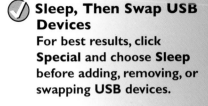

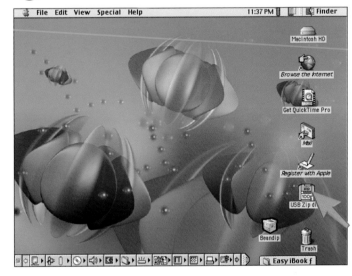

Sleep, Then Swap USB Devices

For best results, click **Special** and choose **Sleep** before adding, removing, or swapping **USB** devices.

Restart After USB Software Is Installed

You need to power off your iBook only after you first install the **USB** software. After the software is installed, you can swap **USB** devices.

When to Remove USB Software

If you decide you no longer want to use a certain **USB** device with your iBook, uninstall the **USB** software, then disconnect the cable and **USB** device from your iBook.

5 Connect the USB device to your iBook (in this case, insert the USB Type A connector end of the zip drive cable into your iBook's USB port).

6 Insert a zip cartridge into the drive.

7 Power on your iBook.

8 Use the zip disk in the same way you use your Macintosh hard drive to store files and folders.

There are several ways to connect a printer to your iBook—the easiest is over an Ethernet network. You can also purchase a printer that has a **USB** port. If you have a printer with a parallel connector, you can use a **USB-to-parallel port** adapter with a parallel printer as long as you also have Macintosh printer software that works with your printer.

(✓) **USB Adapters**
You can connect printers that use the serial port if you use a **USB-to-serial** port adapter.

(✓) **Uninstalling Printer Software**
To remove a printer, remove the printer software, and then disconnect the printer cables from the other **USB** devices connected to your iBook.

Task 2: Connecting a Printer

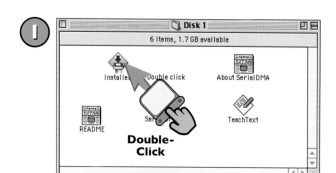

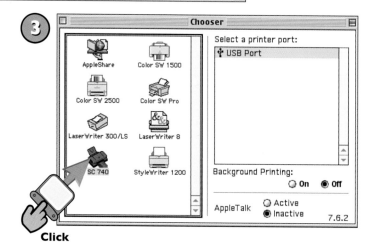

① Install the printer software on your iBook (in this case, the software is for the Epson Stylus Color 740 printer).

② After you physically connect the printer to your iBook, power on your iBook and the printer.

③ Open the **Chooser** and select the printer (in this case the **SC 740** printer driver). Then print a document to the printer to ensure that it works.

Task 3: Replacing the Battery

Start Here

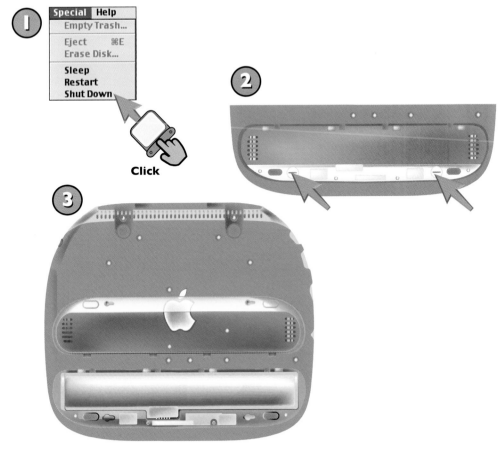

Special	Help
Empty Trash...	
Eject	⌘E
Erase Disk...	
Sleep	
Restart	
Shut Down	

Click

The battery in your iBook gives it the power to go—for about six hours. As the battery wears down, you can either plug it back into a wall-based power outlet to recharge it, or you can plug it into a wall-based outlet and swap batteries. Be sure to put your iBook to sleep before swapping out the battery. This task explains how to replace your iBook's battery.

① Click **Special** and choose **Shut Down** to power off your iBook.

② Turn your iBook over and turn the two screws located toward the bottom-front of the iBook.

③ Remove the current battery, put in a new one, and re-tighten the screws.

✓ **Keep a Second Battery Around**
Your iBook uses a lithium ion battery. It's a good idea to keep a spare battery around, especially if you use your iBook for extended periods of time.

✓ **You Have the Power**
Plug the power cable into a wall power source, then connect your power adapter to your iBook before changing the battery.

End Task

Task 4: Charging the Battery

One of the great things about your iBook is that you can charge the battery whenever you like. You don't need to wait for the charge to run down or run an application before charging the battery. Just plug the iBook's power adapter into a wall power source, then into your iBook, and your battery will start recharging.

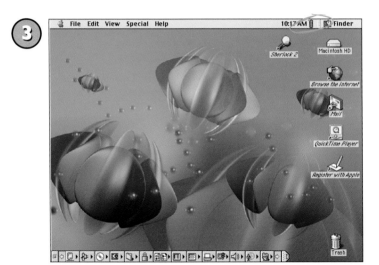

✓ **When to Charge**
When you purchase a new battery, it usually is not fully charged. You should let your iBook sit for at least a few hours to let the battery fully charge. After that, you can recharge it as often as you like.

✓ **Learn More About Your Battery**
For more information about how to work with your iBook's battery, see Part 10, Task 2, "Viewing a Battery's Life."

① Connect a power cable to your iBook's power adapter. Connect the other end of the power cable to a wall power source.

② Connect the cable from your power adapter to your iBook and recharge the battery.

③ Start up your iBook and check the battery level in the menu bar. After the battery is recharged, your iBook is ready to be used while you're on the go.

Task 5: Connecting to a Network

Start Here

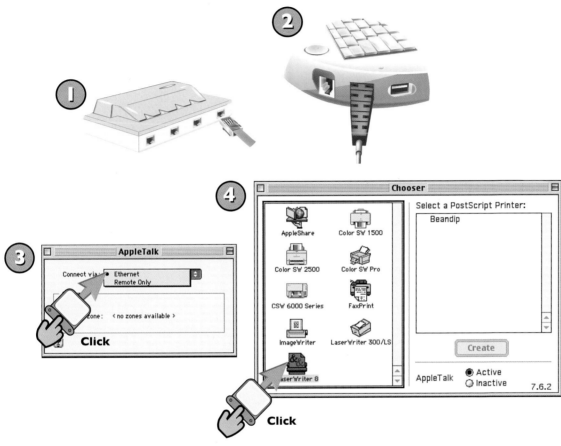

To add your iBook to a 10/100BASE-T Ethernet network, simply plug in the 10BASE-T connector into the iBook's 10/100BASE-T port. If you are setting up an Ethernet network, you will need a 10BASE-T or 100BASE-T Ethernet hub to connect with each computer on the network.

✓ Ethernet Versus Modem Port
The 10BASE-T connector looks similar to a telephone or modem connector, but is slightly larger.

✓ Crossover Cables
It is possible to use a 10BASE-T cable to connect two computers together to create a network between them, or to connect your iBook to a printer. However, you need to purchase a special patch cable—called a *crossover cable*—that twists one of the wires inside the Ethernet jack so you can bypass using an Ethernet hub. A traditional 10BASE-T cable will not work.

① Plug one end of the 10BASE-T connector into an Ethernet hub. Connect any other network devices to the hub, such as another computer or a printer.

② Connect the other end into your iBook's Ethernet port.

③ Open the AppleTalk control panel (click the **Apple** menu, choose **Control Panels**, and then choose **AppleTalk**), click the **Connect via** pop-up menu, and choose **Ethernet**.

④ Click the **Apple** menu, select **Chooser**, and then click the **LaserWriter8** icon.

Task 6: Networking with AirPort

AirPort is iBook's most amazing new technology. It brings wireless networking to your iBook, with the ease and use of a Macintosh. Although the AirPort card is not included with your iBook, it is an affordable must-have accessory if you have access to a network. The AirPort card enables an iBook to connect to an AirPort Base Station if the AirPort card is within 150 feet of the Base Station, which in turn is connected via Ethernet or modem to a network or to the Internet.

✓ **Can't Block This**
AirPort uses radio waves to transmit your network data. So, your iBook does not need a direct, unblocked connection to the AirPort base unit to connect to its network.

✓ **AirPort Software**
If you purchased your AirPort card separately from your iBook, install the AirPort software onto your iBook, and then follow the steps in this task to set up your iBook for the AirPort.

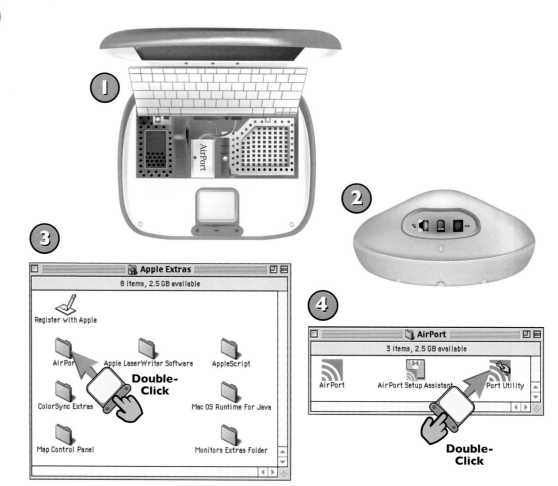

1. Install the AirPort card into your iBook.

2. Connect the Ethernet or modem connection to the AirPort Base Station.

3. Click on the **Macintosh HD** icon, and then double-click the **Apple Extras** folder. Double-click the **AirPort** folder icon.

4. Double-click the **AirPort Utility** icon.

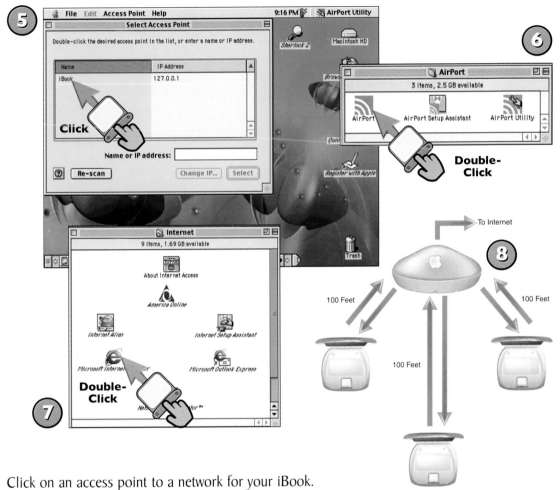

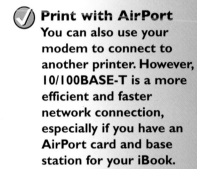

5 Click on an access point to a network for your iBook.

6 Double-click the **AirPort** application icon.

7 Double-click the **Microsoft Internet Explorer** icon and go to a Web site.

8 Take your iBook within AirPort base range and work with your iBook while connected to the network.

End Task

✓ **Print with AirPort**
You can also use your modem to connect to another printer. However, 10/100BASE-T is a more efficient and faster network connection, especially if you have an AirPort card and base station for your iBook.

❗ **Check for a Green Light**
If you are unable to select Ethernet in the AppleTalk control panel, check the Ethernet cables and make sure the light on the Ethernet port is lit on your Ethernet hub (indicating that it senses a connection). Try unplugging and replugging the 10BASE-T connector on your iBook and on the hub to make sure it is connected correctly.

Task 7: Connecting Your Palm Device

Why use a Palm device if you have an iBook? Why not? Palm devices are even smaller than an iBook, and can come in handy when you don't have your iBook ready to go. This task shows you how to connect your Palm device to your iBook.

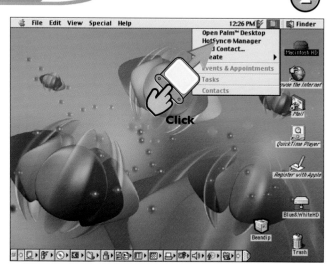

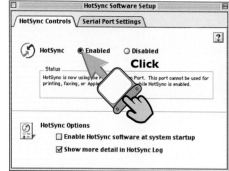

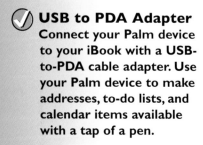

✅ **USB to PDA Adapter**
Connect your Palm device to your iBook with a USB-to-PDA cable adapter. Use your Palm device to make addresses, to-do lists, and calendar items available with a tap of a pen.

 Plug the USB cable from your Palm charger into your iBook. You can also use a USB-to-PDA cable adapter with your Palm cradle cable.

 Click the **Palm Desktop** icon in the menu bar and choose the **HotSync Manager** menu command.

 Click on the **HotSync Controls** tab. Then click on the **Enabled** option button.

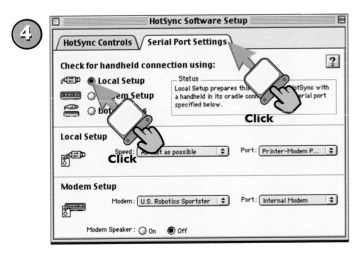

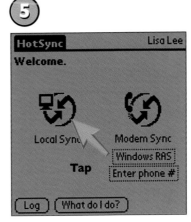

4 Click on the **Serial Port Settings** tab and choose the **Local Setup** option button, and select a port from the **Port** pop-up menu.

5 Tap on the **Local Sync** button on your Palm device. If your iBook is on a network, tap on the **Network Sync** button. Your Palm device will synchronize its data with your iBook.

6 Click on the **Palm Desktop** icon, and choose **Open Palm Desktop** to view the data from your Palm device.

Task 8: Adding Memory

DRAM (dynamic random-access memory) and SDRAM (synchronous dynamic RAM) are the two key kinds of memory in your iBook. DRAM (memory) is used to run Mac OS and any Mac OS applications. SDRAM video memory also works with Mac OS and applications, but does so to bring more colors—at a fast rate—to your screen. Your iBook comes with 4MB of SDRAM video memory, which is a healthy amount to have on any computer. Your iBook also comes with 32MB of DRAM, which you might consider upgrading to 64MB or 96MB. Of course, if you are able to do all your computing with 32MB, then you can skip this task. Your iBook uses synchronous dynamic random-access memory modules that are supplied in small outline dual inline memory modules (SO-DIMMs). The iBook logic board has one slot for memory. It contains a 32MB memory chip and its expansion slot can be used to add more memory.

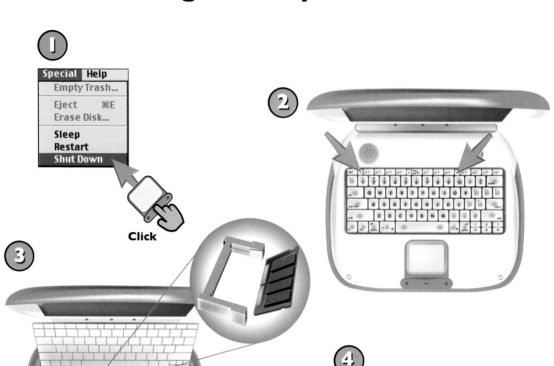

Start Here

Click

Power off your iBook.

Press down on the tabs at the top of the iBook keyboard and lift it open. (Go to **http://til.info.apple.com/techinfo.nsf/artnum/n60427** for Apple's detailed instructions.)

Install the memory into the empty socket on the logic board, and then close the iBook case.

Power on your iBook.

End Task

Task 9: Checking iBook Memory

Start Here

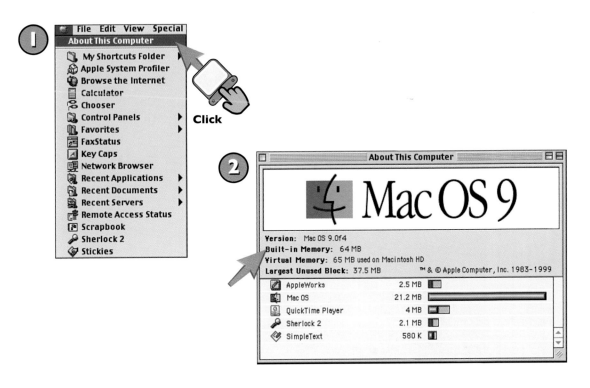

Click

Whether you have or have not added more memory into your iBook, you can always find out exactly how much memory is already there. Keep in mind that Mac OS is always running. So, if you are considering purchasing more memory, check to see how much memory Mac OS is using on your iBook, then add any additional memory required by the applications you will be using.

① Click the **Apple** menu and choose **About This Computer**.

② The amount of built-in memory should reflect the amount of memory you have just installed.

 Two Kinds of Memory
The iBook can use two kinds of memory: physical and virtual. Physical memory is the actual DIMM referred to in the previous task. Virtual memory is a software feature in which your hard disk is used to store data that is used in conjunction with the physical memory installed in your iBook.

End Task

Task 10: Troubleshooting iBook Hardware

In general, adding software and hardware to an iBook is easy and trouble-free. When an iBook does appear to have some sort of problem, don't panic. There are some easy steps you can take to isolate the cause of the problem. The first thing to try (if the problem does not involve data loss) is to reproduce the problem.

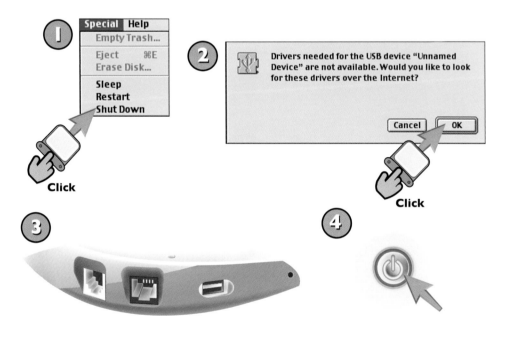

Help Is on the Menu
Don't forget about the **Help** menu on your iBook. The information in the Help Center, Tutorial, and **Mac OS Help** software are invaluable.

Check for Software Updates
You should periodically check Apple's Web site (www.apple.com) for software updates for your iBook.

① Power off your iBook. Connect a USB device to your iBook.

② Power on your iBook. If you do not have USB software installed, you will see a dialog box asking you to install the software for the USB device (in this case, the software for the USB zip drive—see Task 1).

③ If you have installed all software to use a USB device with your iBook, disconnect any additional USB devices from your iBook.

④ Power on your iBook and try to reproduce the problem. If it is no longer reproducible, check to see if each USB cable works correctly.

Next Step

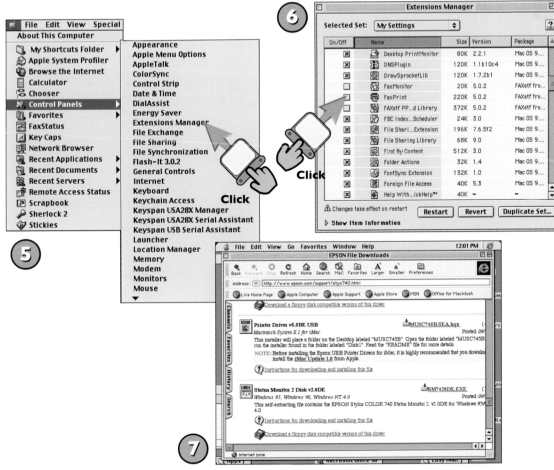

Learn Even More About Your iBook
For more information about maintaining your iBook, see Part 10, "Maintaining Your iBook."

Swap Cables
You might want to use a cable from a working computer to make sure you are not using a cable that does not work correctly.

Hold Down That Shift Key at Startup
If the problem continues to occur after you have removed any additional hardware on your iBook, try starting up your iBook with the **Shift** key pressed down to disable extensions to see whether the problem goes away. If it does, you might have an extensions conflict in your System folder.

⑤ If the problem still occurs, click the **Apple** menu, choose **Control Panels**, and then choose **Extensions Manager**.

⑥ Turn off any USB-related software, including software for any ADB, serial, or network devices, by deselecting the boxes next to their names.

⑦ Restart your iBook and see whether the problem goes away. If not, check for a software update from the manufacturer's Web site (in this case, Epson).

Using iBook Applications

Applications, also called programs, let you do specific tasks with your iBook. Applications are easy to open and use. You can create and save data in a file with different names and in any particular location on your hard drive. You can open a document at any time to view, edit, or print it.

There are other kinds of software, such as control panels, extensions, shared libraries, and desk accessories. But of all these kinds of software, applications provide the richest set of features that let you do some of the most amazing things with your iBook. Part of the magic of applications is that they can use shared libraries as well as settings in control panels and extensions to optimize a particular feature in the application. The best part about using applications on your iBook is that almost all of them use the same, great, easy-to-use interface the Macintosh is famous for.

Tasks

Task #		Page #
1	Starting an Application from the Apple Menu	78
2	Starting an Application from an Alias	80
3	Starting an Application and Opening a Document	81
4	Switching Between Applications	82
5	Switching Between Open Documents	83
6	Saving a Document	84
7	Opening a Document	86
8	Creating a New Document	88
9	Selecting Text	89
10	Copying Text	90
11	Moving Text	92
12	Copying Data Between Documents	94
13	Closing a Document	96
14	Quitting an Application	97

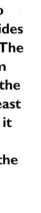

Task 1: Starting an Application from the Apple Menu

Start Here

There are many ways to start an application besides double-clicking its icon. The easiest is to start it from the **Apple** menu. After the application has run at least once, you can also start it from the **Recent Applications** folder in the **Apple** menu.

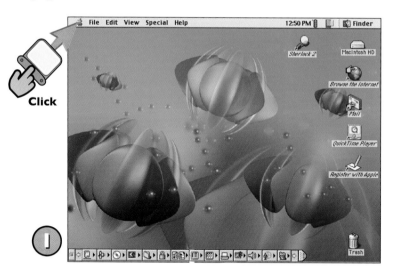

Click

①

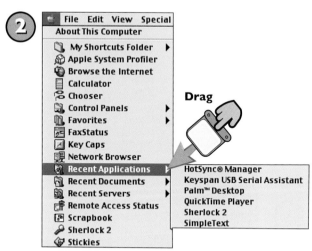
②

Drag

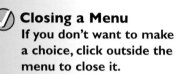

Closing a Menu
If you don't want to make a choice, click outside the menu to close it.

① Click the **Apple** menu.

② Select the **Recent Applications** menu item.

Next Step

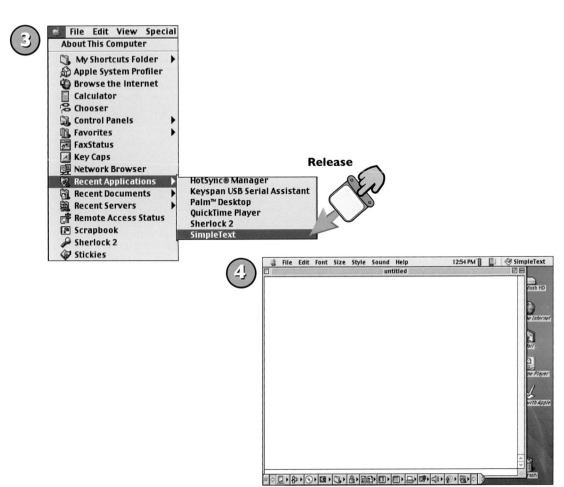

Release

Select the application you want to start.

The application opens in its own window.

Recent Applications Limit

Click on the **Apple** menu, choose **Control Panels**, and then select **Apple Menu Options.** Type in a number between **0** and **9999** to set the maximum number of applications listed in the **Recent Applications** folder in the iBook's Apple menu. You can also set limits for **Recent Documents** and **Servers** that appear in the Apple menu, too.

End Task

Task 2: Starting an Application from an Alias

In addition to the Apple menu, you can also start an application by clicking on its alias. An *alias* is an icon that points to an original file, folder, or networked hard disk. You can create an alias, or shortcut, to an application. Then double-click the alias whenever you want to start the application.

Start Here

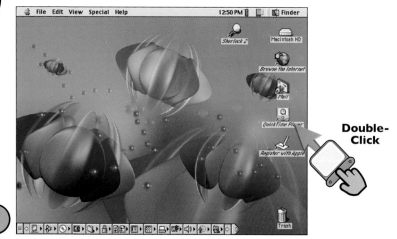

Double-Click

1

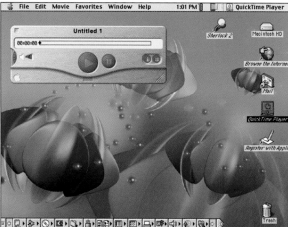

2

1

Double-click the **QuickTime Player** application alias icon on the desktop.

2

The application starts and displays its own menu bar and window.

Learn More About Aliases

To find out how to create an alias to an application, see Task 1, "Adding Aliases," of Part 8, "Setting Up Applications."

End Task

Task 3: Starting an Application and Opening a Document

Start Here

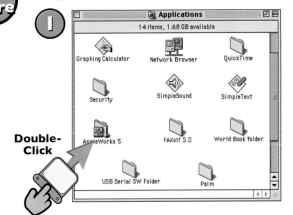

Double-Click

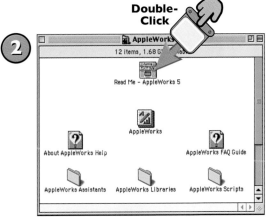

Double-Click

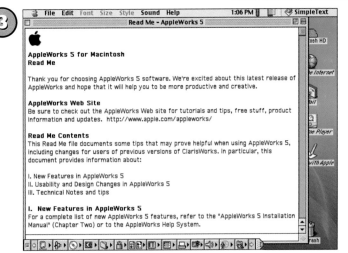

If you want to work on a document you recently created in AppleWorks, you can use an alias to both start an application and open a document. You can also start the document and its related application by clicking on the **Apple** menu and choosing the document in the Recent Documents folder. It can show anywhere from 0 to 9999 recently opened documents.

① Double-click the **Macintosh HD** icon, and then double-click the **Applications** folder icon. Double-click the **AppleWorks 5** icon.

② Double-click the **Read Me—AppleWorks 5** icon.

③ The application for that document starts (in this case, SimpleText), and the document is opened.

✓ **Can't Find an Application?**
Whether you download a file from the Internet, or get an enclosure in email, it might have been created by an application that is not installed on your iBook. Try opening the file with SimpleText. If you use a lot of files regularly, you might want to consider purchasing a document translator.

End Task

Task 4: Switching Between Applications

Working with more than one application at a time can be like working in a jungle. Fortunately, the Applications menu provides a neat list of which applications are currently open on your iBook. You can switch between applications to share data or simply keep busy.

✓ **Applications and Memory**

The number of programs you can have open at any one time depends on the amount of RAM (random access memory) in your system. The amount of hard drive space can also affect how many applications you can run at the same time.

✓ **What Applications Are Open?**

You can tell what programs are open by viewing the **Applications** menu. The Applications menu is located in the upper-right corner of the iBook's menu bar. Each menu item is an application currently running on your iBook.

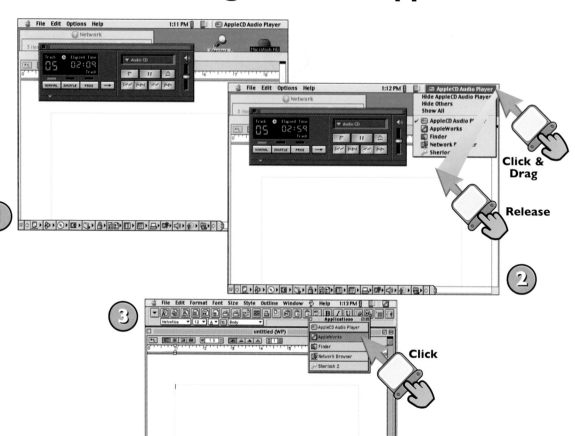

Start Here

Click & Drag

Release

Click

① Start more than one application. The name of the active application (in this case, **AppleCD Audio Player**) appears on the menu bar.

② Click the **Applications** menu button to see a list of other open applications. Click and drag the **Applications** menu away from the menu bar to turn it into a floating window.

③ Click **AppleWorks**. AppleWorks becomes the active application.

End Task

Task 5: Switching Between Open Documents

Start Here

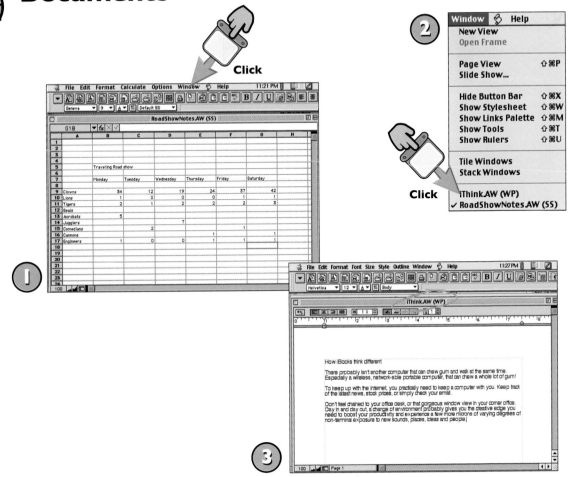

Click

Click

Most applications let you create and open more than one document at a time. To open a document, click **File** and choose the **Open** command. You can open as many documents as your iBook's memory, hard disk, and application will allow. Then you can switch between any of the open documents.

✓ **Applications Versus Documents**
Don't confuse switching between documents with switching between applications. For more information, refer to Task 4, "Switching Between Applications." When you switch between documents you remain in the same application. Switching between applications is the task of selecting a different application from the Applications menu.

✓ **Active Window Behavior**
The active document's title bar will be a different color from the other documents' title bars.

① Click on the **Window** menu in AppleWorks.

② Notice the active document has a check mark next to its name in the menu. Click the document you want to switch to (in this case, the document is called **iThink.AW**).

③ The document you just selected in the **Window** menu becomes the active document.

Task 6: Saving a Document

Most applications let you type, draw, copy, or paste to your heart's content. If you want to take a break and store your changes, you need to save the document to your hard disk. The first time you save a file, you need to give it a name and save it to a folder (or location) on your hard disk. This task shows you how to save a document in AppleWorks.

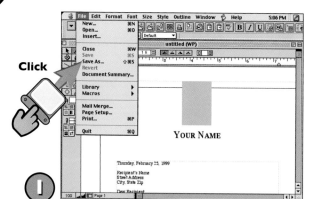

Click

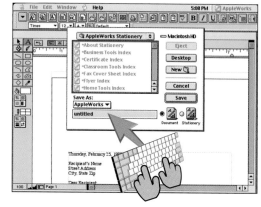

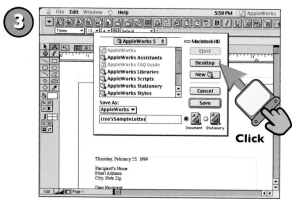

Click

✓ **Save Command**
After you've saved and named a file, you can simply click **File** and select **Save** to resave that file to the same location with the same name. Any changes you have made since the last save are reflected in the file.

① Click **File**, and then click **Save As**.

② The application might suggest a name for the file. You can either accept this name or type a new name.

③ Click on the **Desktop** button to save the document to another disk or network server.

Next Step

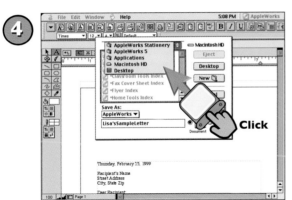

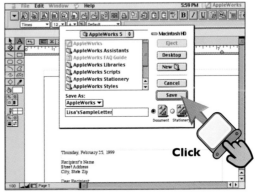

Click

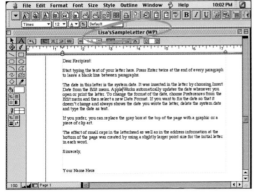

Click

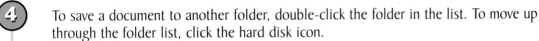

(4) To save a document to another folder, double-click the folder in the list. To move up through the folder list, click the hard disk icon.

(5) Click the **Save** button.

(6) The application saves the file and returns to the document window. The document name appears in the window title bar.

✓ **Save As Command**
To save the file with a different name or in a different location, use the **Save As** command in the **File** menu and enter a different filename or folder.

End Task

Task 7: Opening a Document

You can open documents created on any other Macintosh, and in some cases, you can also open documents created on other computers. The whole point of saving a document is so that you can access it later. Click on the **File** menu and choose **Open** to open any document you want to view.

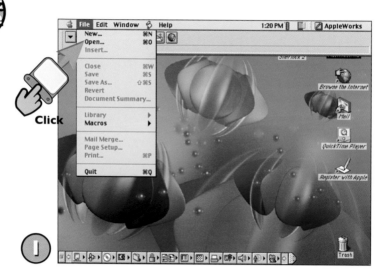

Click

Need a Clue?

If you can't find the file you want to work with, it could be because you did not save it where you thought you did. Try looking in a different drive or folder. If you still can't find it, try searching for the file (for more information about searching for files, see Part 5, "Working with Disks, Folders, and Files").

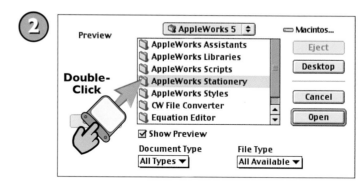

Double-Click

(1) Click **File** and then select **Open**.

(2) If the file you want is listed in the dialog box, double-click it and skip the remaining steps.

Next Step

Click

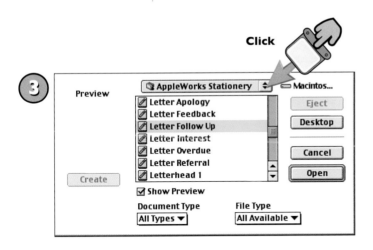

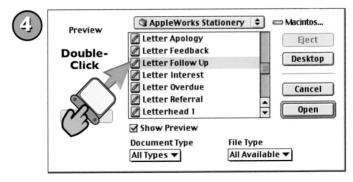

③ If the file is not listed, click the drop-down list and select another folder to view. Double-click the folder name where the file was saved.

④ Double-click the file you want to open.

Task 8: Creating a New Document

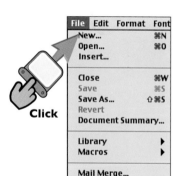

Applications create documents, which enable you to store all kinds of data, similar to a blank sheet of paper waiting for you to write something on it. Most smaller applications, such as SimpleText, automatically create a new document when you start the application. AppleWorks enables you to create text, paint, and create database and spreadsheet documents all within the same application. More complex applications, such as FileMaker Pro and Microsoft Word, add more features and enable you to create larger, more complex documents.

 Duplicate an Existing File

You can also create a new document file by creating a copy of another document file in Finder. Just click on a file and then choose the **File** menu and select the **Duplicate** menu command or simply press **Command+D**.

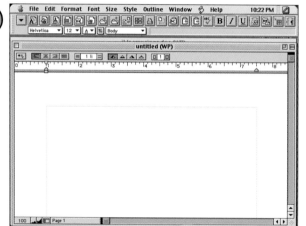

Click **File**, and then click the **New** command.

In the AppleWorks window, select the kind of application you want to use. Be sure the **Create New Document** option button is selected. Click the **OK** button.

A new, blank document is displayed.

Task 9: Selecting Text

Start Here

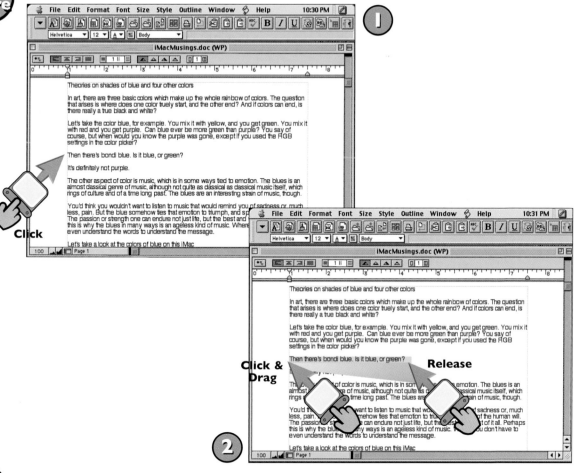

1

Click

Click & Drag

Release

2

One of the basic skills you need for working with data is knowing how to select what you want to work on. After you select the text you want, you can delete it, copy it, move it, change its appearance, and so on. If you prefer to use your iBook keyboard, you can also select text using keyboard controls.

① Click at the start of the text you want to select.

② Hold down the mouse button and drag across the text, then release the mouse button. The selected text appears highlighted.

✓ **Select Text Using the Keyboard**
If you prefer to use the keyboard to select text, hold down the **Shift** key and use the arrow keys to highlight the text you want to select.

✓ **Deselecting Text**
To deselect text, click outside the selected text.

End Task

Task 10: Copying Text

Even though you might think different, one of the best forms of flattery is seeing your work copied. One of the most common editing tasks is to copy text, then paste it into the current document or into another document.

Start Here

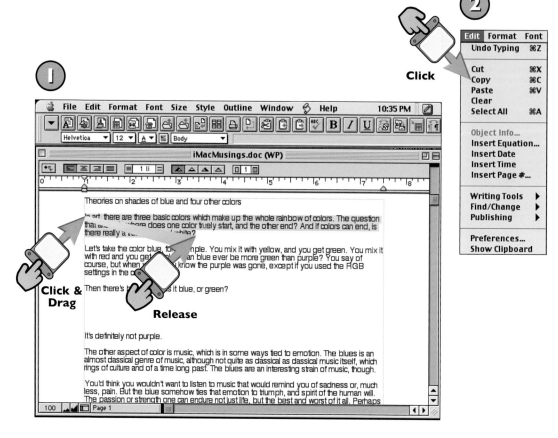

Click

2

Edit	Format	Font
Undo Typing		⌘Z
Cut		⌘X
Copy		⌘C
Paste		⌘V
Clear		
Select All		⌘A
Object Info...		
Insert Equation...		
Insert Date		
Insert Time		
Insert Page #...		
Writing Tools		▶
Find/Change		▶
Publishing		▶
Preferences...		
Show Clipboard		

Click & Drag

Release

Copying Data

To copy data from one open document to another, select the text, click the **Edit** menu, and choose **Copy**. Then use the **Window** menu to choose a document. Finally, select a location in the document where you want to paste the text. Then click **Edit** and choose **Paste**.

1 Select the text you want to copy.

2 Click **Edit**, and then select the **Copy** command. iBook copies the text and places it on the Clipboard, a temporary holding place.

Next Step

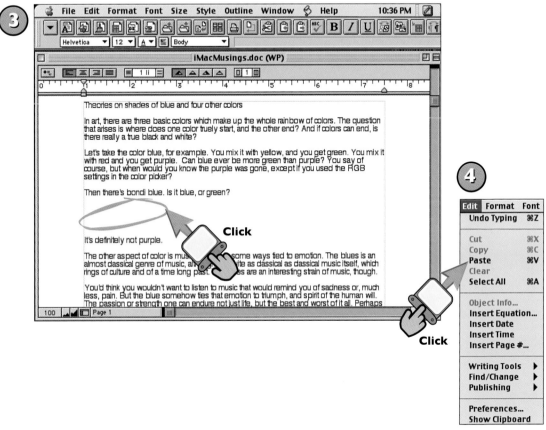

③ Click the spot in the document where you want to put the copied data.

④ Click **Edit**, and then select the **Paste** command.

Learn More About Copying Data

For more information about copying data between documents, see Task 12, "Copying Data Between Documents."

End Task

Task 11: Moving Text

Text in your documents is almost as mobile as your iBook. You can move text within a document or from one document to another. Moving text is similar to copying text except the text is deleted from its original location.

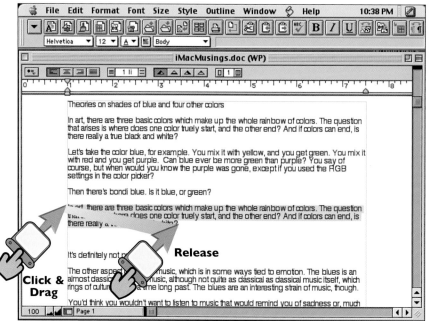

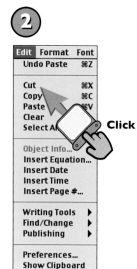

✓ **Learn More About Moving Data**
For help on moving data from one document to another, see Task 12, "Copying Data Between Documents."

✓ **Undo a Paste Command**
You can undo a paste command if you change your mind. Click **Edit** and then select the **Undo Paste** command to remove the text you just pasted.

 Select the text you want to move.

Click **Edit**, and then click the **Cut** command. iBook deletes the data from the document and places it in the Clipboard, a temporary holding spot.

Next Step

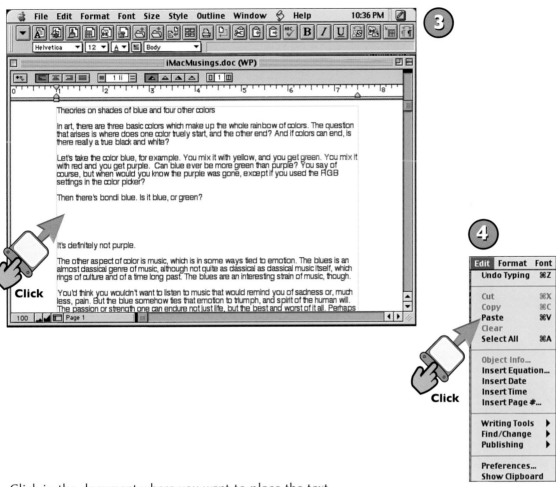

Click

Click

③ Click in the document where you want to place the text.

④ Click **Edit**, and then select the **Paste** command.

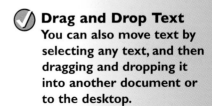
Drag and Drop Text
You can also move text by selecting any text, and then dragging and dropping it into another document or to the desktop.

Task 12: Copying Data Between Documents

You can copy data from a document in one application and paste it into another document in another application to save time typing. Not only can you copy text, but you can copy spreadsheets, images, charts, clip art, and so on. Get more work done with your iBook by copying and pasting text and graphics in your documents.

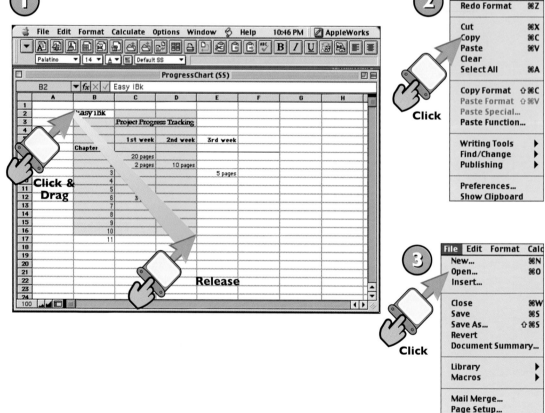

✓ **Copy and Paste Shortcuts**
You can also use the keyboard shortcut **Command+C** to copy and the keyboard shortcut **Command+V** to paste. Also look for toolbar buttons for **Copy** and **Paste** buttons.

1. Select the data you want to copy.

2. Click **Edit**, and then click the **Copy** command.

3. Click **File**, and then click the **Open** command.

Next Step

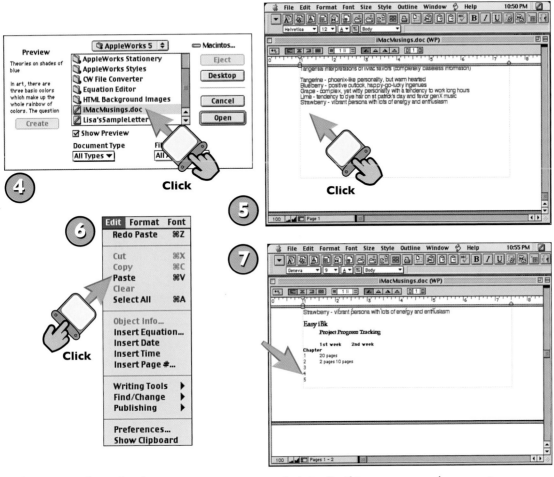

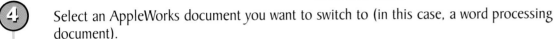

(4) Select an AppleWorks document you want to switch to (in this case, a word processing document).

(5) In the word processing document, click the location where you want to paste the copied data.

(6) Click **Edit**, and then click the **Paste** command.

(7) The data is pasted into the document.

 What? No Paste Command?
If the Paste command is grayed out, it means you have not copied anything. Be sure to click **Edit** and select the **Copy** command before you try to paste the text or graphic.

Task 13: Closing a Document

After you save a document, it remains open so that you can continue to work on it. You can easily close a document by clicking on its Close box. If you are no longer using a document, you should close it to free up memory and reduce window clutter.

✓ **Closing a Document Does Not Quit an Application**
If you click the **Close** button on the document window, the application name remains visible in the menu bar and the application is still open. To quit the application, press **Command+Q**.

✓ **Document Window Controls**
In most programs, the document window has its own set of controls— separate from the controls for the application window. You can move, resize, restore, collapse, and close the document window using the skills you learned in Part 1, "Getting Started."

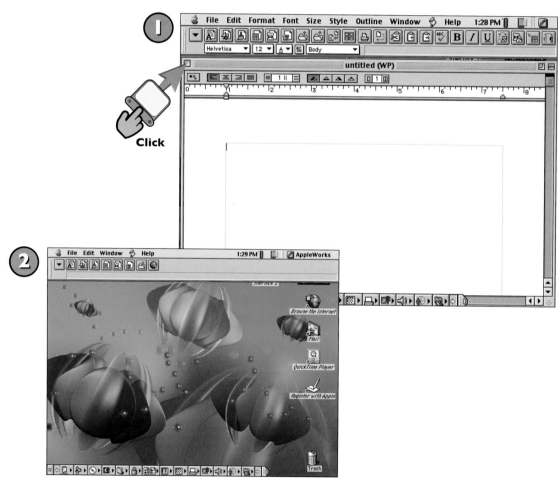

Click

① Click the **Close** button.

② The document is closed, but the application remains open. You can create a new document or open an existing document or you can close the application by selecting **File** and then **Quit**.

Task 14: Quitting an Application

Start Here

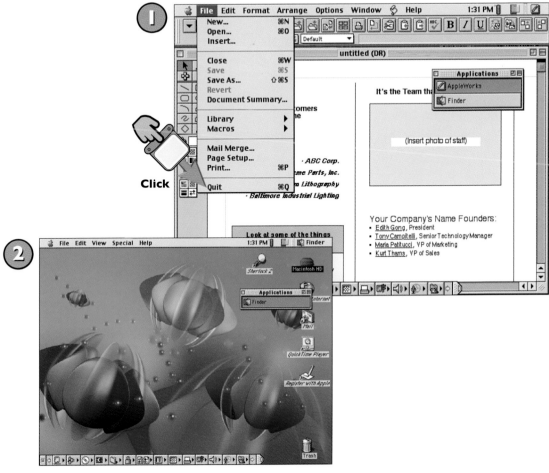

Click

Click **File** and then click **Quit**.

The application is closed. Notice that the taskbar button for AppleWorks has disappeared from the floating Applications menu.

When you finish working in an application, you should close it to free system memory. Too many open applications can occupy both memory and hard disk space on your iBook. This can slow down your iBook and use up more battery power.

✓ **Quit Command Shortcut**
To close an application, you can also press **Command+Q**.

✓ **Save Documents Before You Quit an Application**
If you have not saved a file and choose to close that file's application, a message box appears asking whether you want to save the file. If you do, click **Yes**; if not, click **No**. If you want to return to the document, click **Cancel**.

✓ **Don't Quit, Just Sleep**
If you use an application frequently, you can leave it open and put your iBook to sleep instead of quitting the application.

Working with Disks, Folders, and Files

All the software you use on your iBook is stored on your hard disk. When you start an application, some of its code runs in memory, but the application file is stored on your hard disk. A hard disk is similar to a big filing cabinet. Mac OS creates a directory and tracks every file and folder you create and delete on your hard disk. As you use your iBook, Mac OS and any applications you use create additional files in addition to any document files or folders you might create yourself.

The more you work on your computer, the more files and folders you add. After a while your computer will become cluttered and you'll need a way to keep these files organized. Mac OS provides features that can help you find, organize, and manage your files. You can copy, rename, move, delete unnecessary files, and more.

Tasks

Task #		Page #
1	Navigating Your Hard Disk with the Trackpad	100
2	Opening and Closing Folders	101
3	Changing the View for a Folder	102
4	Sorting Window Contents	104
5	Changing View Options	105
6	Finding Files and Folders with Sherlock 2	106
7	Using Sherlock 2 to Search File Contents	108
8	Selecting Folders or Files	110
9	Selecting All Folders and Files	112
10	Creating a Folder	113
11	Copying Folders and Files	114
12	Moving Folders and Files	115
13	Renaming Folders and Files	116
14	Creating a Pop-up Folder Window	117
15	Creating an Alias to a File or Folder	118
16	Changing a Folder or File Label	119
17	Synchronizing Folders and Files with Your Desktop	120
18	Deleting Folders and Files	121
19	Emptying the Trash	122

You can view the contents of your hard disk in a variety of ways. The easiest way is to use what Apple calls a *click-and-a-half* on your hard disk icon. This changes the arrow cursor into a magnifying glass, and then opens any hard disk icon or folder over which you hold the magnifying glass. Using a click-and-a-half, you can navigate your hard disk without having to open and close windows to get to what you want.

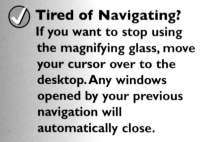

Tired of Navigating?
If you want to stop using the magnifying glass, move your cursor over to the desktop. Any windows opened by your previous navigation will automatically close.

What's a Click-and-a-Half?
A click-and-a-half is the same as a double-click, except you keep the mouse button held down on the second click.

Task 1: Navigating Your Hard Disk with the Trackpad

Start Here

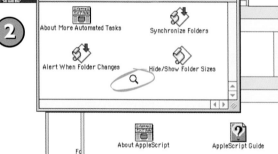

 Click once on the hard drive icon on your desktop, then click again and hold down the mouse button. The hard drive's window will automatically open.

 Open any folders in the window by moving the magnifying glass cursor over the folder icon.

End Task

Task 2: Opening and Closing Folders

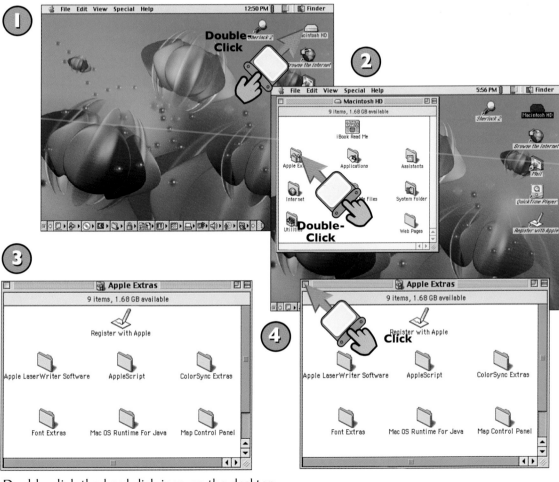

Folders contain files, applications, or other items that you can use to do work in Mac OS. You can display the contents of a folder to work with the files—move a file, create a shortcut icon, start a program, and so on. When you've finished working with a folder window, close it.

✓ **Window Controls**
Remember that you can use the scrollbars to scroll through the window. Also, you can move and resize the window as needed.

✓ **Navigate a Window**
Hold down the **Command** key, and then click in any window. The arrow cursor changes into a hand, and you can navigate within a window as you drag the cursor up, down, or sideways within the open window.

✓ **Option-Close All Windows**
To close a window and all its associated windows, hold down the **Option** key and click the **Close** button.

1 Double-click the hard disk icon on the desktop.

2 Each icon you see represents a folder on your hard drive. Double-click any of the folders.

3 Each file folder icon represents groups of files and folders. Each page icon represents a document.

4 Click on the window's **Close** box to close the folder.

Task 3: Changing the View for a Folder

There are three kinds of window views. The default view is Icons. The List view provides the most infor-mation and the most flexi-bility for displaying file and folder information. The Buttons view is another way you can view files and folders on your hard drive. When you select a window view, it affects only the frontmost window you have selected in Finder.

Start Here

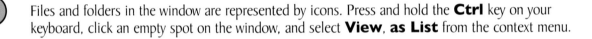

✓ **Desktop View Options**
Any folder window can be viewed in Icons, List, or Buttons mode. However, you can view icons on the desktop only as icons or as buttons.

1 Double-click the hard disk icon on the desktop.

2 Files and folders in the window are represented by icons. Press and hold the **Ctrl** key on your keyboard, click an empty spot on the window, and select **View**, **as List** from the context menu.

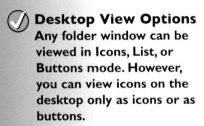

Next Step

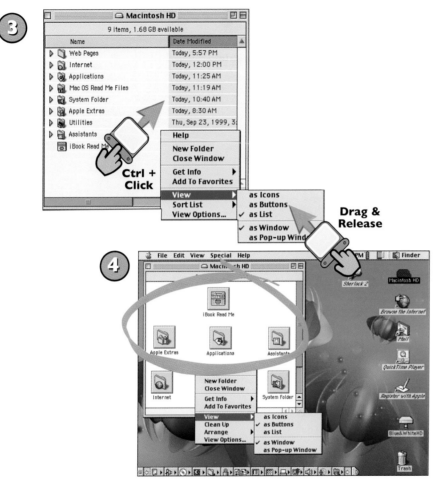

Ctrl + Click

Drag & Release

3 Hold down the **Ctrl** key, click an empty spot on the window, and select **View, as Buttons** from the context menu.

4 All files and folders in the window are represented by buttons.

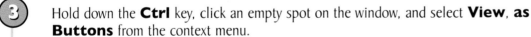

Practice Your Double-Click
If nothing happens when you double-click an icon, it might be because you did not click quickly enough or because you single-clicked, moved the mouse, and single-clicked again. You have to click twice in rapid succession.

Task 4: Sorting Window Contents

Sort the contents of a window in List view so that you can more easily find the files you want. Mac OS enables you to arrange the files in a folder by name, type, date, and size. You can move the columns to the left or right of each other and view the items in ascending or descending order.

✓ **All Sorts of View Options**
You can sort icons in Icons or Buttons mode, too. Choose the **View, Arrange** command to sort the items in the onscreen window. You can sort files viewed as large, medium, or small icons.

✓ **Move Any Column in List View**
You can move any columns in List view by clicking the top of the column and dragging it to the desired location.

✓ **Arrange Your Desktop View**
You can arrange items on the desktop by name, size, date, and so on.

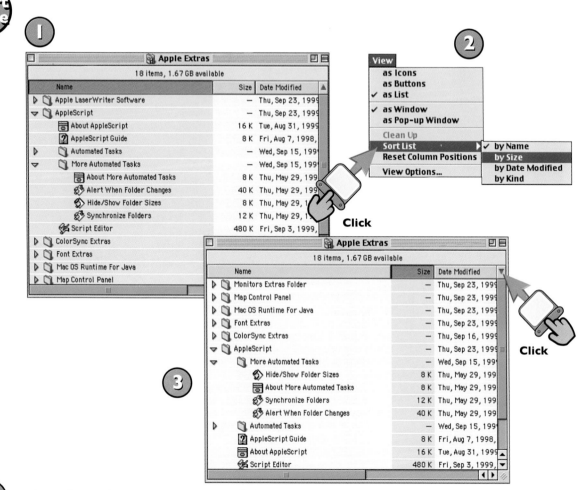

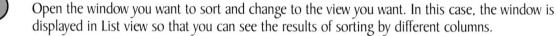

1 Open the window you want to sort and change to the view you want. In this case, the window is displayed in List view so that you can see the results of sorting by different columns.

2 Click **View**, select the **Sort List** command, and choose the sort order you want (in this case, **by Size**). Mac OS sorts the files in the selected order.

3 To change the ascending or descending sort order in a window in List view, click the arrow icon above the top of the right scrollbar.

Task 5: Changing View Options

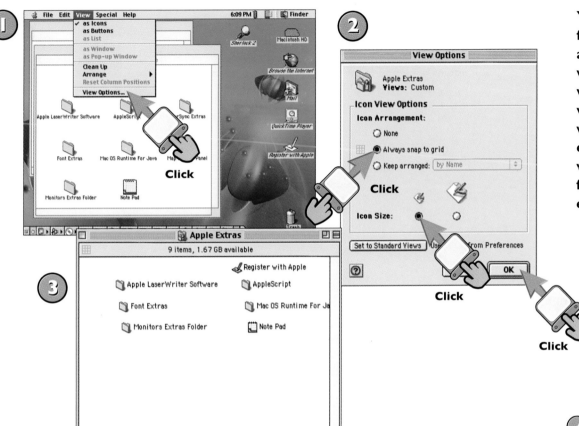

You can customize the way folders and files appear in a window by changing the window's view options. Each window can have a different view. For example, a folder with two files might be easier to navigate in Icons view, while a folder with 30 files and folders might be easier to view in List view.

1. Click **View** and select the **View Options** command.

2. Click the small **Icon Size** option button and the **Always snap to grid** option button. Click **OK**.

3. The contents of the window are displayed in Small Icon view and are mapped to the grid. You might need to resize the window.

✓ **Default Window View**
The default view for windows is Icons view.

⚠ **Button Behavior**
You cannot select a file or folder if a window is in Buttons view. Clicking once on a button icon opens a folder or starts an application.

Task 6: Finding Files and Folders with Sherlock 2

After you've worked for months with your applications, your computer will become filled with various folders and files, which can make it nearly impossible for you to know where everything is. Luckily, Mac OS includes Sherlock 2, which helps you quickly locate specific files or folders by name, file type, size, location, and so on. This can save time and battery power.

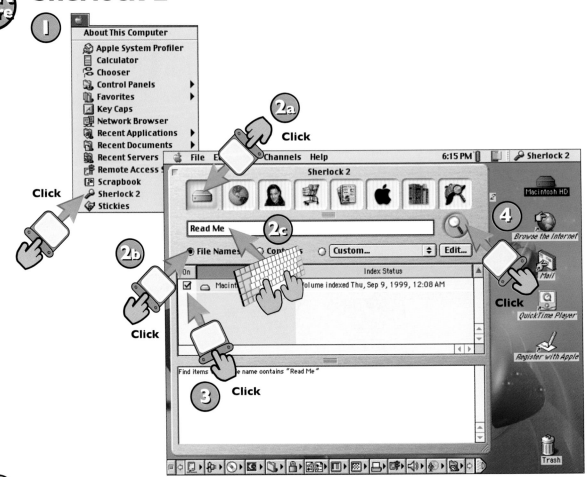

Start Here

Click

2a Click

2b Click

2c

3 Click

4 Click

Click

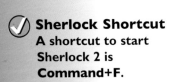

Sherlock Shortcut
A shortcut to start
Sherlock 2 is
Command+F.

1. Click the **Apple** menu and select the **Sherlock 2** command, or double-click the **Sherlock 2** icon on your desktop.

2. Click on the hard disk icon in the toolbar, then click on the **File Names** option button. Type one or two words you want to search for.

3. Click on a check box next to the hard drive you want Sherlock 2 to search.

4. Click the **Search** button.

Next Step

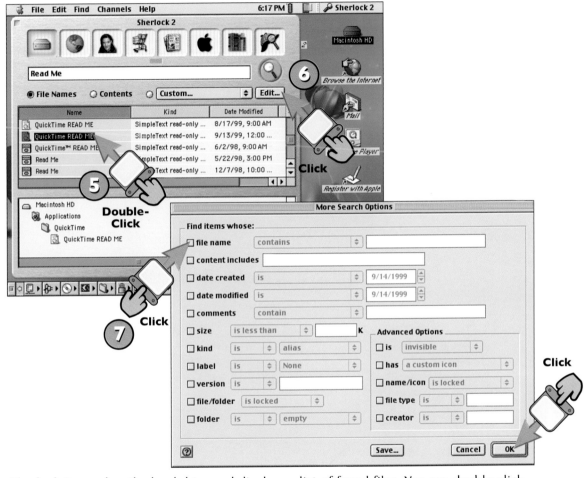

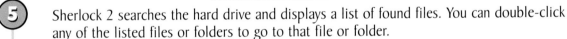

(5) Sherlock 2 searches the hard drive and displays a list of found files. You can double-click any of the listed files or folders to go to that file or folder.

(6) Click on the **Edit** button to view the More Search Options window.

(7) Click on a check box to choose the search options you want. Click **OK** to close the More Search Options window.

 More Than Just a Name
If you do not know the name of the file but you know what type of file it is, click the check box to select **Kind** or **Size** in the More Search Options window.

You can use Sherlock 2 to search your hard drive for any text contained within a document. As you use your hard disk, click the Update Index button to keep Sherlock 2 current with the latest files on your hard disk.

✅ **Close Sherlock 2 with One Click**
Close Sherlock 2 just as you do any other application: Select the **Quit** command from the **File** menu. You can also close Sherlock 2 by clicking the **Close** button in the application's title bar.

✅ **Sherlock 2 Shortcuts**
A shortcut to start Sherlock 2 is **Command+F**. Subsequent content searches can be executed by pressing **Command+G**. The first time you press **Command+G**, Sherlock will open in Find by Content mode.

Task 7: Using Sherlock 2 to Search File Contents

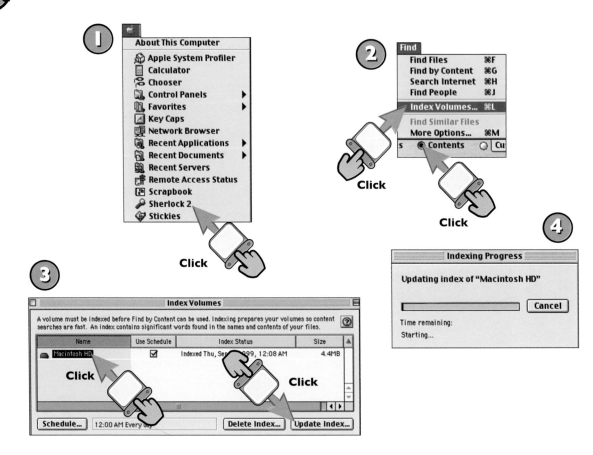

Click the **Apple** menu and select the **Sherlock 2** command, or double-click the **Sherlock 2** icon on your desktop, to open Sherlock 2.

Click on the **Contents** option button. Click on the **Find** menu, and then choose the **Index Volumes** menu command.

Click on a hard drive you want to index, and then click on the **Create Index** button. In this case, I am updating my index, so I click on the **Update Index** button.

Wait for the index to complete.

Next Step ▶

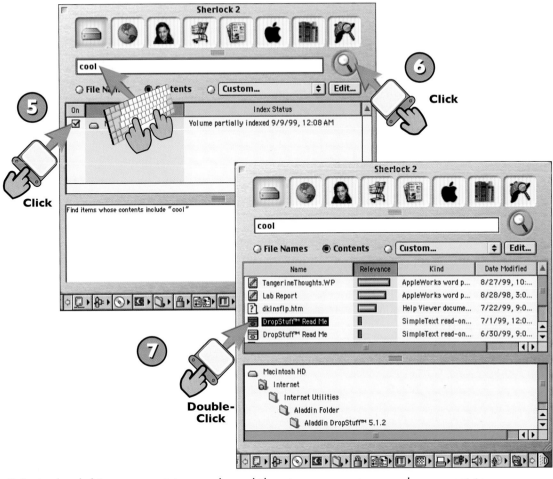

Click

Click

Click

Double-Click

5 Select a hard drive you want to search, and then type one or two words you want to search for.

6 Click the **Search** button.

7 Review the list of files in the Sherlock 2 window. Double-click a file you want to open.

✓ **Double-click an Item**
You can double-click to open any of the folders shown in the results window to view any items within the folder.

✓ **Click and Drag Any Item**
You can drag any item out of the results window to move it to the desktop or a new location.

✓ **Sort Your Results**
Click on any column in the Sherlock 2 window to change the sort order of your search results.

Task 8: Selecting Folders or Files

When you want to work on folders or files (copy, move, print, delete, and so on), you start by selecting the folders or files you want. You can select a single file or folder, select a group of files and folders in a window, or pick and choose any combination of file or folder in a window.

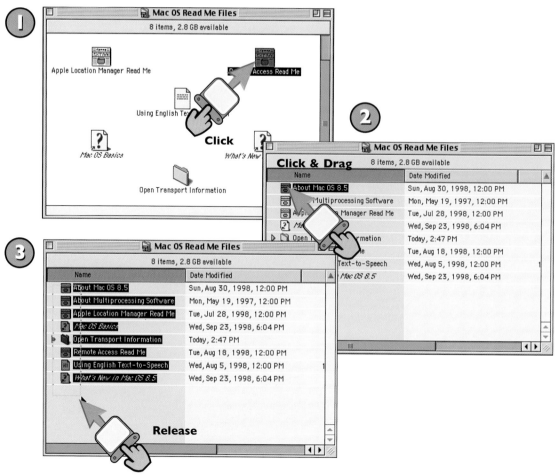

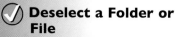

Deselect a Folder or File
To deselect one or several folders or files, click outside a highlighted file or folder.

Select by Typing a Name
You can select a single file in a window by typing one or several characters of the filename.

1 Click the folder or file you want to work with. That folder or file is selected.

2 To select adjacent items, click next to the first folder or file of the group that you want to select, and then drag the mouse around the items you want to select.

3 Release the mouse after you highlight all the items in the window; the first and last folder or file—as well as all the folders and files between—are selected.

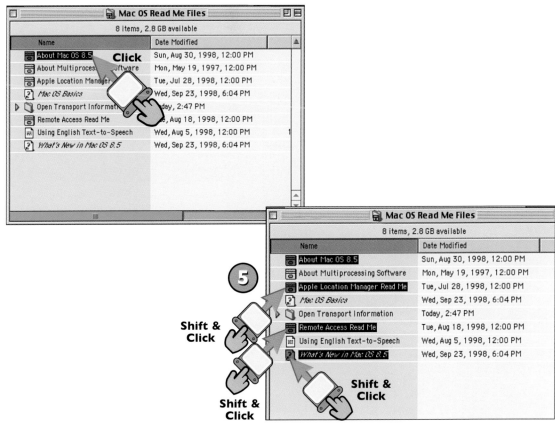

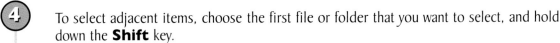

4 To select adjacent items, choose the first file or folder that you want to select, and hold down the **Shift** key.

5 While holding down the **Shift** key, click each file or folder that you want to select. Each file you click remains selected.

Watch Where You Click

If your window is in Buttons view, you must click the folder or file button name to move the icon. Clicking the button opens a folder or starts an application.

Task 9: Selecting All Folders and Files

When you feel the need to do a massive reorganization of your iBook's hard drive, you can select all items in a folder and then move, copy, or delete everything you've selected.

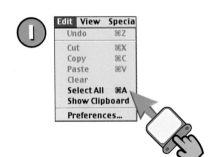

Start Here

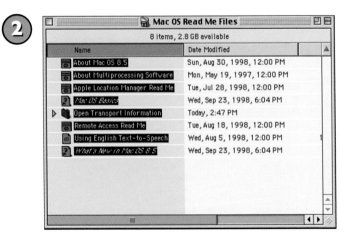

Click

✓ **Menu for Select All**
After you've selected all items in a window, hold down the **Control** key to view a menu of commands you can use on the selected items. You can open, delete, categorize, or assign the same label color to all selected folders and files.

! **System Files**
Be careful when opening the System Folder folder. If you move any files or folders out of the System Folder folder, your iBook might not have all the software it needs to run properly.

1 Click **Edit**, and then choose the **Select All** command.

2 All files and folders are selected.

✓ **Select All Shortcut**
Click in any window and press **Command+A** to select all items in the window.

End Task

Task 10: Creating a Folder

Start Here

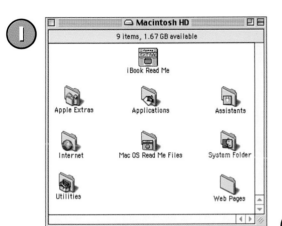
①

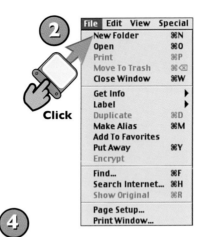
②
Click

③
My New Folder

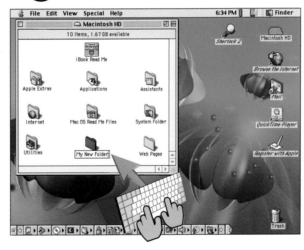
④

Working with your files is easier if you group related files into folders. For example, you might want to create a folder in your word-processing program's folder to hold all the documents you create with that program. Creating a folder enables you to keep your documents separated from the program's files so you can easily find your document files.

Deleting a Folder
If you change your mind about the new folder, you can always delete it. To delete the folder, select it and then press the **Command+Delete** keys on your keyboard. Click the **Yes** button to confirm the deletion.

What's in a Folder Name?
The folder name can contain as many as 31 characters and can include spaces.

① Open the window for the folder or disk in which you want to create the folder.

② Click **File** and select the **New Folder** command.

③ The new folder appears in the drive window.

④ To change the name of the folder, type a new name and press **Return** to create the new folder.

End Task

Task 11: Copying Folders and Files

The iBook makes it easy for you to copy a file or folder to a new location. You can, for example, copy a file or folder to another location on the hard drive if you want to revise the original file or folder for a different use. You also can use AirPort to copy a file or folder to another iBook.

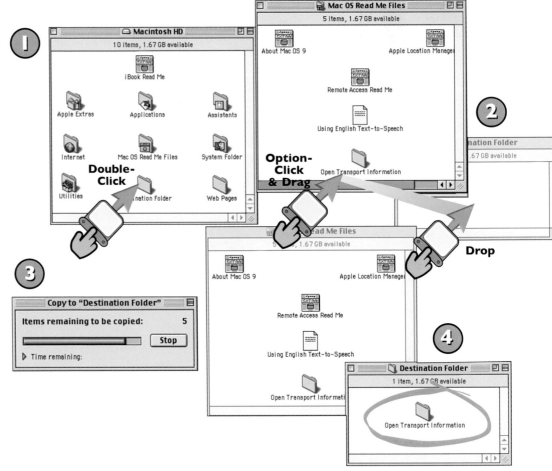

✓ **Copy by Dragging**
You can copy a file or folder by first opening both the window that contains the file or folder (the source) and the window to which you want to copy the file or folder (the destination). Click the file or folder in the source window and drag it to the destination window.

✓ **Duplicate Command**
You can also use the **Duplicate** command or **Option+click** the file or folder to create a copy.

① Double-click to open the folder you want to copy files or folders to. Then go to the source folder and select the folder or file you want to copy.

② Press the **Option** key and drag the folder or file to the destination folder.

③ Observe the copy dialog box as it copies your file or folder to the new folder.

④ The copy of the file or folder appears in the destination window.

Task 12: Moving Folders and Files

Start Here

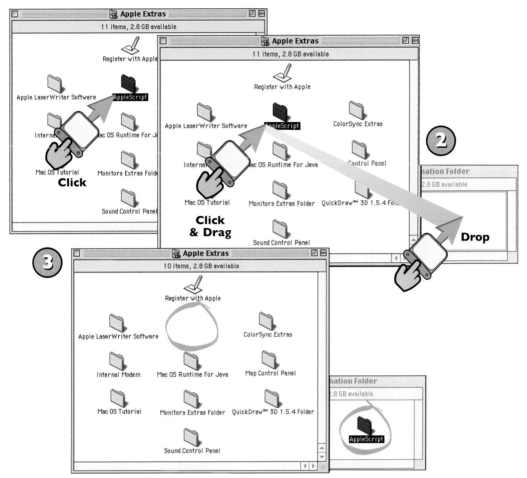

Click

Click & Drag

Drop

Move a file or folder to another folder so that you can reorganize your hard drive. For example, you might want to move all related files and folders to the same place on your hard drive so you can find them quickly and easily.

1. Select a folder or file that you want to move.

2. Open the destination window you want to move the selected folder or file to. Click and drag the folder to the destination window or folder icon, and then release the mouse button.

3. Mac OS moves the folder to the new location.

✓ Put Away Command
If you move a file or folder from a window to the desktop, you can return it to its original location by clicking **File** and selecting the **Put Away** command.

⚠ System Files
Be careful when opening the System Folder folder. If you move any files or folders out of the **System Folder** folder, your iBook might not have all the software it needs to run properly.

End Task

Task 13: Renaming Folders and Files

As you add more and more folders and files to your computer, you will eventually need to rearrange and reorganize them. In addition to needing to know how to copy and move folders and files, you'll need to know how to rename them (for instance, in case you want to give a folder a more descriptive name). Your iBook enables you to easily rename files and folders.

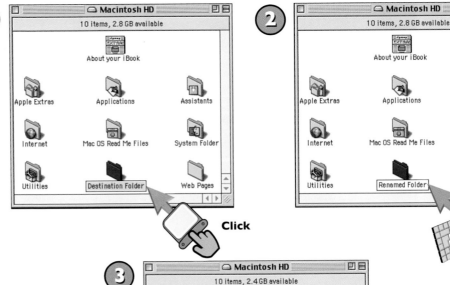

Click

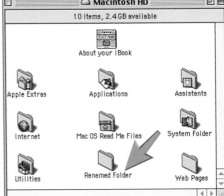

① Click on the name of the folder or file that you want to rename.

② Wait for about one second or press the **Return** key. Type a new name for the folder, and press **Return**.

③ The folder is renamed.

Task 14: Creating a Pop-up Folder Window

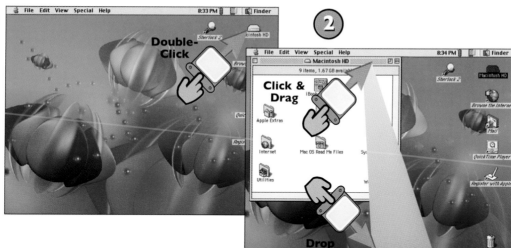

If you use a folder frequently, you can move it to the bottom of the desktop window to turn it into a pop-up folder. You can access a pop-up folder from Finder or any application.

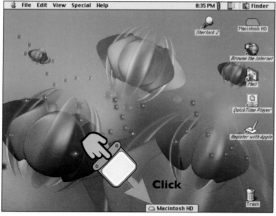

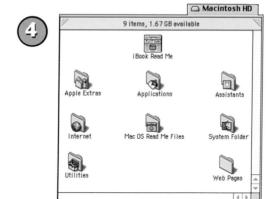

Double-click the hard disk icon on the desktop.

Move the window to the bottom of the desktop by clicking the window title bar and dragging. The window title bar turns into a tab.

Click the pop-up window tab.

The window pops up to display its contents.

View a Folder's Path
If you forget where a pop-up folder resides on your hard disk, you can **Command+click** the title bar of the pop-up window to view the path of the folder on your hard disk.

Maximum Pop-Up Windows
You can place as many pop-up windows at the bottom of your desktop as will fit. After the bottom of the screen has filled with pop-up menu tabs, the next time you drag a window to the bottom of your desktop, Finder will ask you to remove a pop-up window if you want to add a new one.

Task 15: Creating an Alias to a File or Folder

If you often use the same file or folder, you might want fast access to it. If so, you can create a shortcut, or alias icon, for the file or folder on the desktop. Double-clicking a file's alias icon opens the file in the application you used to create the file. Double-clicking a folder displays the contents of the folder in a window.

✓ **Delete an Alias**
To delete an alias icon, move it to the Trash. Don't worry—you are only deleting the alias, and not the original file or folder.

✓ **Finding the Original of an Alias**
You can find the original file of the alias by **Ctrl+clicking** the alias and selecting **Show Original**.

✓ **An Alias for the Alias**
To rename an alias icon, click it, and then wait for the text to highlight it. Type a new name and press **Return**.

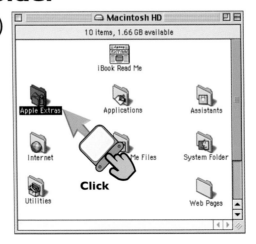

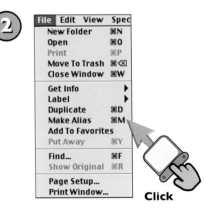

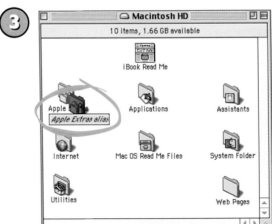

1 Select the folder or file you want to create an alias for.

2 Click **File** and select the **Make Alias** command.

3 Mac OS creates an alias to the folder or file. Move the alias to your desktop or to a folder that contains other aliases.

Task 16: Changing a Folder or File Label

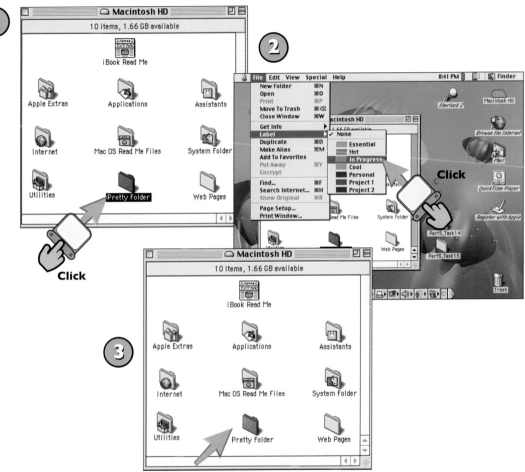

You can group or label files or folders with a color. Color labels can help you more easily identify a particular file or folder in a window or on the desktop.

1 Click on a folder or file in a window. Here I have selected a folder.

2 Click **File** and select a color from the **Label** submenu.

3 Mac OS adds the label to the folder.

✔ Customize Your Labels

You can change the label colors and names by clicking **Edit** and selecting the **Preferences** command. In the Preferences window, select the **Labels** tab and click on a color you want to change. To change the color, select a different color from the color wheel.

Task 17: Synchronizing Folders and Files with Your Desktop

Start Here

If you use another Macintosh computer to do your work and share common folders between the two machines, you can easily synchronize them using the File Synchronization control panel. You can synchronize data so that one machine always updates the other, or so that both machines share mutual contents. This task shows you how to use the File Synchronization control panel with two Macs connected on an Ethernet network.

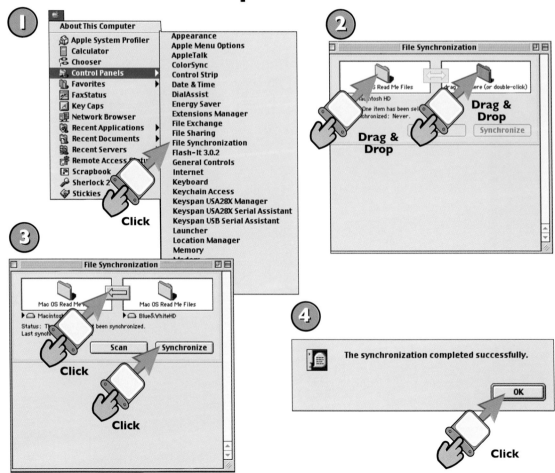

✓ **When to Synchronize**
If you travel frequently, or change several files often, synchronize at least once a day, or as often as possible. If you do not rely on your desktop computer to contain the same data as your iBook, you don't need to synchronize as often.

① Click on the **Apple** menu, choose **Control Panels**, and then select **File Synchronization**. The File Synchronization window opens.

② Drag a folder to the left window, and a second folder you want to synchronize with to the right window.

③ Click on the arrow button to select a synchronization direction, and then click on the **Synchronize** button.

④ Click **OK** on the Synchronization Completed Successfully dialog box. Open one of the synchronized folders to verify its contents have been updated.

End Task

Task 18: Deleting Folders and Files

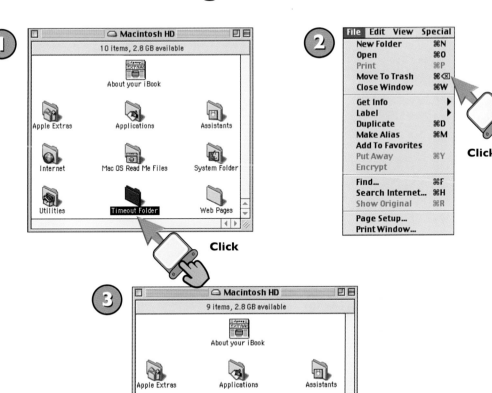

Eventually, your iBook will become full of files and folders, and you'll have a hard time organizing and storing them all. You might need to clean house by deleting files and folders you no longer need. Mac OS 9 keeps folders and files that you want to delete in the Trash.

✓ **Empty the Trash, Too**
Files placed in the Trash are not deleted until you empty the trash. See Task 19, "Emptying the Trash," for information about permanently deleting files and folders from your iBook.

✓ **Shortcut to the Trash**
You can move any item to the Trash by **Ctrl+clicking** an icon and selecting the **Move to Trash** command.

✓ **Drag File to the Trash**
You can move any item to the Trash by selecting a file or folder, dragging it to the Trash icon, and then dropping it.

1 Click the folder or file that you want to delete.

2 Click **File** and select the **Move to Trash** command.

3 The folder or file is moved to the Trash.

PART

Task 19: Emptying the Trash

If you want to permanently remove from your system the folders and files in the Trash, you can empty it.

✓ **Shortcut to Empty the Trash**
An alternative way to empty the Trash is to click on the **Trash** icon, and then press the **Ctrl** key and select **Empty Trash**.

✓ **Cancel to Save Your Data**
If you change your mind about deleting the folder, click the **Cancel** button in the Confirmation Alert dialog box after selecting **Empty Trash** from the **Special** menu.

① When the Trash icon appears to be brimming with garbage, it means that there is at least one file or folder in the Trash.

② To empty the Trash, click **Special** and select the **Empty Trash** command.

✓ **Unerase Files**
If you have Norton Utilities 4.0 (or higher), you can use the Norton FileSaver control panel and Norton's UnErase feature to recover many files after you've emptied the Trash.

Next Step

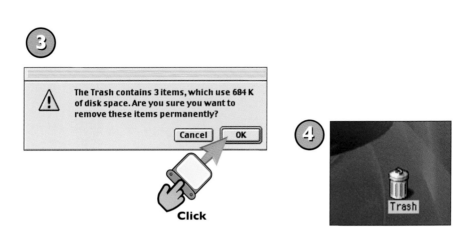

Click

Trash

 Mac OS displays an alert asking you to confirm whether you want to delete all the files in the Trash; click **OK**.

 The Trash is emptied; notice that the Trash icon no longer appears to overflow with garbage.

✅ **Turn Off the Trash Warning**
If you select **Get Info on the Trash**, you can turn off the warning message that appears whenever you empty the Trash.

PART 6

Printing with Your iBook

Your iBook uses Mac OS as its operating system, which in turn enables you to use any Mac OS application on your iBook. All Mac OS applications use the same setup for your printer, which saves time and ensures that you can print from any Mac OS application without reselecting for each program. Mac OS 9 includes printer software for Apple and PostScript printers. If needed, you can install additional printer software, or set up more than one printer. In addition, you can easily manage printing for all your applications.

You print a document from the application in which you created it. When you send a file to the printer, the file first goes to a **_print queue_**, or holding area. The print queue can contain one or many files at any time, and you can make changes to this print queue. While a file is in the print queue, you can pause, restart, and even cancel the print job. This part shows you how to control and manage printing with your iBook.

Tasks

Task #		Page #
1	Selecting a Printer	126
2	Setting the Default Printer	127
3	Printing a Document	128
4	Viewing the Print Queue	129
5	Pausing and Restarting a Print Job	130
6	Canceling a Print Job	131
7	Changing Printer Settings	132
8	Adding a Desktop Printer	134
9	Deleting a Desktop Printer	135

Task 1: Selecting a Printer

Before you can actually print a document, you need to select a printer. When you select a printer, Mac OS works with its printer driver software to identify which kind of printer is connected to your iBook. If the printer is connected to the network, Mac OS will know where the printer lives in your network neighborhood.

✓ A Word About Printer Software

If you have a PostScript printer, Mac OS 9 has the latest LaserWriter printer driver installed. However, if you want to use a USB printer or other direct-connect printer with your iBook, you will need to install software from the printer vendor so that Mac OS can recognize the new printer.

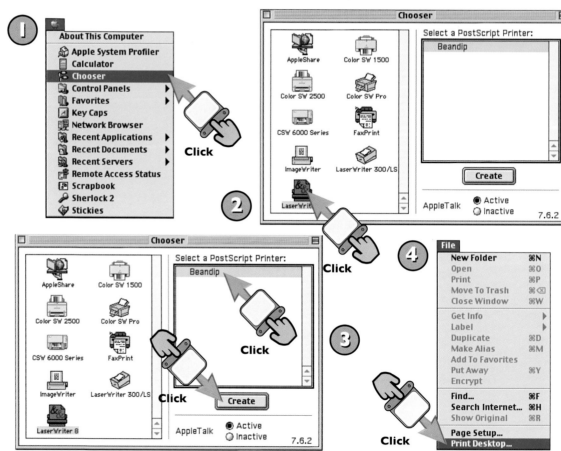

 Click the **Apple** menu, and then select **Chooser**.

 Click on the printer driver icon for your printer. In this case, I've selected the **LaserWriter 8** printer driver.

 Select a printer from the right side of the Chooser window. Click **Create** to setup a new printer. Then close the Chooser window.

 In Finder, click **File** and choose **Print Desktop**. A picture of your desktop should print to the printer you just selected in Chooser.

Task 2: Setting the Default Printer

Start Here

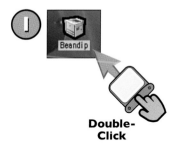

①

Beandip

Double-Click

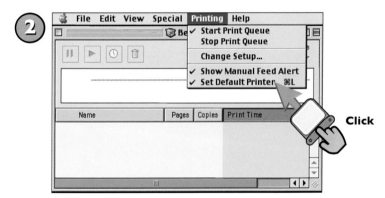

②

File   Edit   View   Special   **Printing**   Help

✓ **Start Print Queue**
  Stop Print Queue

  Change Setup...

✓ **Show Manual Feed Alert**
✓ **Set Default Printer**   ⌘L

Name   Pages Copies Print Time

Click

If you have more than one printer connected, you must select one as the default. The default printer you set in Mac OS is the printer your applications automatically use when you choose to print.

✅ **Use a Nondefault Printer**
To use a different printer, you can select and drag a document to any other desktop printer icon.

✅ **Change the Default Printer**
You can change the default printer by double-clicking any desktop printer icon, or selecting any desktop printer icon and pressing Command+L.

① Double-click a desktop printer icon on the desktop.

② Click **Printing** and select the **Set Default Printer** command.

End Task

Task 3: Printing a Document

After you've set a default printer, you can print from any application using this printer. Printing your documents gives you a paper copy you can proofread, use in reports, give to co-workers, and so on.

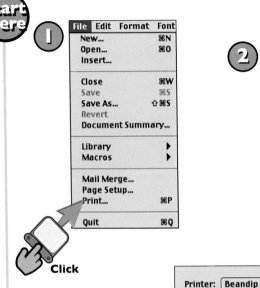

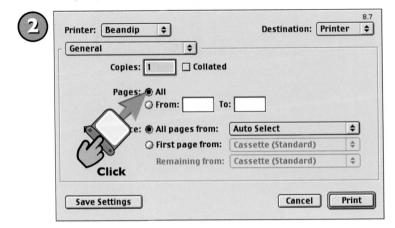

Click

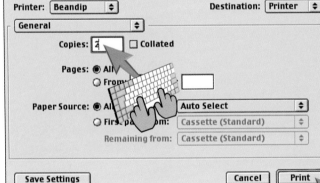

First Turn on Your Printer
Be sure that your printer is plugged in, online, and has paper.

Send the Job to Any Printer
If you want to use a printer other than the default, choose the printer you want to use from the **Printer** pop-up menu list in the **Print** dialog box.

1 In an application, click **File**, and then click the **Print** command.

2 In the Print dialog box, specify a page range.

3 Enter the number of copies you want printed.

4 Click the **Print** button.

Task 4: Viewing the Print Queue

Start Here

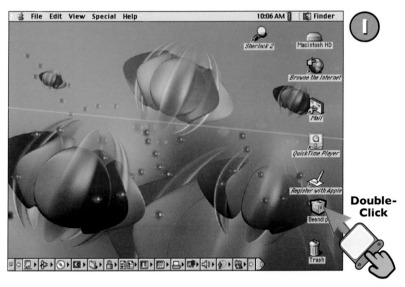

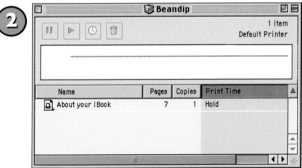

You can print directly to the printer or you can print in the background. The default setting for the iBook is to print to the background, which enables you to spool several documents to a print queue. The print queue lists the documents that have been sent to a printer and shows the progress of the printing.

1 Double-click the printer icon on the desktop. (**Beandip** is the name of the icon for my LaserWriter 12/640 printer, which uses the LaserWriter 8 printer driver software.)

2 The printer window displays a list of the documents in the queue, as well as information about the document being printed.

✓ **Background Printing**
The controls for choosing foreground or background printing vary, depending on the kind of printer you are using. For example, if you are using the LaserWriter 8 printer driver, you can choose foreground or background printing in the Print dialog box. If you are using a **USB** printer, you can turn off background printing from the Chooser.

End Task

Task 5: Pausing and Restarting a Print Job

You might want to pause printing when you have to make a change in the text or when you want to load a different paper type. You can easily stop the printing from the Printing menu, and can restart it at any time.

Short Jobs Print Quickly

You have to be quick to pause or stop a short print job. If nothing appears in the print queue, it probably means that the entire print job has already been sent to the printer.

Control Print Jobs with Buttons

You can use the button controls in the print queue window to pause printing on a specific job (if, for example, you have sent several jobs to the printer but want to pause and change paper for a particular job). Select the job you want to pause, and click the **Pause** button icon at the top of the print queue window.

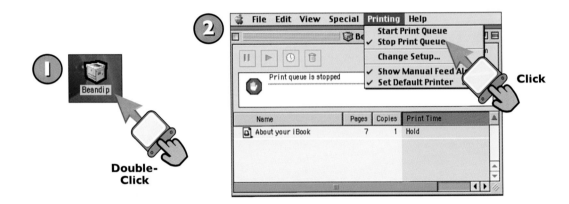

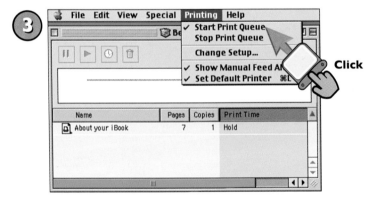

Double-Click

Click

1. Double-click the desktop printer icon.

2. Click **Printing**, and then choose the **Stop Print Queue** command.

3. Click **Printing**, and then click the **Start Print Queue** command to resume printing.

Task 6: Canceling a Print Job

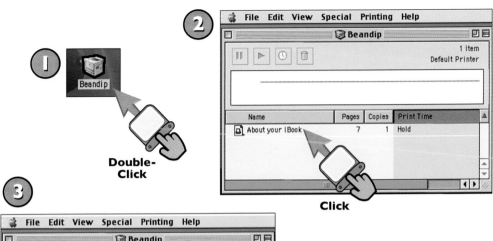

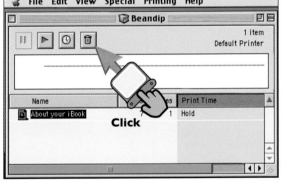

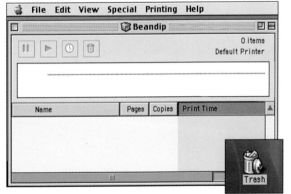

Double-Click

Click

Click

Save paper and time by canceling a print job. If you discover an error in the job you are printing or if you decide that you need to add something to it, you can cancel the print job.

① Double-click the desktop printer icon to open the print queue window.

② Select the document you want to cancel.

③ Click the **Trash** icon in the toolbar.

④ The item is removed from the print queue and placed in the Trash.

Start Here

End Task

Small Documents Print Quickly
Depending on your computer and your printer, the print job might be listed in the print queue for only a few seconds before it is sent to the printer. You might not be able to cancel it in time.

Task 7: Changing Printer Settings

You can easily change printer settings. You might, for example, switch to a different printer driver so that your printer works better with your applications. Alternatively, you might change the paper tray, the printer description file, or specify whether you want double- or single-sided printing (whether these types of options are available depends on the printer you use).

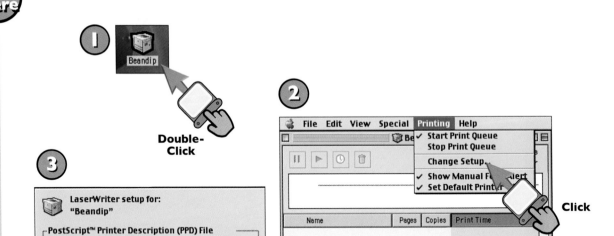

Double-Click

Click

Click

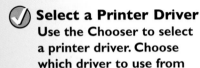
Select a Printer Driver
Use the Chooser to select a printer driver. Choose which driver to use from the left window.

① Double-click a desktop printer icon.

② Open the **Printing** menu and choose the **Change Setup** command.

③ Adjust printer settings as desired. When finished, click **OK**.

Next Step

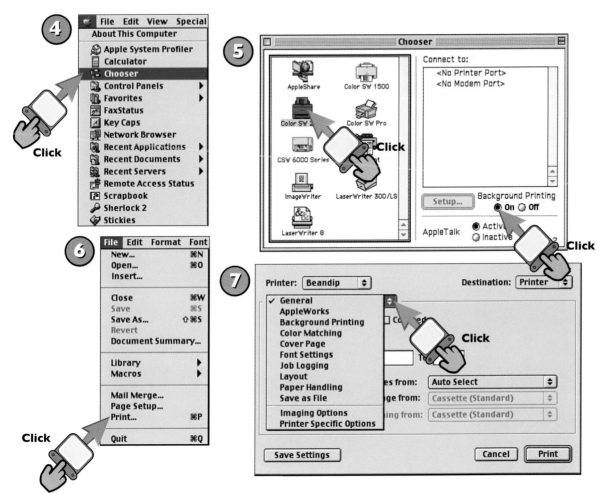

(4) Open the **Apple** menu and click **Chooser**.

(5) Select a printer, then click the **On** button to turn on background printing. You can specify whether background printing is enabled, and you can select the printer port.

(6) Close the Chooser by clicking its **Close** box. In an application, click **File** and then click **Print**.

(7) Print options vary from printer to printer (in this case, the LaserWriter 8 Print dialog box has many options to choose from).

More About Step 5
In step 5 of this task, no ports are available for the selected printer because the iBook has only one USB port.

Task 8: Adding a Desktop Printer

Your iBook gives you fast access to your printer by enabling you to add a printer icon to your desktop. You can then double-click this icon to view the print queue. You can also drag documents from a file window to the desktop printer icon to print the documents.

If you disable the desktop printing extensions by moving them out of the system folder, you can only print to the printer selected in Chooser. With desktop printing, you can use multiple printers without having to open Chooser each time you want to change the printer.

✓ **Organize Desktop Printers**
If you have more than one desktop printer, you can move a desktop printer you might not use very often to a different folder to reduce desktop clutter.

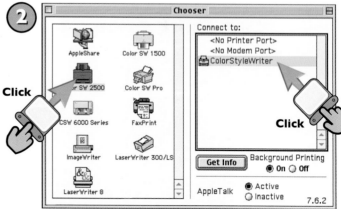

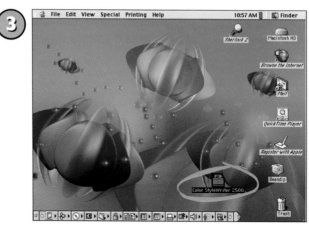

Click the **Apple** menu and click **Chooser**.

Click the printer icon and then the printer name. If you are adding another LaserWriter printer, choose the **Create** button.

The desktop printer icon appears on the desktop.

Task 9: Deleting a Desktop Printer

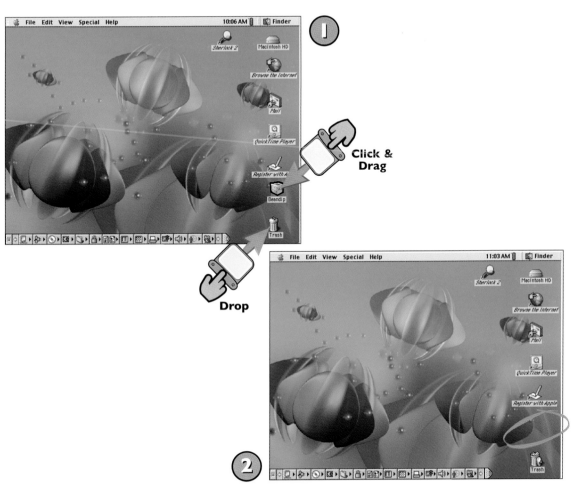

Click & Drag

Drop

If you get a new printer, you can delete the setup for the old printer so that you don't get confused about which printer is which. Deleting a printer removes it from the desktop.

Click on a desktop printer icon that you would like to delete and drag and drop it over the **Trash** icon.

The printer is deleted.

 Accidentally Delete a Printer?
If you delete a printer by mistake, you can always add it back by using the Chooser.

Personalizing Your iBook

Apple has made it easy for you to customize many software features on your iBook. For example, you can assign an application or alias to a function key on your keyboard, assign a color to the scrolling controls on windows, change the font used to display file and folder names, and customize Mac OS settings to match the location of your iBook. You can adjust colors used for onscreen elements such as sliders, progress bars, and labels. You can change how the trackpad and mouse work, when and what sounds are played, and more. Mac OS 9 includes many options for setting up your work environment just the way you want. This part shows you how to customize Mac OS.

Tasks

Task #		Page #
1	Showing and Hiding Applications	138
2	Moving the Applications Menu	139
3	Choosing a Desktop Picture	140
4	Choosing a Desktop Pattern	142
5	Choosing a Theme	143
6	Changing Highlight Colors on Your iBook	144
7	Synchronizing Colors on Your iBook	145
8	Using Energy Saver	146
9	Tweaking Your Monitor	148
10	Using the Control Strip	149
11	Changing How Your Sound Works	150
12	Recording an Alert Sound	152
13	Changing the System Alert Sound	154
14	Changing How Your Trackpad Works	155
15	Changing the System Date and Time	156
16	Using Location Manager	158
17	Customizing Your Keyboard Controls	160

Task 1: Showing and Hiding Applications

Mac OS shows the application icon and name in the menu bar at all times as a default setting. To view another application running under Mac OS, open the **Applications** menu and click the application you want. The name of the previous application disappears from the menu bar and the current, newly selected application icon and name appears.

✅ **What Is Finder?**
Finder is one application that is always open with Mac OS. When you select it in the **Applications** menu, you can view the desktop and any open windows.

❗ **Control Panels and the Applications Menu**
Most, but not all, control panels appear in the Applications menu when opened. For example, Color Sync, **General Controls, Numbers, QuickTime Settings, Speech,** and **Text** do not appear on the Applications menu.

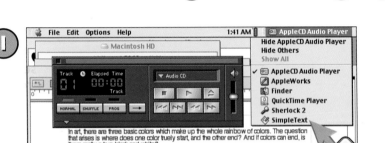

Click

1 With several applications open, click the **Applications** menu and choose a different application.

2 Mac OS switches to the application you chose. The name of the application appears in the **Applications** menu area.

Task 2: Moving the Applications Menu

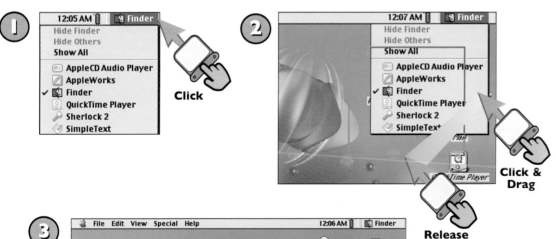

Click

Click & Drag

Release

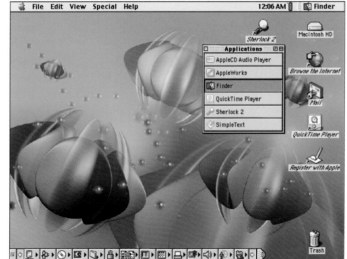

You can configure the Applications menu to "float" over your desktop so that you can switch to any other application with a single click of the mouse. You can also collapse the floating Applications menu to maximize the amount of screen space available to another document window.

1. Open the **Applications** menu.

2. Drag the **Applications** menu away from the menu bar by clicking and holding down the mouse in a gray area of the menu.

3. The Applications menu becomes a floating window, showing all open applications.

Resize Applications Buttons, Too
You can resize the Applications menu button so that the application name does not appear—just drag the left edge of the **Applications** menu button to the right. You can also drag the right edge of the floating **Applications** window to customize the amount of information you can view in this window. Clicking its **Zoom** box reduces the window to its minimum size.

Task 3: Choosing a Desktop Picture

You can personalize your desktop in Mac OS by adding a desktop picture. Mac OS 9 offers many colorful desktop picture options, including photos of landscapes, flowers, and buildings; 3D art; convergent colors; and ensembles.

✓ **Patterns versus Pictures**
You can also add a pattern to the desktop as covered in the next task.

✓ **Select a Picture to Fit Your Screen**
If the image you selected is blurry, it might be because Mac OS has scaled a smaller image to fit the size of your screen. Deselect **Scale to Screen** to view the image at its original size on the desktop.

✓ **See the Picture Tiled**
If your desktop picture doesn't fit your entire screen, you might want to choose **Tile on Screen** to turn a desktop picture into a large pattern.

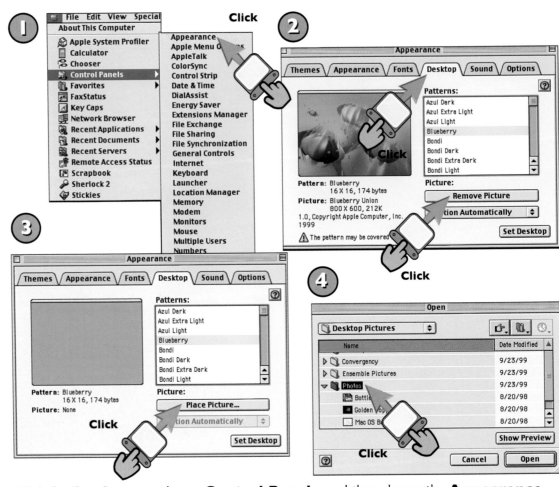

① Click the **Apple** menu, choose **Control Panels**, and then choose the **Appearance** control panel.

② Select the **Desktop** tab and click on the **Remove Picture** button.

③ Click on the **Place Picture** button.

④ In the Open window, click on a picture file.

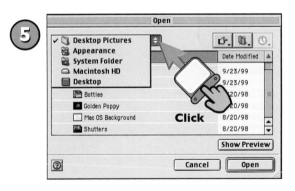

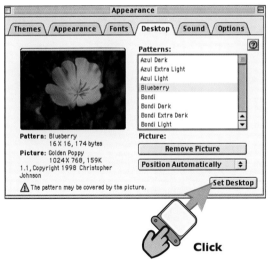 

Click

Click

Click

✓ **Preview Desktop Pictures**
Click **Show Preview** to preview images in the Open window. The preview will show you a snapshot image of the picture and can help you choose the picture you want.

✓ **More Desktop Pictures on iBook CD-ROM**
More desktop pictures are available on the iBook Software Install CD-ROM. You can preview the pictures by inserting the iBook Software CD-ROM while the Appearance control panel is open. Use the Open window, go to the Additional Desktop Pictures folder, and preview any image in that folder.

5 To choose a picture in a different folder, navigate to it using the pop-up menu, or use the **Shortcuts**, **Favorites**, or **Recent** button.

6 After you have selected a file, click the **Open** button.

7 Click the **Set Desktop** button.

8 The picture you selected is displayed on the desktop.

End Task

Task 4: Choosing a Desktop Pattern

If you don't like the selections for desktop pictures, you might want to experiment with a pattern. A pattern can range in size from an 8×8-pixel to a 128×128-pixel image. The pattern is repeated across the entire desktop both horizontally and vertically, producing a tile effect.

✓ **Remove a Pattern**
To remove a pattern from the Pattern list, select the pattern you want to remove and press **Command+X**.

✓ **Add a Pattern**
To add a desktop pattern to the list of patterns in the Desktop tab of the Appearance control panel, click the pattern in the Scrapbook file and drag it to the desktop. Mac OS will convert that pattern into a picture clipping file. Drag the picture clipping file over the Pattern window.

To add a desktop pattern on the CD-ROM to the list of patterns in the Desktop tab of the Appearance control panel, copy the **Additional Desktop Pattern** file to your hard disk.

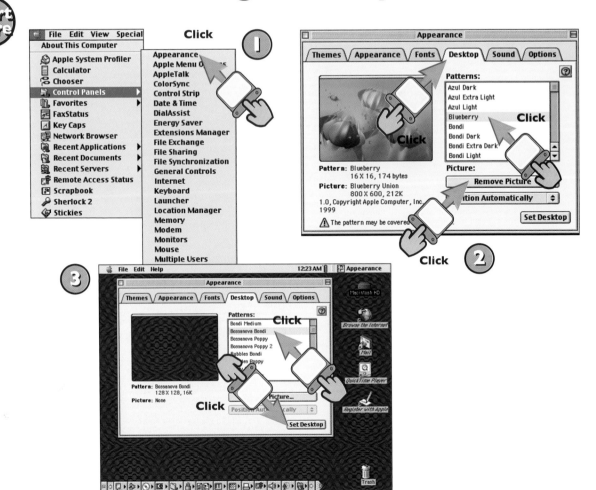

Click the **Apple** menu, choose **Control Panels**, and then choose the **Appearance** control panel.

Click on the **Desktop** tab, and then choose a pattern from the **Patterns** list. Click the **Remove Picture** button if a desktop picture is visible in the left window.

When you find one you like, click **Set Desktop**. Mac OS uses the pattern on your desktop.

Task 5: Choosing a Theme

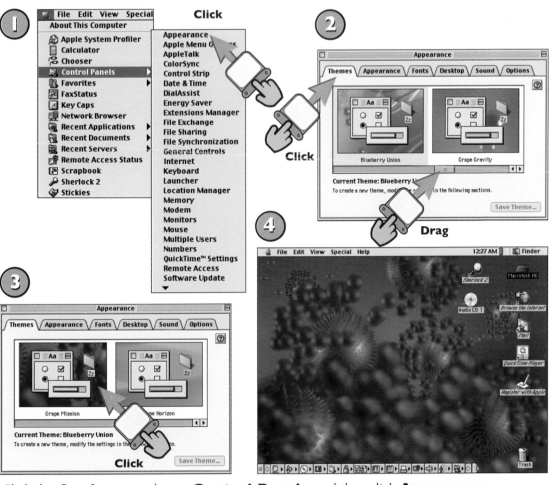

You can change one or many appearance settings in the **Appearance** control panel. Any combination of appearance settings can be saved as a theme. A *theme* consists of the colors, font, desktop image, sound settings, and window settings chosen in the Appearance control panel. A theme lets you quickly switch from one set of custom settings to another.

✓ **Save Your Themes**
You can create your own theme by choosing your settings in the **Appearance** control panel, selecting the **Themes** tab, and clicking **Save Theme**.

1. Click the **Apple** menu, choose **Control Panels**, and then click **Appearance**.

2. Click the **Themes** tab, and view the various available themes by clicking and dragging the scrollbar.

3. Click on a theme.

4. Mac OS changes the fonts, colors, desktop picture, and window and sound settings for the theme (in this case, **Grape Mission** is the name of the theme I selected).

✓ **What's My Theme?**
If you can't remember the default theme for your iBook, Blueberry Union is the theme for blueberry iBooks. Tangerine Fusion is the theme for tangerine iBooks.

Task 6: Changing Highlight Colors on Your iBook

There are two different color-related control panels in Mac OS 9: Appearance and ColorSync. The Appearance control panel lets you choose the highlight color you see when you select text in Mac OS and its applications.

Start Here

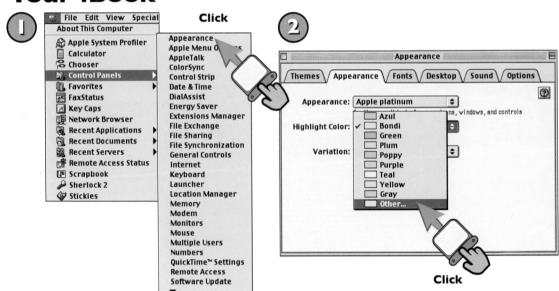

Click

① View Your Highlight Color

The highlight color is the color of a highlighted item, such as text or graphics, in an application. You can easily view the highlight color by typing in a SimpleText application and then selecting some text.

② Exit Without Saving

To recover the original colors or settings, click **Cancel** instead of **OK**. If you have already closed the dialog box, you can revert to one of the standard themes in the Themes tab of the Appearance control panel.

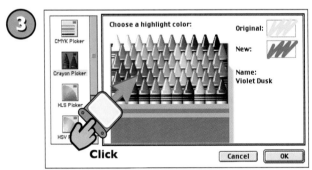

Click

1 Click the **Apple** menu, choose **Control Panels**, and then select the **Appearance** control panel.

2 Click the **Appearance** tab and choose **Other** from the **Highlight Color** pop-up menu.

3 Select a color from the Color Picker window, and click **OK**. If you can't decide on a color, click the **Crayon Picker** in the Color Picker window and select a crayon color.

End Task

Task 7: Synchronizing Colors on Your iBook

Start Here

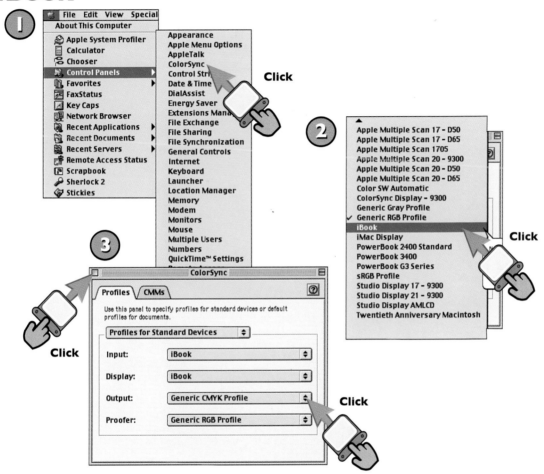

Click

Click

Click

Click

ColorSync is Apple's color-management technology, which enables color synchronization between the iBook's screen, printers, scanners, and cameras. ColorSync lets your iBook use the correct color on paper as well as on your screen. For example, if you have a color printer connected to your iBook, the color document on your iBook screen will print with the same color information to your color printer, even though your iBook monitor and printer process color very differently from one another.

1. Click the **Apple** menu, choose **Control Panels**, and then select **ColorSync**.

2. Click on the **Profiles** tab, and then select **iBook** from the pop-up menu.

3. Select an output profile from the **Output** pop-up menu. Click the **Close** button to save your changes.

End Task

Task 8: Using Energy Saver

You can specify when your iBook sleeps (that is, when the iBook dims the display and puts the hard drive into low power mode, also known as *spinning down the hard disk*). These energy-saving features help your iBook reduce wear on the monitor, hard disk, and computer. The iBook also has several new energy saver features that let you save contents in memory or shut down when the iBook goes to sleep.

✓ **More Options with the Detail Button**
To use the display and hard disk features in the Energy Saver control panel, click the **Show Details** button.

✓ **File Sharing Behavior and Sleep**
If your iBook has File Sharing turned on, you can access it while it is sleeping.

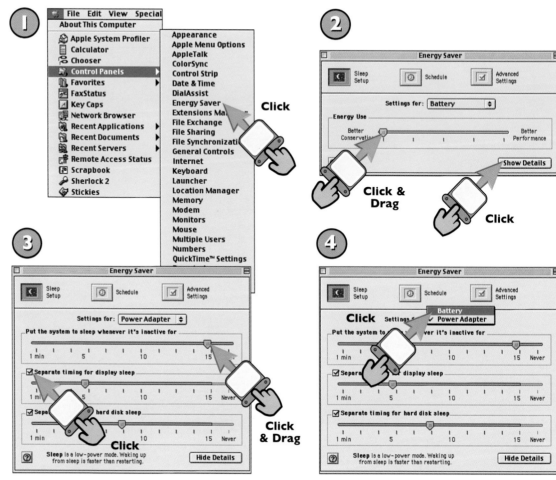

Click the **Apple** menu, choose **Control Panels**, and then click **Energy Saver**.

Move the slider to a setting between **Better Conservation** and **Better Performance**. Click on the **Show Details** button to access more energy-saving options.

Click and drag the slider to set the time when you want your iBook to automatically sleep. Click on a **Separate timing** check box to adjust monitor and hard drive energy-saving options.

Click on the **Settings for** popup menu to select settings for battery or power adapter modes. View and adjust your battery settings for your iBook.

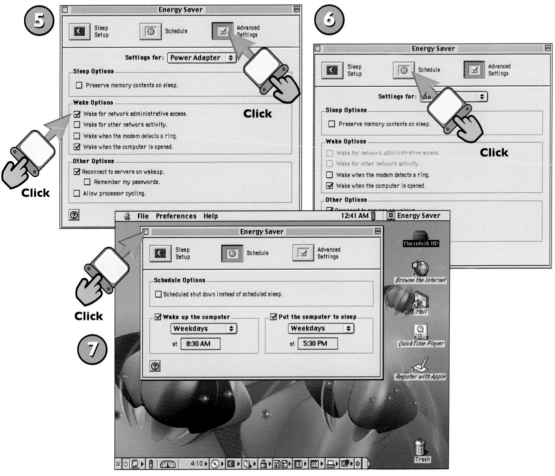

New iBook Sleep Options

Your iBook can do a whole lot more while it's sleeping. Click on the **Advanced Settings** button to preserve memory on shut down when your iBook goes to sleep, or choose from several wake options.

Is It Asleep?

Whenever you put your iBook to sleep, the light located at the back of the iBook handle pulses. If you put your iBook to sleep with the lid open, the same light flashes right below the Apple icon below the iBook screen.

⑤ Click on the **Advanced Settings** button. Click on a check box to turn any feature on or off.

⑥ Click on the **Schedule** button.

⑦ Click on the settings you want to use to wake up or put to sleep your iBook. Click on the **Close** button of the Energy Saver window to save your changes.

Task 9: Tweaking Your Monitor

The iBook monitor enables you to select certain options about how it operates, such as the number of colors it displays or its *resolution*. (Resolution measures the number of pixels or picture elements displayed. An example of a common resolution is 800×600. The larger the resolution, the larger the desktop size; desktop elements, such as icons, appear smaller.) You might need to change your monitor's display properties if you want to use a different size desktop with a partcular application, or if you want to improve the appearance of a high-resolution desktop picture.

✓ **Use the Monitors Control Panel to Change Resolution**
To change the resolution of the iBook monitor, click a resolution from the **Resolution** list box in the Monitors control panel or from the **Control Strip**. Mac OS changes the desktop size to match the resolution you choose.

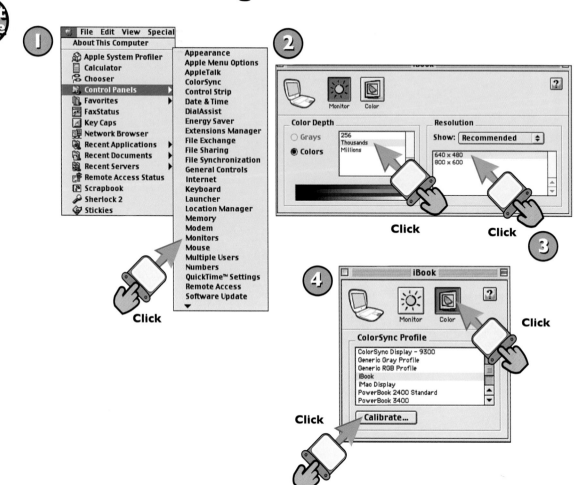

(1) Click the **Apple** menu, choose **Control Panels**, and select **Monitors**.

(2) Select the color depth you want from the **Color Depth** list box on the left.

(3) Click the resolution you want in the **Resolution** list box on the right.

(4) Click the **Color** button to choose and calibrate the ColorSync profile for your monitor.

Task 10: Using the Control Strip

Start Here

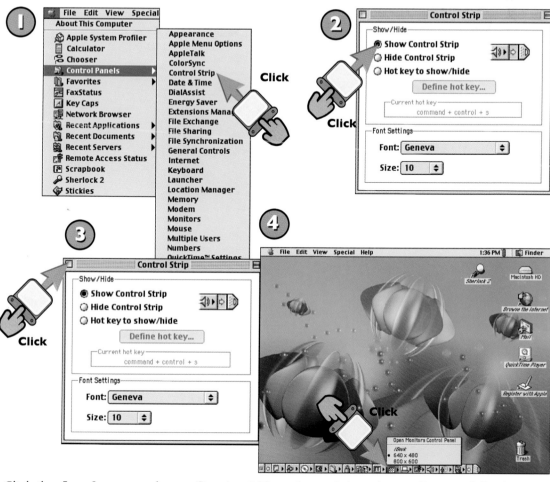

The fastest way to access some of the major Mac OS features on your iBook is to use one of the control strip modules. The control strip appears at the bottom left of your iBook's desktop and is always the foremost window on your screen. Control strip modules let you control your audio CD player, turn file sharing on or off, or change the resolution of your monitor with a click of a button.

✓ **Hide Control Strip**
You can show or hide control strip modules by clicking the right tab of the **Control Strip** window.

✓ **Adjust the Size of Your Control Strip**
You can adjust the viewable area of the **Control Strip** window by clicking and dragging the right tab to the left or right.

① Click the **Apple** menu, choose **Control Panels,** and then choose **Control Strip**.

② Click the **Show Control Strip** radio button.

③ Close the Control Strip window.

④ Click any control strip module to change a setting (in this case, the resolution of your iBook screen).

End Task

Task 11: Changing How Your Sound Works

Another way to customize how your iBook looks and feels is to change the sound your iBook makes when it issues an alert. Other sound settings you can adjust include the sound-input and monitoring source, sound output, external speaker volume, and the sound volume of your iBook.

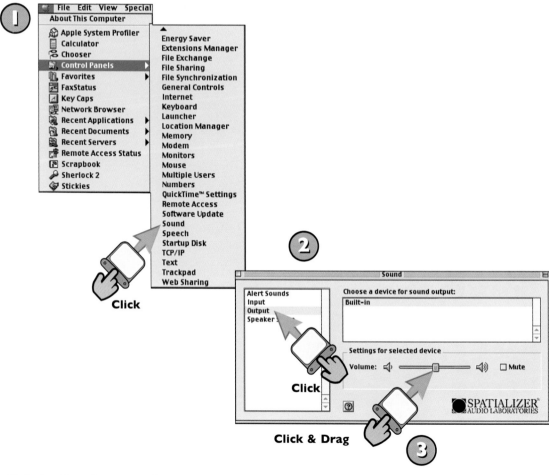

Click

Click

Click & Drag

✓ Sounds Great Without Any Tweaking
You probably won't need to adjust most sound settings on your iBook.

✓ Use Function Keys
Press the **F3** and **F4** keys on your iBook keyboard to decrease or increase the volume.

✓ Test Your Speaker Sound
Click on the **Speaker Setup** item in the window list. Then click **Start Test** to test the sound output on external speakers connected to your iBook.

 Click the **Apple** menu, choose **Control Panels**, and select **Sound**.

 Click on the **Output** item from the window list.

 Adjust the iBook's volume by dragging the slider to the left or right.

Next Step

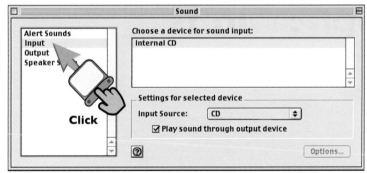

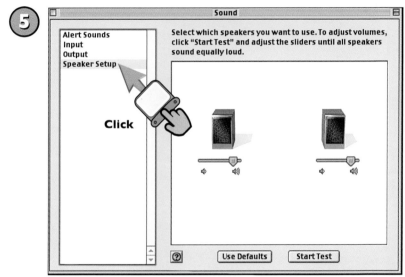

4 Click **Input** to view the sound input source for your iBook.

5 Click on **Speaker Setup** to set the output volumes for external speakers connected to your iBook.

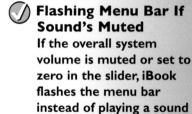

Flashing Menu Bar If Sound's Muted
If the overall system volume is muted or set to zero in the slider, iBook flashes the menu bar instead of playing a sound to issue an alert.

Task 12: Recording an Alert Sound

Your iBook provides a healthy collection of multimedia software, such as SimpleText, QuickTime Player, and Simple Sound, which enable you to add sound to presentations, documents, and Mac OS. This task shows you how to use the Sound control panel to record an alert sound from an audio CD. You can follow these steps with SimpleText and Simple Sound, too.

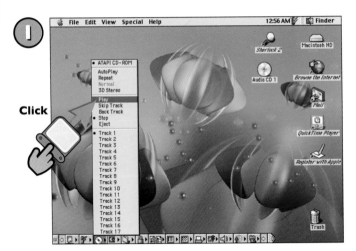

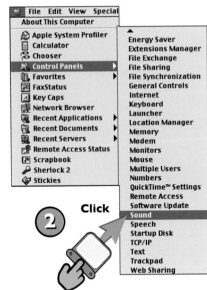

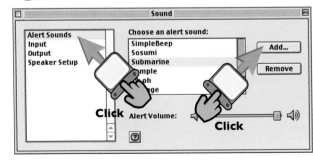

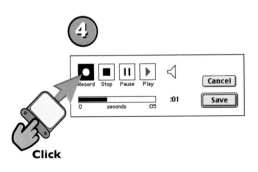

✓ Where's the Microphone?

The iBook does not have a built-in microphone. However, you can create an alert sound on another Macintosh computer and share it with an iBook. Use AirPort to send it from your desktop Mac to your iBook.

1 Insert an audio CD into your iBook's CD-ROM tray. Click on the **CD Control Strip** module and choose **Play**.

2 Click on the **Apple** menu, choose **Control Panels**, and click **Sound**.

3 Click on the **Alert Sounds** item in the window list. Then click on the **Add** button.

4 Click on the **Record** button to record audio from the CD-ROM. Click on the **Stop** button to stop recording audio.

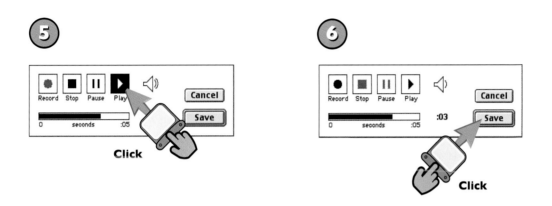

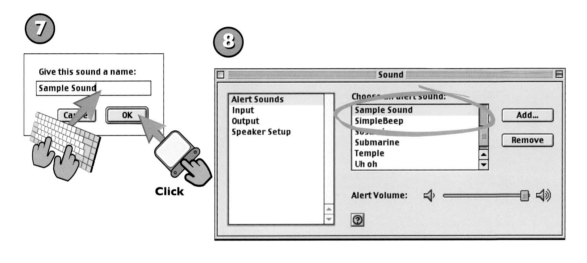

5 Click on the **Play** button to listen to your recording.

6 Click on the **Save** button to save the sound.

7 Type a name for the sound and click the **OK** button.

8 The new sound appears in the list of alert sounds.

When you perform certain actions in Mac OS 9, you might hear a sound. You might hear a sound when you receive an email, or as an alert. You can use the default simple beep as your alert sound, or you can select a different sound.

✓ **Add Sounds from the Internet**

You can download sounds from the Internet and drop them on the **System** file to add them to the list of alert sounds available to your iBook.

✓ **Create Your Own Alert Sounds**

Although the iBook comes with several alert sounds from which to choose, you can create your own alert sounds by using an audio CD. For more information about recording sound, see the previous task.

Task 13: Changing the System Alert Sound

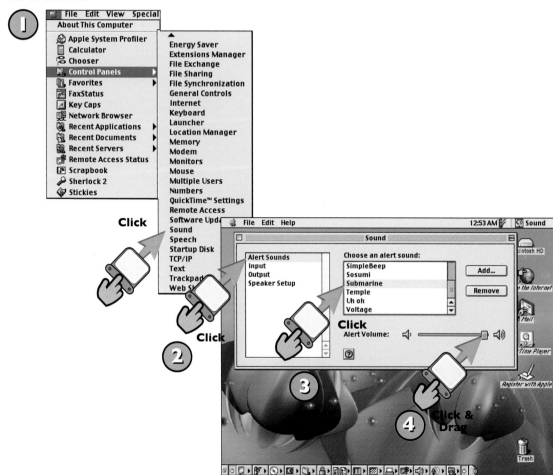

Click

Click

Click

Click & Drag

Start Here

① Click the **Apple** menu, choose **Control Panels**, and select **Sound**.

② Click on the **Alert Sounds** item in the window list.

③ Click on a sound in the list. The sound plays.

④ Click and drag the slider to adjust the volume of the alert sound.

Task 14: Changing How Your Trackpad Works

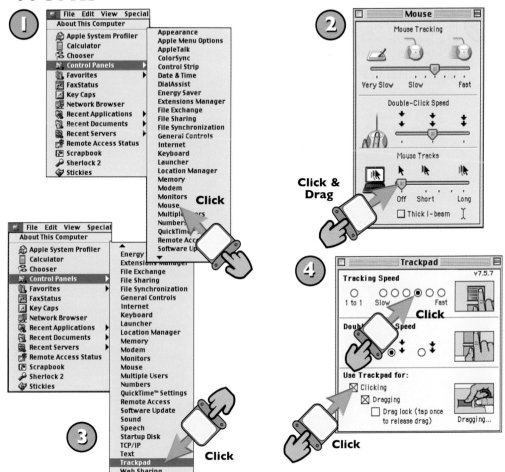

Click

Click & Drag

Click

Click

Click

You can adjust the tracking and double-click speed to make using the trackpad more comfortable for you. In addition, you can decrease your pointer speed so that you can easily find your cursor onscreen when you move it quickly.

✓ **Check Your Double-Click**
You can test the double-click speed by double-clicking a folder icon.

✓ **Trackpad or Mouse?**
You can attach a USB mouse to your iBook and use it in addition to or instead of your trackpad. The trackpad works just as a mouse does, except instead of moving the mouse, you move your finger along the trackpad.

✓ **Faster Is Better**
If you would like to cross the entire desktop with minimal mouse movement, select a faster tracking speed.

1. If you have a USB mouse attached to your iBook, click the **Apple** menu, choose **Control Panels**, and then click **Mouse**.

2. Click and drag a slider to adjust the **Mouse Tracking** or **Double-Click Speed** for a mouse, or the **Mouse Tracks** feature for your trackpad.

3. Click on the **Apple menu**, choose **Control Panels**, and then choose **Trackpad**.

4. Adjust your trackpad settings for **Double-Click Speed** and **Tracking Speed**. Click on the **Clicking** check box to enable your trackpad to support dragging and clicking.

 End Task

If your iBook's clock (or date) is wrong, you should correct it because Mac OS stamps the time and date on every file you save, including email files.

Task 15: Changing the System Date and Time

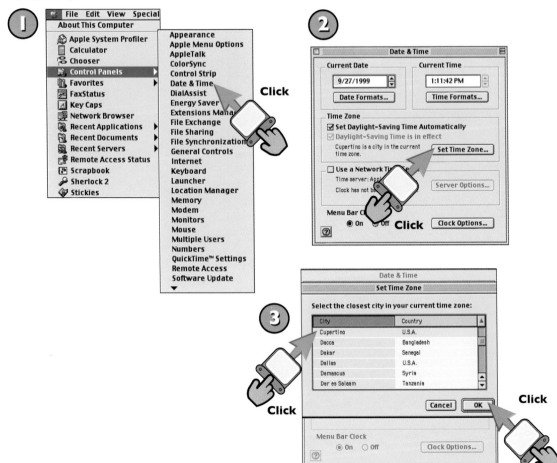

Get a Date from the Menu Bar
You can click the time in the menu bar to display the current date.

Time Zone Affects Email
Some email applications use the **Time Zone** setting to determine what time to stamp on your email.

① Click the **Apple** menu, choose **Control Panels**, and then click **Date & Time**.

② Click the **Set Time Zone** button in the Date & Time control panel.

③ In the Set Time Zone dialog box, choose the city and country in the same time zone you are in, and click **OK**.

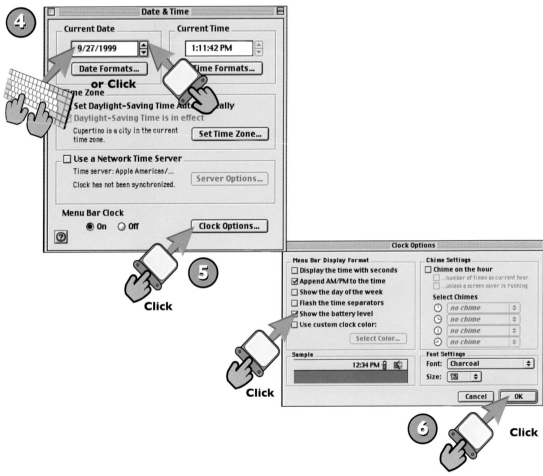

Date & Time

Current Date
9/27/1999

Current Time
1:11:42 PM

Date Formats...

Time Formats...

or Click

Time Zone

Set Daylight-Saving Time Automatically

Daylight-Saving Time is in effect

Cupertino is a city in the current time zone.

Set Time Zone...

☐ Use a Network Time Server

Time server: Apple Americas/...

Clock has not been synchronized.

Server Options...

Menu Bar Clock

◉ On   ○ Off

Clock Options...

Click

Clock Options

Menu Bar Display Format

☐ Display the time with seconds
☑ Append AM/PM to the time
☐ Show the day of the week
☐ Flash the time separators
☑ Show the battery level
☐ Use custom clock color:

Select Color...

Chime Settings

☐ Chime on the hour
  ☐ ...number of times as current hour
  ☐ ...unless a screen saver is running

Select Chimes

🕐 no chime
🕐 no chime
🕐 no chime
🕐 no chime

Sample

12:34 PM 🔋 📶

Font Settings

Font: Charcoal
Size: 12

Cancel   OK

Click

Click

Click

4 Use the spin controls or type the correct numbers into the date and time fields.

5 Click the **Clock Options** button.

6 Customize the clock in the **Menu Bar Display Format**, **Chime Settings**, and **Font Settings**. Click **OK**. Click the **Close** button in the Date & Time control panel.

✓ **Adjust Time from the Internet**

If your iBook has access to the Internet, you can use a network server to set the time on your iBook. Click the **Use a Network Time Server** check box in the Date & Time control panel, and click the **Server Options** button to configure your use of this feature.

End Task

Task 16: Using Location Manager

When you're on the go, Apple provides Location Manager to store different software settings for different locations. For example, you can save your AppleTalk network or Extensions Manager sets for a particular location. Location Manager can save you the time of manually changing these settings in your iBook as you move from place to place.

✓ **Deactivate Location Manager**
Click on the **None** set in the **Current Location** pop-up menu to turn off Location Manager. You can also uncheck the Location Manager extension and control panel to prevent Location Manager from loading at startup.

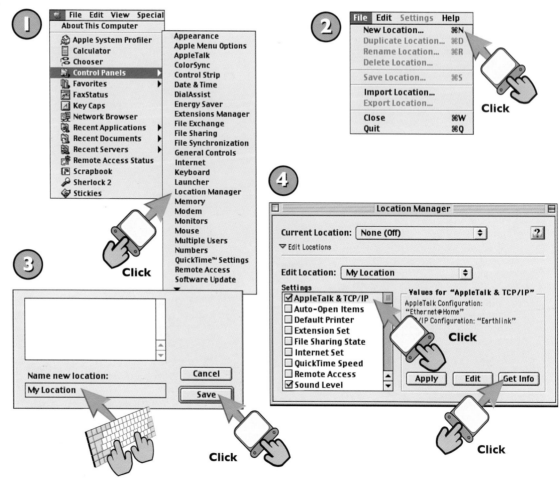

① Click on the **Apple** menu, choose **Control Panels**, and then select **Location Manager**.

② Click **File** and choose **New Location**.

③ Type the name of the new location, and then click the **Save** button.

④ Select software and its settings for that location. Location Manager saves the current setting of the selected software. Click on the **Get Info** button to find out more about an item.

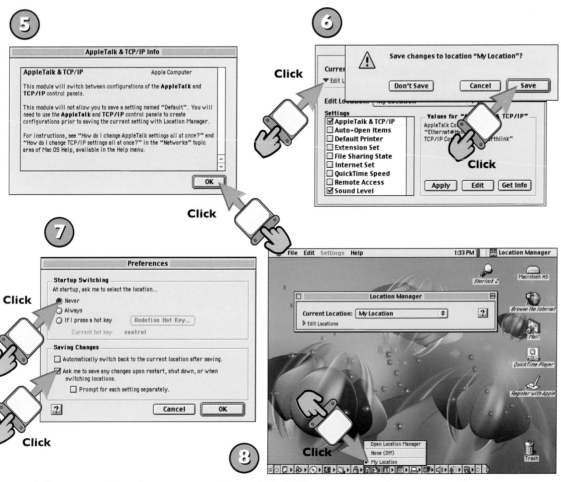

Click

Click

Click

Click

Click

Click

Click

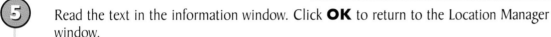

⑤ Read the text in the information window. Click **OK** to return to the Location Manager window.

⑥ Click the **Edit Locations** button arrow, and then click the **Save** button.

⑦ Click **Edit** and choose **Preferences** to customize Location Manager to the way you want it to behave. Click on a check box or radio button to choose a setting you want.

⑧ To change to a particular Location Manager set, click on the pop-up menu in the Location Manager window, or click on the **Location Manager Control Strip** module.

Task 17: Customizing Your Keyboard Controls

A full set of function keys is included with your iBook. You can assign a particular function to the F7–F12 keys. When you press the function key, you can start an application, open a document, or run an AppleScript. Configure your function keys with the Keyboard control panel.

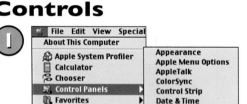

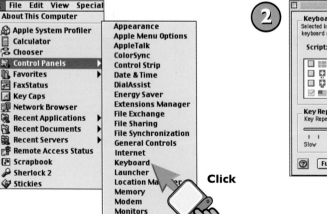

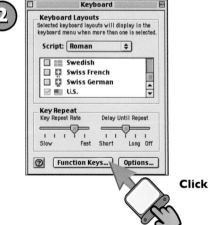

Click

Click

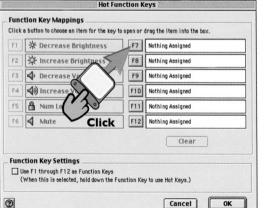

Click

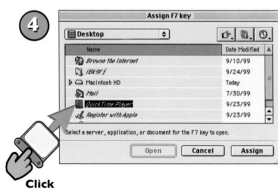

Click

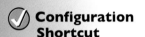

✓ **Configuration Shortcut**
Assign a file or folder to a function key by dragging and dropping the item over the function key's text field in the Hot Function Keys window.

Click on the **Apple** menu, choose **Control Panels**, and then select **Keyboard**.

Click on the **Function Keys** button.

Click on a function key you want to modify. In this case, I've selected the **F7** key.

Click on an item you want to assign to the function key. In this case, I've chosen the **QuickTime Player** alias.

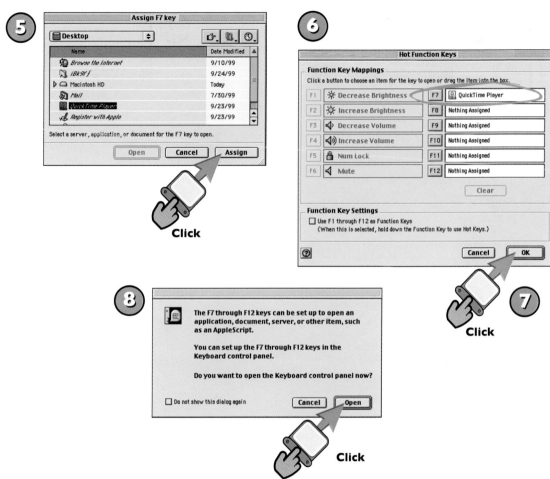

Click (step 5)

Click (step 7)

Click (step 8)

⑤ Click on the **Assign** button.

⑥ The function key is assigned to the selected item.

⑦ Click on the **OK** button to exit the Keyboard control panel.

⑧ Press an unassigned function key as a shortcut to access the Hot Function Keys window. Click **Open** in the window to go to the Keyboard control panel.

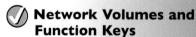

Network Volumes and Function Keys
If you use a file or access a folder over the network frequently, you might want to assign a function key to access it quickly.

Setting Up Applications

Most of the time you spend using your iBook will be spent using an application. Whether you're starting, setting up, installing, or de-installing an application, Apple makes all this as easy as possible. Mac OS provides many ways you can work with applications. You can create shortcuts, or **aliases**, to an application and place the alias on the desktop to make it more accessible. You can install new applications and remove applications that you no longer use. This part shows you how to accomplish all these setup tasks and more.

Tasks

Task #		Page #
1	Adding Aliases	164
2	Renaming an Alias	165
3	Deleting Aliases	166
4	Adding Applications to the Apple Menu	167
5	Deleting Applications from the Apple Menu	168
6	Adding Folders to the Apple Menu	169
7	Rearranging the Apple Menu	170
8	Starting an Application When You Start Mac OS	171
9	Installing Applications	172
10	Uninstalling Applications	173
11	Using AppleScript	174
12	Using File Sharing	176

Task 1: Adding Aliases

You can create aliases and place them on the desktop or in the Apple menu to provide quick access to applications. You then double-click an alias to quickly start that program—without having to open menus and folders.

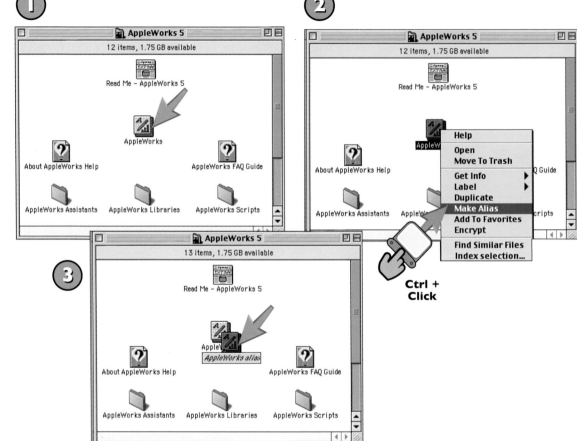

Ctrl + Click

✅ **Fixing a Broken Alias**
If an alias cannot find its original application, you can search for it. Click **Fix Alias**, and then use the Fix Alias window to locate the application corresponding to the alias.

❗ **Don't Delete the Original, Only the Alias**
You can't replace an application with an alias. Do not delete the application after creating an alias to it.

① In an open window, display the application file for which you want to create an alias icon.

② Holding down the **Ctrl** key, click the icon and choose **Make Alias**.

③ Mac OS adds the alias to your desktop.

Task 2: Renaming an Alias

Start Here

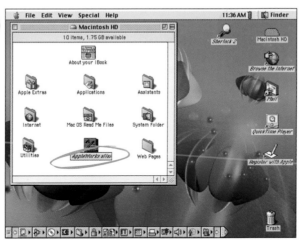

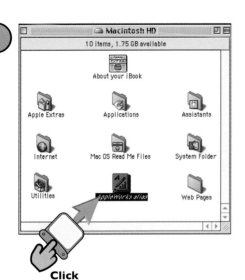

Click

When you create an alias, your iBook will assign a name to the icon. Nonetheless, you might want to use a different name. For instance, rather than the name **System Folder alias,** you might prefer **Mac OS Folder.** You can rename any of the alias icons anywhere on your hard drive.

① Click the name area of the alias icon you want to rename.

② Wait about one second; the text becomes highlighted.

③ Type a new name for the alias and press **Enter**.

 For Aliases Only
Alias icons are always named with text formatted in *italic*.

End Task

Task 3: Deleting Aliases

You can use aliases to quickly open the program you need. But as time passes, your needs for programs might change, and your desktop might become cluttered with application icons you no longer need. Just as you can create new aliases as you add new applications, you can delete aliases you no longer use.

✓ **Original Remains If Alias Is Deleted**
Deleting an alias does not delete that application from your hard drive. To delete the application, you must uninstall it. Uninstalling applications is covered in Task 10, "Uninstalling Applications."

✓ **Undelete an Alias**
If you change your mind about deleting an item, you can move the alias out of the Trash. To do so, double-click the **Trash** icon and click and drag the alias to the desktop.

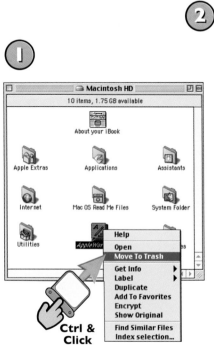

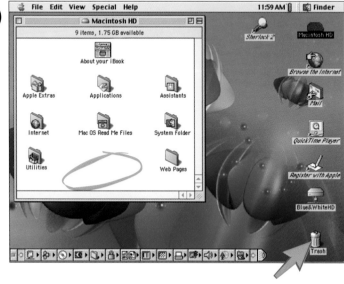

 Holding down the **Ctrl** key, click the icon, and choose **Move To Trash**.

 Mac OS moves the alias to the Trash. The alias will be deleted from the hard drive the next time **Empty Trash** is chosen from the **Special** menu.

Task 4: Adding Applications to the Apple Menu

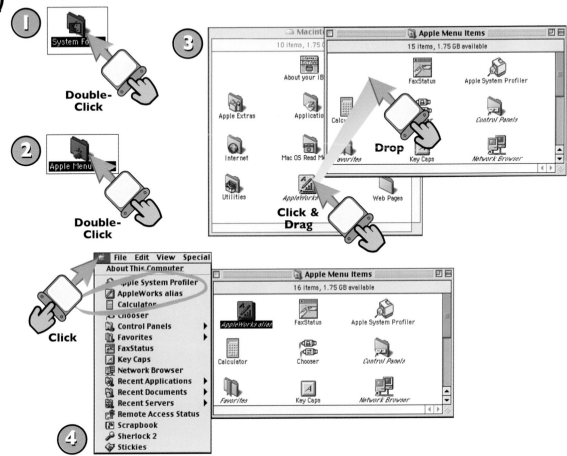

Double-Click

Double-Click

Click

Click & Drag

Drop

With most applications, you need to tunnel through several folders to open the application. You can add an alias to an application to the Apple menu to enable quick, easy access.

✅ **Recent Applications Folder**
The Apple Menu Options control panel adds an alias for any application you start to the **Recent Applications** folder in the Apple menu. This enables you to add several applications to the **Apple** menu without affecting the menu's length.

✅ **Create an Apple Menu Alias**
Click on the **Apple Menu Items** folder, click on the **File** menu, and then choose **Make Alias (or press Command+M)** to create an alias of your Apple menu folder. Select the alias and drag to your desktop, to quickly access any item in that folder.

① Double-click the **System Folder** icon.

② Double-click the **Apple Menu Items** folder icon.

③ Select an application's alias file and drag it to the Apple Menu Items folder window.

④ Click on the **Apple** menu to access the alias.

Task 5: Deleting Applications from the Apple Menu

At first, you might add all kinds of icons to the Apple menu. However, after you use the iBook more and more, you might want to streamline the Apple menu and weed out programs that you don't use. If your Apple menu becomes cluttered, you might want to delete icons for applications that you don't use.

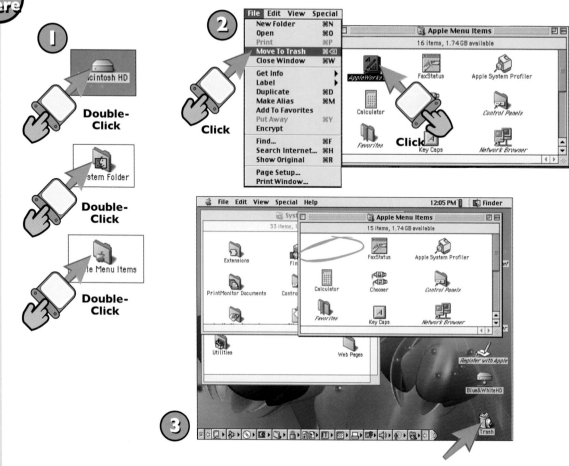

Start Here

Double-Click

Double-Click

Double-Click

Click

Click

① ② ③

✓ **Delete a Folder, Too**
You can also follow this procedure to remove a folder from the Apple menu. Simply select the folder and select **Move To Trash** from the **File** menu.

1 Double-click the hard drive icon, and then double-click the **System Folder** icon. Double-click the **Apple Menu Items** folder icon.

2 In the Apple Menu Items window, click the application icon you want to delete (in this case, **AppleWorks**), click **File**, and then choose **Move To Trash**.

3 Mac OS moves the file from the Apple Menu Items folder to the Trash.

End Task

Task 6: Adding Folders to the Apple Menu

When you install a new application, that application's installation sets up application folders and icons for itself. If you don't like the arrangement of the folder and icons, you can change it. For instance, if more than one person uses your iBook, you might set up folders for each person and then add the applications that a certain person uses to his or her folder.

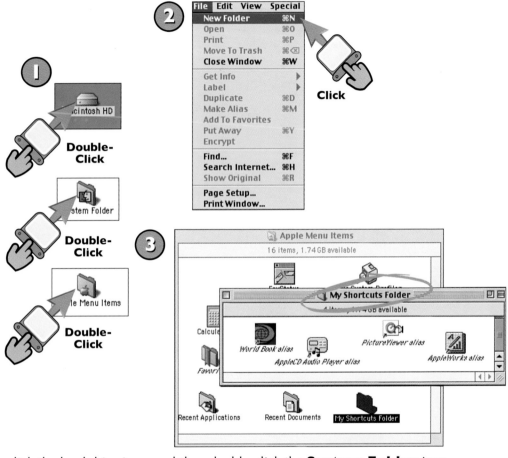

Double-Click

Double-Click

Double-Click

Click

File   Edit   View   Special
New Folder   ⌘N
Open   ⌘O
Print   ⌘P
Move To Trash   ⌘⌫
Close Window   ⌘W

Get Info   ▶
Label   ▶
Duplicate   ⌘D
Make Alias   ⌘M
Add To Favorites
Put Away   ⌘Y
Encrypt

Find...   ⌘F
Search Internet... ⌘H
Show Original   ⌘R

Page Setup...
Print Window...

1 Double-click the hard drive icon, and then double-click the **System Folder** icon. Double-click the **Apple Menu Items** folder icon.

2 Click **File** and choose **New Folder** to create a new folder in the Apple menu.

3 Use drag and drop to add any aliases to applications to this folder, and then name the folder according to its contents (in this case, **My Shortcuts Folder**).

 Delete Folders with Contextual Menus
You can delete folders. To do so, simply hold down the **Ctrl** key and click the folder you want to delete. Then choose the **Move To Trash** command.

Task 7: Rearranging the Apple Menu

After you set up folders, you can organize your Apple menu, putting the program icons in the folder and order you want.

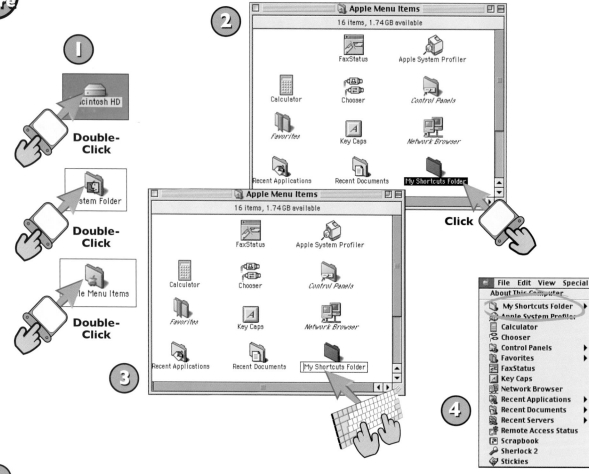

✓ **Put a Folder in the Apple Menu**

If the Apple menu becomes cluttered with too many icons, create a folder and place any group of icons in it. Placing several icons in one folder makes it easier for you to find items in the Apple menu.

1 Double-click the hard drive icon, and then double-click the **System Folder** icon. Double-click the **Apple Menu Items** folder icon.

2 Click on the file or folder that you want to appear at (or near) the top of the Apple menu (in this case, **My Shortcuts Folder**).

3 Press the **left arrow** key once, and then press the **spacebar** once. Press the **Enter** key to save the filename.

4 Click the **Apple** menu. Note that the **My Shortcuts Folder** icon appears at the top of the menu.

Task 8: Starting an Application When You Start Mac OS

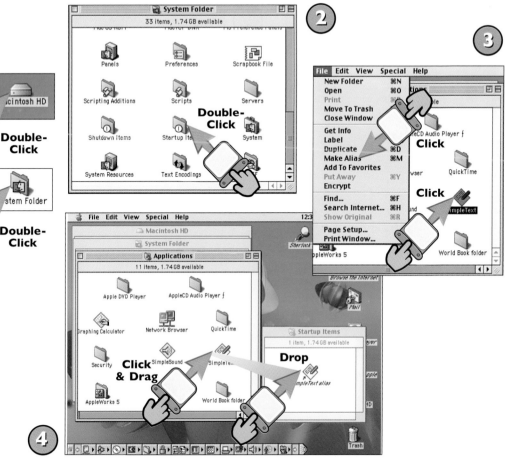

Mac OS enables you to start one or more applications at the same time that you start Mac OS by turning your iBook on. Applications you might want to open automatically include those that you use everyday or those that you use first thing every morning.

Double-Click

Double-Click

Double-Click

Double-Click

Click

Click

Click & Drag

Drop

---

① Double-click the hard drive icon, and then double-click the **System Folder** icon.

② Double-click the **Startup Items** folder icon.

③ Find and select the application you want to run at startup, and then create an alias by selecting **Make Alias** from the **File** menu.

④ Drag the alias to the Startup Items folder. Restart Mac OS, and the application will open after Mac OS starts up.

✓ **Wake Up Faster**
If you put your iBook to sleep and don't shut it down at night, these applications will not be started each morning. They are started only when you start up your iBook.

✓ **Using the Shut Down Items Folder**
You can also run applications when you shut down Mac OS. Instead of placing an alias in the Startup Items folder, place the alias in the Shutdown Items folder.

Task 9: Installing Applications

When you bought your iBook, it came with certain applications already installed. If you want to add to these, you can purchase additional programs and add them to your iBook. Installing a new program basically copies the program files to a folder on your hard drive and, in some cases, might add an alias icon to the Apple menu for starting the application. The application's installation might also make changes to other files or programs on your hard drive, including the System Folder folder.

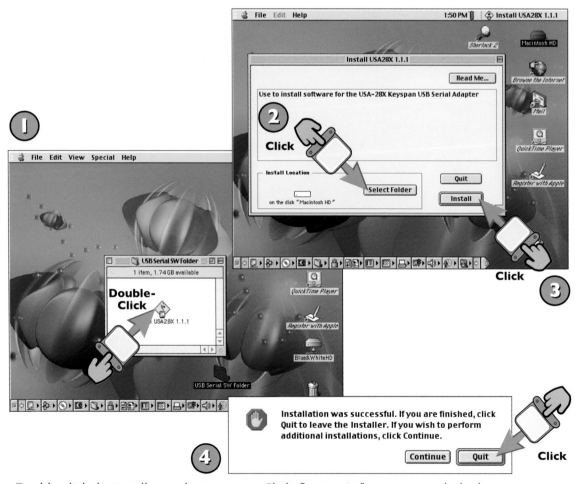

✅ **Various Installers**
Some installation applications might vary from the steps in this procedure. If an easy installation of the software is not available, choose the typical or default installation for the software.

1 Double-click the installer application icon. Click **Accept** if you agree with the licensing agreement for the software you are installing.

2 Click the **Select Folder** button (or pop-up menu) to choose where you want the application installed on your hard drive.

3 Click the **Install** button and follow any instructions presented in the installer application.

4 Click the **Continue** button if you need to install additional applications. Click **Quit** or **Restart** to complete the installation.

Task 10: Uninstalling Applications

Start Here

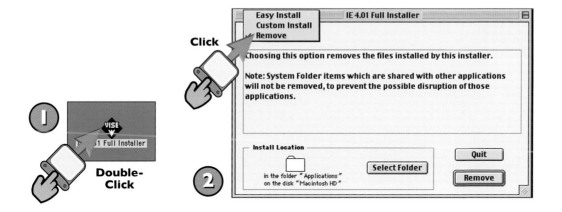

Click

Double-Click

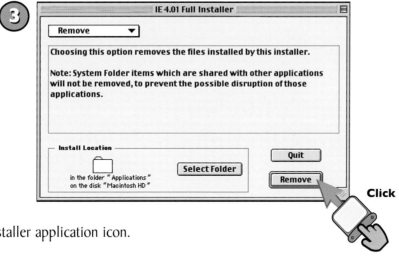

Click

You can remove an alias icon from the Apple menu, but doing so leaves that application on your hard drive. When you want to get rid of the application and its files entirely, you can uninstall it. This removes the application and all its related files and folders from your hard drive. However, first you should move any data files you want to keep from your application's folders. You might also want to create a backup of the application before you uninstall it.

1 Double-click the installer application icon.

2 Click the pop-up menu and choose **Remove**.

3 Click the **Remove** button. The installer application uninstalls the files and returns you to the installer application window.

☑ **No Uninstall?**
Some programs do not include an uninstall option in their installer applications. In most cases, you can move the application folder to the Trash to uninstall it.

End Task

Task 11: Using AppleScript

Mac OS includes a scripting language, AppleScript. If you have applications that support AppleScript, you can automate tasks in those applications by creating an AppleScript script. The Script Editor application is located in the AppleScript folder, which is installed by Mac OS in the Apple Extras folder.

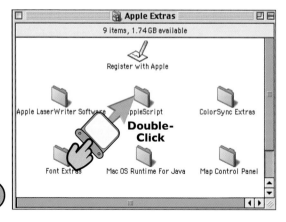

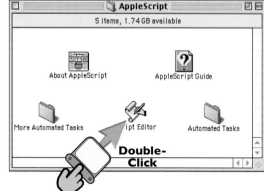

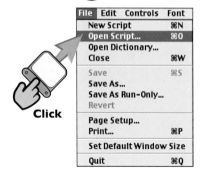

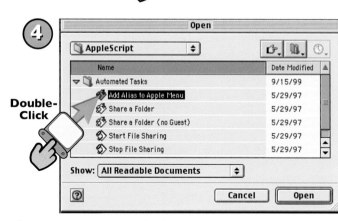

✓ Basic AppleScript Commands

Most applications support a core set of AppleScript commands, such as opening and quitting an application.

✓ Automated Tasks in Mac OS

Mac OS comes with several AppleScripts, which are located in the Automated Tasks and More Automated Tasks folders in the AppleScript folder.

① Double-click the hard drive icon, then the **Apple Extras** folder icon, and finally the **AppleScript** folder icon.

② Double-click the **Script Editor** application icon.

③ Click **File** and choose the **Open Script** command.

④ Double-click the **Automated Tasks** folder, and then double-click an AppleScript file (in this case, the **Add Alias to Apple Menu** script).

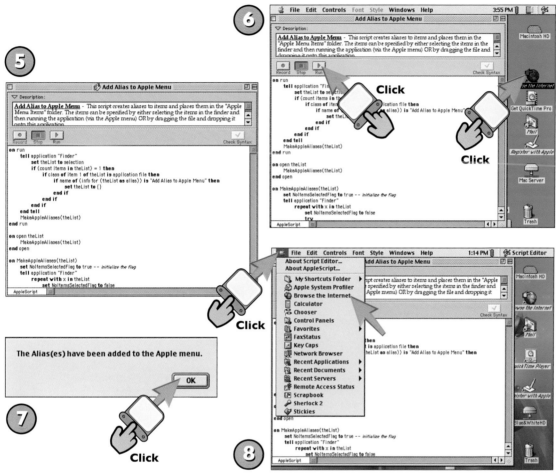

Modify the AppleScript
You can modify the AppleScript in the Script Editor. The Script Editor can help you use the AppleScript programming language to complete your AppleScript scripts.

Add Onto an Existing AppleScript Script
You can use an existing AppleScript script to create your own. After you are able to successfully run your own AppleScript, you can add it to the Automated Tasks folder in the AppleScript folder.

Use Different Dictionaries in AppleScript
You can change the AppleScript dictionary to create scripts for different applications. Click the **File** menu and choose **Open Dictionary** to choose a dictionary you want to use with your AppleScript script.

⑤ View the contents of the Add Alias to Apple Menu file in the Script Editor window.

⑥ Select an icon you want to add to the Apple menu (in this case, the **Browse the Internet** alias on the desktop). Click the **Run** button.

⑦ Mac OS runs the AppleScript. Click the **OK** button to close the dialog box.

⑧ Click the **Apple** menu. Note that the item has been added to the Apple menu.

Task 12: Using File Sharing

Whether your iBook is on a wired or wireless network, you can share files with other computers on the network. If another Macintosh is on the network, using either Chooser or Network Browser, the other Mac can directly access the iBook on the network using File Sharing.

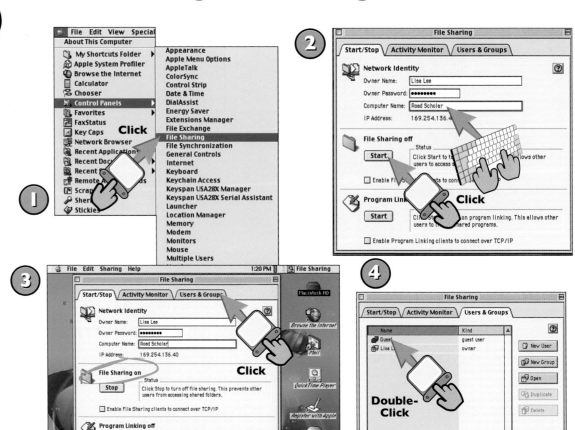

✅ **Personal Versus Public**
Most networks have servers that support both Mac and PC files. If you do not want to share your iBook on the network, you can copy a file or folder to a public server on the network instead of using File Sharing.

① Click the **Apple** menu, choose **Control Panels**, and click **File Sharing**.

② Type in the owner name, the owner password, and the computer name in the appropriate fields. Click on the **Start** button under **File Sharing off**.

③ Wait for **File Sharing on** to appear. Click the **Users & Groups** tab in the File Sharing control panel.

④ Double-click on the **Guest** icon.

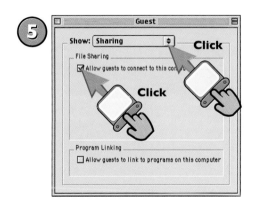

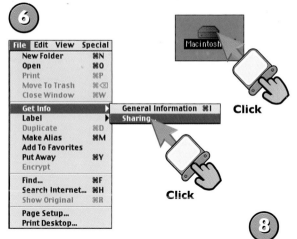

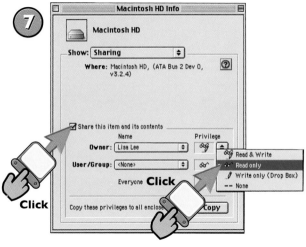

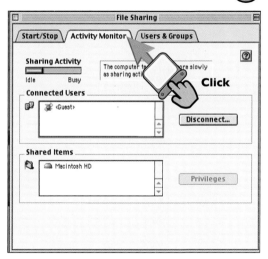

(8)

Can't Rename That Folder?

If you share a folder, you won't be able to rename it until you turn off File Sharing privileges to the folder. Click on the **File** menu, choose **Get Info**, and then select **Sharing** to turn off File Sharing access to a folder or hard disk.

File Sharing Slows Down Your iBook

If you leave File Sharing on, it will use additional memory and will have a considerable performance impact on your iBook whenever another Macintosh accesses your iBook over the network. For optimal performance, turn on File Sharing only when you need to share a file on your iBook.

(5) Click **Sharing** in the **Show** pop-up menu. Click the **Allow guests to connect to this computer** check box.

(6) Find and select the folder you want to share. In this case, I've selected the **Macintosh HD**. Click the **File** menu, choose **Get Info**, and then choose **Sharing**.

(7) Click the **Share this item and its contents** check box. The folder is now shared on the network. Click on the **Privilege** pop-up menu to assign access privileges to the selected folder.

(8) Click on the **Activity Monitor** tab to view Sharing activity and a list of Connected Users and Shared Items.

Using iBook Accessories

iBook provides several accessories that you can use to help you in your work. Many of these accessories—such as Key Caps—do not have quite as many features as other applications, such as SimpleText. But they are useful for specific jobs on your iBook. Accessories include a calculator, a graphing calculator, and Keychain Access, as well as more feature-laden applications such as SimpleText, Sherlock 2, Stickies, and various Internet applications. (The Internet applications are discussed in Part 2, "Connecting to Online Services and the Internet.") iBook also includes some multimedia applications for playing CDs and for editing and playing back media files.

Tasks

Task #		Page #
1	Creating Multiple User Accounts	180
2	Using Stickies	182
3	Typing Text in Stickies	183
4	Creating Text Documents with SimpleText	184
5	Viewing Fonts with Key Caps	185
6	Viewing an Image with SimpleText	186
7	Formatting Text in SimpleText	187
8	Using Scrapbook	188
9	Using Sherlock 2	190
10	Playing an Audio CD	191
11	Changing the Volume	192
12	Playing a Media File	193
13	Editing Audio and Video with QuickTime Player	194
14	Editing a QuickTime Movie Using QuickTime Player	196
15	Using Calculator and Graphing Calculator	198
16	Selecting Network Devices with Chooser	200
17	Surfing the Net with Network Browser	202
18	Using Keychain Access	204

Task 1: Creating Multiple User Accounts

If you would like to share your iBook with others, you might want to create multiple user accounts. The **Multiple Users control panel** enables you to customize access to your iBook for three different kinds of user accounts. Each account has its own login name and password. Each time a person logs in, all the settings for a particular account will be used.

Start Here

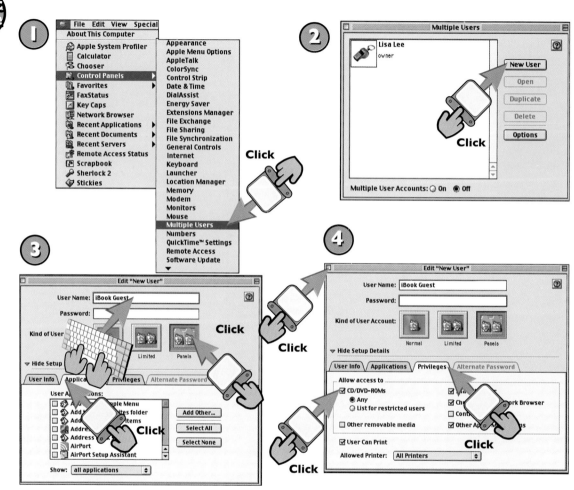

About Kinds of Accounts

Users can have a Normal, Limited, or Panels account. A normal account gives a user full access to your iBook. Limited access lets you choose which folders the user can access. If others will be using your iBook, be careful about which folders and software applications you give them access to.

① Click the **Apple** menu, choose **Control Panels**, and then choose **Multiple Users**.

② Click the **New User** button.

③ Type the user's name and a password. Choose the **Kind of User Account**. I chose **Panels**. Click the **Applications** tab to configure the applications for that user.

④ Click on the **Privileges** tab. Then click on a check box to select or deselect features for the new user. Click on the **Close** box to save your changes.

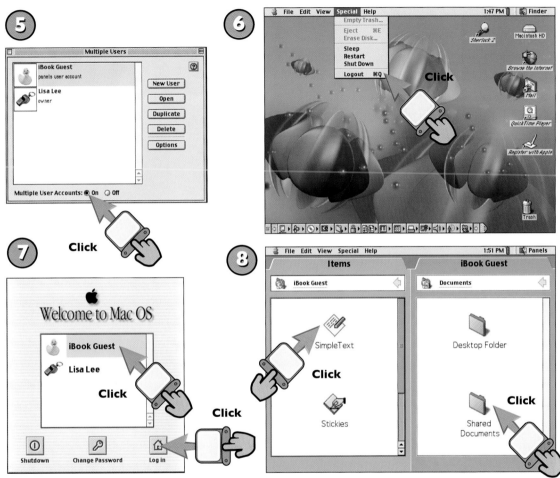

⑤ Click the **On** radio button to activate **Multiple User Accounts**.

⑥ Click on the **Special** menu and choose **Logout**.

⑦ Click on a username, and then click on the **Log in** button.

⑧ Click on an icon in the **Items** or **iBook Guest** panels to access an application or folder.

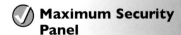 **Maximum Security Panel**
The most secure account to create for your iBook is a Panels account.

Task 2: Using Stickies

As you browse the Internet or work on a document, you may want to save small sections of text to another window for future use. iBook provides Stickies and Note Pad as applications that can be used to store text.

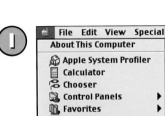

✓ **More Than One Color**
Change the color of a sticky note by clicking the **Color** menu and choosing the color you want.

✓ **Startup Stickies**
The first time you quit Stickies, you will be asked if you want Stickies to open whenever you start your iBook. If you choose **Yes**, an alias to Stickies is placed in the Startup Items folder of your System folder. If you do not want Stickies to open at startup, move its alias out of the Startup Items folder.

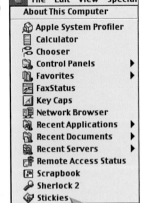
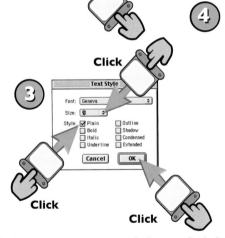
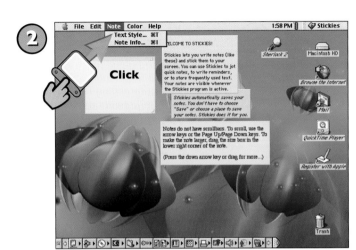

1. Click the **Apple** menu and choose **Stickies**.

2. To change text styles, click the **Note** menu and choose **Text Style**.

3. Choose a font, size, and style, and then click **OK**.

4. Type text into any Stickies window. Any changes you make to a Stickies note are saved automatically.

Task 3: Typing Text in Stickies

Start Here

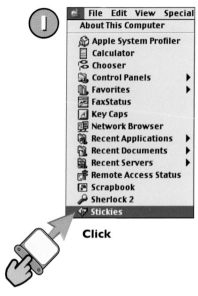

Click

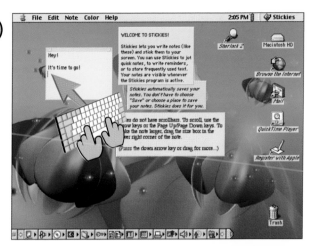

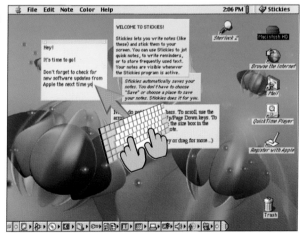

You can add or delete text anywhere in a Stickies window. To do this, use the arrow keys and alphanumeric keys in combination with the mouse.

Correct Mistakes
If you make a mistake while typing, press the **Delete** key to backspace and remove one character at a time. Then retype the text.

Save Your Work!
Although Stickies automatically saves your documents, most applications, such as SimpleText, save a document only when you select the **Save** command. Be sure to periodically save your document. See Task 6, "Saving a Document," in Part 4, "Using iBook Applications."

Selecting Text
If you're not sure how to select text, refer Part 4, Task 9, "Selecting Text."

① Click on the **Apple** menu, and then choose **Stickies**.

② Type some text. To start or end a paragraph and start a new one, press **Return**. The insertion point moves to the next line.

③ To move to a different location in the document, click the spot where you want to place the insertion point.

④ To add text, start typing. To remove text, press the **Delete** key on your keyboard.

End Task

The most common type of simple file is the text file. You can find instructions on how to install an application and other information in text files; some configuration files are also text files. To edit and work with this type of file, you can use SimpleText, which has text-editing features similar to AppleWorks and Stickies. You can use SimpleText to save each text file as an individual file on your hard drive. Plus, it has the capability to find and replace text in a document. SimpleText can also read many more types of files, such as QuickTime movies, sound files, QuickDraw 3D files, and Read Me files, included with most Macintosh applications products.

✓ Another Way to Open a File

You can drag and drop a text, PICT, 3D, or QuickTime file over SimpleText to open it.

Task 4: Creating Text Documents with SimpleText

Double-Click

Double-Click

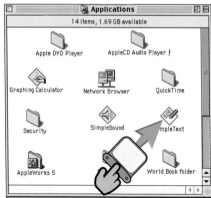
Double-Click

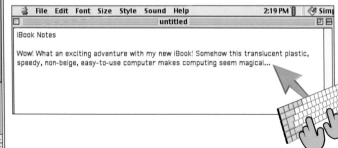

 Double-click the hard drive icon.

 Double-click the **Applications** folder.

 Double-click the **SimpleText** icon.

 The SimpleText window opens; type whatever text you want.

Task 5: Viewing Fonts with Key Caps

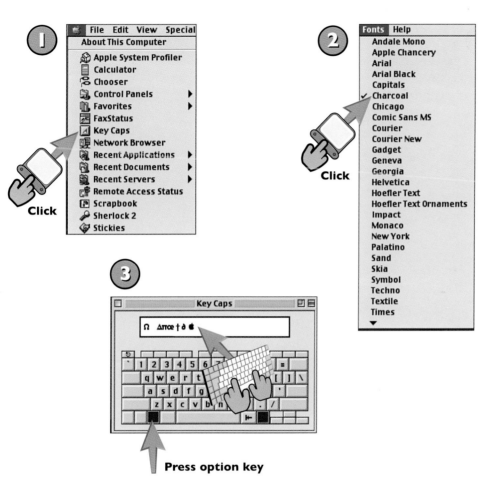

Click

Click

Press option key

Several fonts are installed in your System folder on your iBook. A *font* consists of a core set of characters, usually consisting of the alphabet. Additional characters can be viewed using the Key Caps application. These additional characters can be typed by holding down the **Option** or **Ctrl** keys while typing on the alphanumeric keys on the keyboard.

1 Click the **Apple** menu and choose **Key Caps**.

2 Click the **Font** menu and choose a font.

3 Type text in the Key Caps window to view the font style.

✓ **Even Bigger Keys**
You can resize the Key Caps window by clicking the Zoom box in the Key Caps window title bar.

SimpleText can open several kinds of image documents, including those in **PICT, JPEG, 3DMF,** and **GIF** file formats.

 Create a Screenshot
You can create a screenshot of your iBook screen by pressing **Command+Shift+3**. Mac OS names the screenshot **Picture 1** and saves it to your hard drive folder.

 Even More About Screenshots
You can create a custom screenshot and choose only part of the screen to capture by dragging your mouse. Press **Command+Shift+4**, then select the part of the screen you want to capture. Mac OS names the screenshot **Picture 1** and saves it to your hard drive folder. If you hold down the **Ctrl** key, you can save the screen shot to the **Clipboard** and paste it into an application such as **Scrapbook**, or use it as a desktop pattern.

Task 6: Viewing an Image with SimpleText

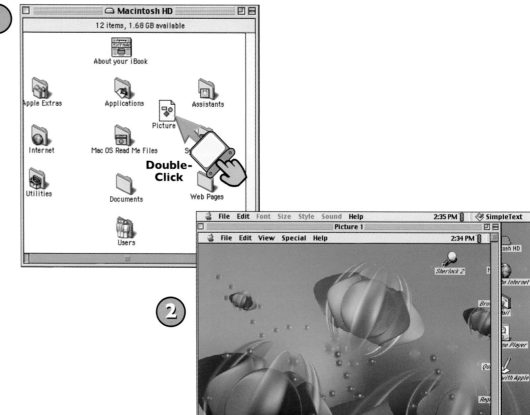

Press **Command+Shift+3** to create a screenshot of your desktop. Double-click the **Macintosh HD** icon, then double-click the image document.

The image opens in SimpleText

Task 7: Formatting Text in SimpleText

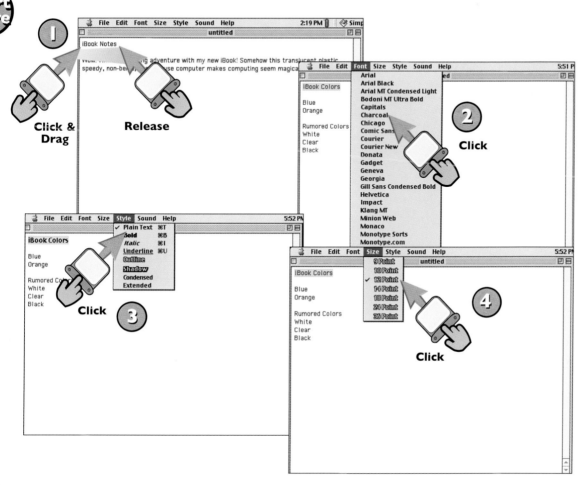

You can easily make simple changes to the appearance of the text by using the SimpleText application. For example, you can change the font or font size, and you can make text bold, italic, or underlined. This task touches on just a few of the formatting changes you can make. Experiment to try out some of the other available formatting features.

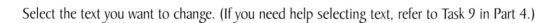

1. Select the text you want to change. (If you need help selecting text, refer to Task 9 in Part 4.)

2. To use a different font, click the **Font** menu and choose the font you want.

3. To make text bold, italic, underline, and so on, select the text you want to change, click the **Style** menu, and choose the desired font style.

4. To change the font size, select the text you want to change, click the **Size** menu, and choose the font size you want.

✓ Why Format Text?
Formatting text can make it easier for people reading your document to comprehend what they are reading.

❗ Don't Overdo It
Using too many customizing features can be hard on the eyes. Although these features can enhance the appearance of the document, they can cause more harm than good if you overdo it.

Task 8: Using Scrapbook

You can use Scrapbook to store snippets of text, art, or sounds. Scrapbook is an application that stores several kinds of data.

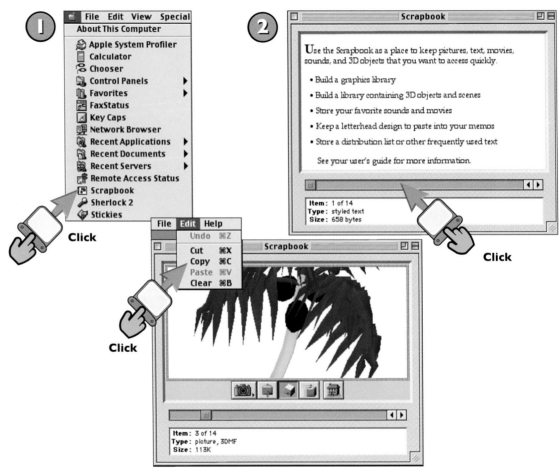

Click

Click

Click

Item: 1 of 14
Type: styled text
Size: 658 bytes

Item: 3 of 14
Type: picture, 3DMF
Size: 113K

✓ **Check It Out**
Mac OS includes several images in Scrapbook.

✓ **Transfer Files with Scrapbook**
Drag and drop any item from Scrapbook. Then drag and drop or cut and paste it into another application.

① Click the **Apple** menu and choose **Scrapbook**.

② Click on the right or the left side of the scrollbar thumb to view each piece of data stored in the Scrapbook.

③ To copy an item from Scrapbook, scroll to an item in the Scrapbook window, click **Edit**, and choose **Copy**. Go to another application, click on **Edit**, and choose **Paste**.

Next Step

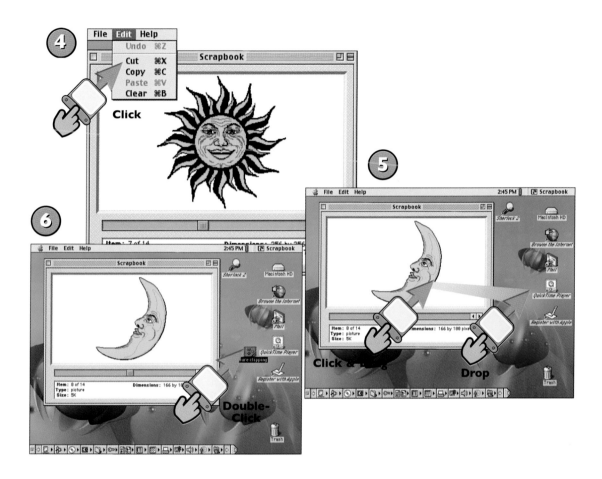

Click

Double-Click

Click & Drag

Drop

To remove an item from the Scrapbook, click **Edit** and choose **Cut** to paste the data to another document or **Clear** to remove the item from the Scrapbook.

To move an item out of the Scrapbook, select the item and drag it to the desktop.

Mac OS converts the image into a clipping file—in this case, the name of the file is **Sample Image**. Double-click the clipping to view it.

 Give Scrapbook More Memory

If you use Scrapbook to store a lot of data, you may eventually need to increase the amount of memory allocated to the Scrapbook application as the Scrapbook file grows larger. For more information about how to increase application memory, see Task 12, "Increasing Application Memory," in Part 10, "Maintaining Your iBook."

Task 9: Using Sherlock 2

Using Sherlock 2, you can find files on any hard drive or network server, or you can index your hard drive so that you can search it (Sherlock 2 can search a 4GB hard drive in about 90 seconds).

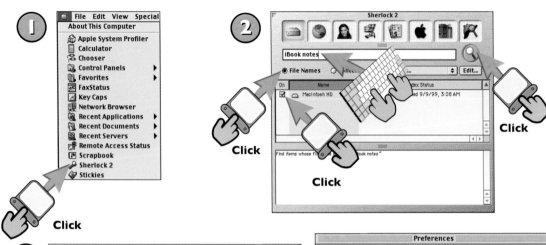

Start Here

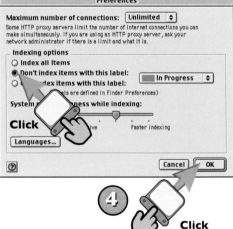

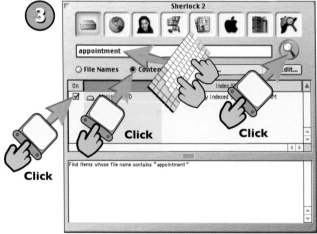

Plug into Sherlock 2
If you have Internet access, you can download Sherlock 2 plug-ins for several Internet sites so that you can search the Internet quickly before you actually log in to it.

✓ **Save Your Search Criteria**
You can save and open search criteria with Sherlock 2. Click **File** and choose **Open Search Criteria** to open any previously saved search criteria.

① Click the **Apple** menu and choose **Sherlock 2**. You can also start Sherlock 2 by double-clicking the **Sherlock 2** icon on your desktop.

② To look for a file or folder, click **File Names**, then type a word or words into the text field. Click on the drive you want to search and click on the **Search** button.

③ To search the contents of your hard disk, click on **Contents**. Type a word or words you want to search for. Click on the drive you want to search and click on the **Search** button.

④ Click **Edit** and choose **Preferences**. Click **Don't index items with this label**, and choose the label you want excluded from the index. Click **OK**.

End Task

Task 12: Playing a Media File

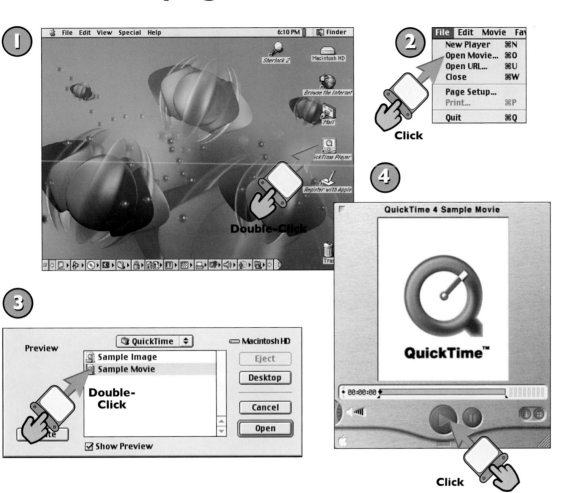

Media files are a combination of text, graphics, sounds, video, and animations. As computers take more and more advantage of the multimedia features of your iBook, you will find more media files for your use. For instance, your iBook provides some sample media files. To play these presentations, you can use QuickTime Player.

✅ **Even More Media Files**
The Internet includes many types of media files you can use with your iBook. For information on browsing the Internet, refer to Part 2, "Connecting to Online Services and the Internet."

① Double-click the **QuickTime Player** icon on the desktop.

② Click **File** and choose **Open Movie**.

③ Double-click the movie file you want to view. In this case, I've chosen **Sample Movie**. If the file is not a native QuickTime movie file, QuickTime will convert the file for you.

! **Before Playing Movies**
Be sure file sharing is turned off when playing a movie with QuickTime Player. Movie playback performance will be slower with file sharing turned on.

④ Click on the **Play** button in QuickTime Player and watch the QuickTime movie.

Apple includes the Quick-
Time Player application
with your iBook. It replaces
the Movie Player application,
which used to ship with
Apple's releases of Quick-
Time. Your iBook comes
with the latest version of
QuickTime: QuickTime 4.0.
This task shows you how to
edit audio and video with
the QuickTime movie
sample file.

Task 13: Editing Audio and Video with QuickTime Player

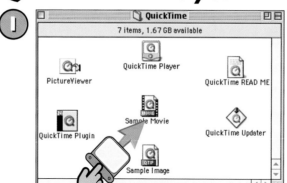

Double-Click

Click

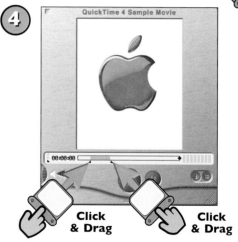

Click & Drag   **Click & Drag**

(!) No Microphone
Your iBook does not have a
built-in microphone.

(!) Register QuickTime
You must register
QuickTime in order to be
able to use the steps in this
task, as well as the
following task.

(1) Double-click a movie file window. In this example, I chose the **Sample Movie** file.

(2) Click the **Play** button.

(3) View the QuickTime 4 Sample Movie. Notice that the audio meter levels change in the QuickTime Player window.

(4) Click and drag the left marker to the right in the QuickTime Player progress bar. Then click and drag the right marker to select a section of the movie to edit.

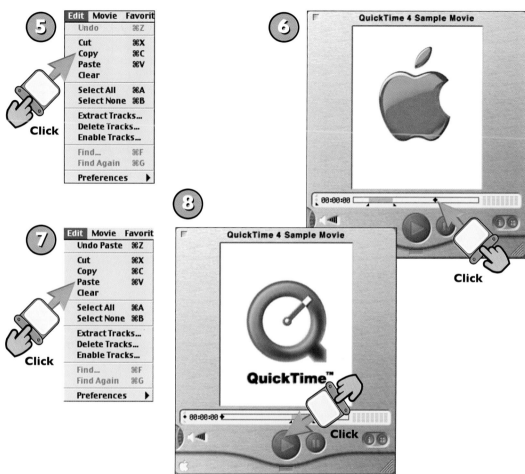

5 Click **Edit** and choose **Copy**.

6 Click on a different location on the progress bar. This is where the edited part of the movie will be pasted to.

7 Click **Edit** and choose **Paste**.

8 Click on the **Play** button. Watch your newly edited QuickTime movie.

✓ **Adjust iBook Volume**
If you can't hear the sound, adjust the volume on your speakers. For more information about how to adjust the volume on your iBook, refer to Task 11, "Changing the Volume."

✓ **Where Sound Files Live**
Open the System file to move or copy the sound for use with an application or document.

End Task

QuickTime Player is one of several media players Apple includes with Mac OS. QuickTime Player, which works with QuickTime 4.0 (Apple's multimedia technology), enables your iBook to open, view, and edit virtually any kind of media file created by computers today.

 Task 14: Editing a QuickTime Movie Using QuickTime Player

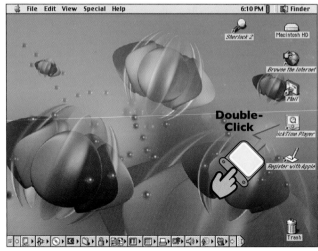

Double-Click

Click

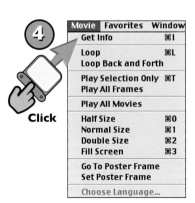

Click

Double-Click

✓ Register QuickTime Player
You need to have a registered copy of QuickTime Player in order to use the editing features covered in this task. You can see whether QuickTime Player is registered by opening the **QuickTime Settings** control panel. Click the pop-up menu and choose **Registration**. If QuickTime Player is not registered, click the **Register Online** button to register QuickTime Player with Apple.

 Double-click the **QuickTime Player** icon on the desktop.

Click the **File** menu and choose **Open Movie**.

Double-click the movie file you want to edit. In this task, I chose the **Sample Movie** file.

Click the **Movie** menu and choose **Get Info.**

Next Step

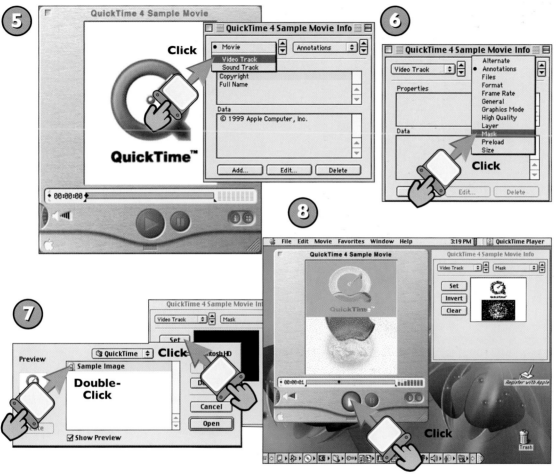

Click the left pop-up menu and choose **Video Track**.

Click the right pop-up menu and choose **Mask**.

Click the **Set** button and double-click the **Sample Image** file.

Click the **Play** button. Notice that the still image is now a part of each frame of the QuickTime sample movie.

✓ **Edit Media Files with QuickTime Player**
You can import, export, and edit audio and video tracks from a wide variety of movie files with QuickTime Player.

✓ **QuickTime Player Tricks**
QuickTime Player can convert most media files to its own QuickTime file format. It can also compress a file to optimize playback performance over the Internet.

! **Blockbuster Editing**
If you are editing large video or movie files, be sure you have enough hard disk space available to work with the file.

Task 15: Using Calculator and Graphing Calculator

If you need to perform a quick calculation, use the Calculator application included with your iBook. You can add, subtract, multiply, divide, and more with this tool. If you want to graph more complex mathematical equations, you can use the Graphing Calculator.

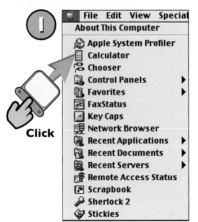

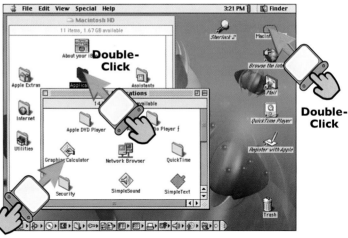

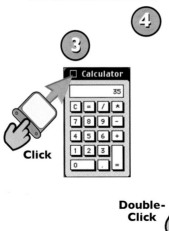

✓ **Built-In Demo**
The Graphing Calculator has a built-in demo. To run the demo, click the **Demo** menu and choose **Full Demo**. Run the demo to review features such as 2D and 3D graphing and animation.

✓ **Change the Background**
You can cut and paste or drag and drop images onto the 3D graphing window of the Graphing Calculator.

1. Click the **Apple** menu and choose **Calculator**.

2. Click the buttons on the calculator to enter an equation. (You can also use the keyboard to enter an equation.)

3. When you are finished, click the **Close** button.

4. Double-click the **Macintosh HD** icon and double-click the **Applications** folder icon. Double-click the **Graphing Calculator** icon.

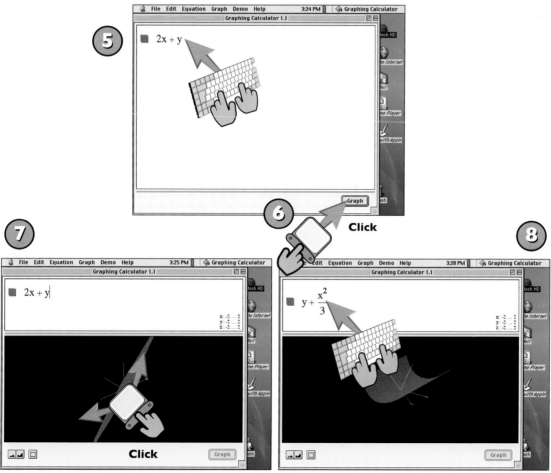

Click

Click

(5) Type a mathematical equation.

(6) Click on the **Graph** button.

(7) The application creates a 3D image of your equation. Click the 3D animation to speed up or slow down the rotation speed of the 3D image.

(8) Type in a different equation, and then press **Return**. View the new 3D graph.

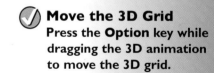

Move the 3D Grid
Press the **Option** key while dragging the 3D animation to move the 3D grid.

End Task

Page
199

Task 16: Selecting Network Devices with Chooser

If your iBook is on a network, or if you have a printer connected to your iBook, you will need to use the Chooser application. Chooser enables you to select a network server or printer to work with your iBook. You can also use the Network Browser in Task 17, "Surfing the Net with Network Browser," to work with network servers connected to your iBook.

Start Here

Click

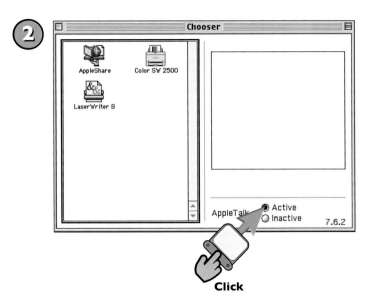

Click

Create an Alias to a Server
You can bypass Chooser to log in to a server by creating an alias to the server after you log in to it. Click on the server and press **Command+M** to create an alias.

Learn More About Chooser
For more information about printing with Chooser, refer to Part 6, "Printing with Your iBook."

1 Click the **Apple** menu, and then click **Chooser**.

2 Click the **Active** radio button to turn on AppleTalk.

Next Step

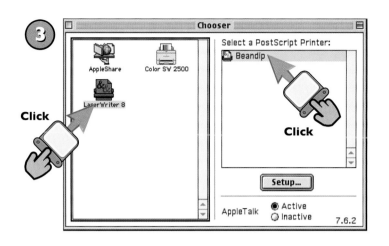

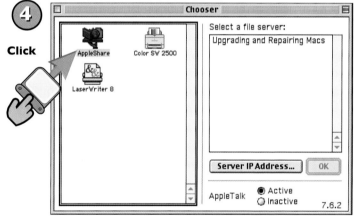

Activating AppleTalk

You can activate AppleTalk from **Chooser**, from the **AppleTalk** control panel, or from the **Control Strip**. Click the **Apple** menu and choose **Control Panels**, and then choose **AppleTalk** to open the AppleTalk control panel. If AppleTalk is inactive, click the **Yes** button when you are asked if you want to make AppleTalk active when closing the control panel.

Network Browser

Chooser shares many of the same network-related features found in **Network Browser**. For more information about Network Browser, see the next task.

What's AppleTalk?

AppleTalk is the name of Apple's network technology. It is software used by Macintosh computers to communicate with other computers on a network.

③ Click a printer driver to choose the default printer device you want to use. (If your network has only one printer, that printer will automatically be selected when you click the printer driver.)

④ Click the **AppleShare** icon to view any network servers available on your local network.

The network browser is a newer version of the network server feature in the Chooser application in Mac OS. The main window of the network browser shows any AppleShare servers on your network, including any Macintoshes that may have file sharing turned on. The network browser lets you view your network servers in a resizable window and access any of your favorite or recent servers with a click of a button.

✓ **Favorite Server Access**
You can select a favorite network server by clicking the **Favorites** folder button.

✓ **Shortcut Button for Shortcuts**
Click the **Shortcuts** button to choose a previously selected network server.

Task 17: Surfing the Net with Network Browser

Start Here

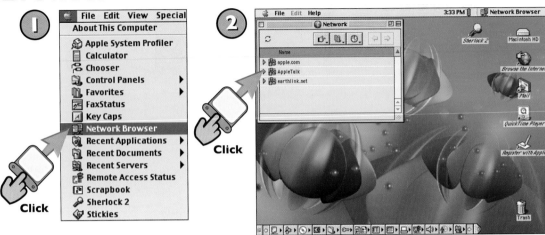

Click

Click

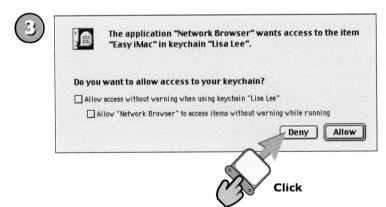

Click

① Connect your iBook to a network. Then click the **Apple** menu and choose **Network Browser**.

② Click on the arrow beside the network server you want to use.

③ Click on the **Allow** or **Deny** button, or select a check box to configure KeyChain Access for the server you are accessing.

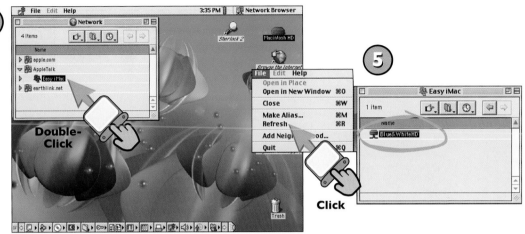

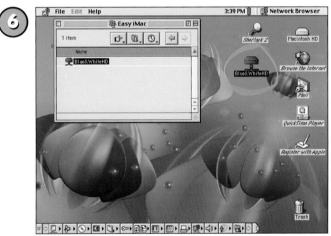

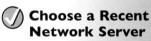

(4) Double-click the server icon. Type your login and password information, and then click on the **Connect** button.

(5) Click **File** and choose **Refresh** to view any network devices added to your local network.

(6) After you enter the login and password information, the server icon will appear on your desktop. You can work with this icon as you would the Macintosh HD icon.

✓ **Choose a Recent Network Server**
Use the **Recents** button to view and choose a network server you previously used.

✓ **Put Away a Network Server**
To remove the network server from your desktop, press the **Ctrl** key and choose **Put Away** from the pop-up menu, or drag the server icon to the Trash.

End Task

Task 18: Using Keychain Access

Store your login name and password to a network server with Keychain Access. If you use several servers in your day-to-day work, you can quickly access them by using Keychain Access instead of using the Chooser or Network Browser.

✓ Change Your Password

Change your password at least every six months. This will help discourage others from trying to log into your server accounts by guessing your password.

✓ Store a Backup

If you have access to a file-sharing server with plenty of hard disk space, you might want to keep a backup of any critical files from your iBook on that server. That way, if something happens to your iBook, you can always restore a backup from the server and not have to start from scratch.

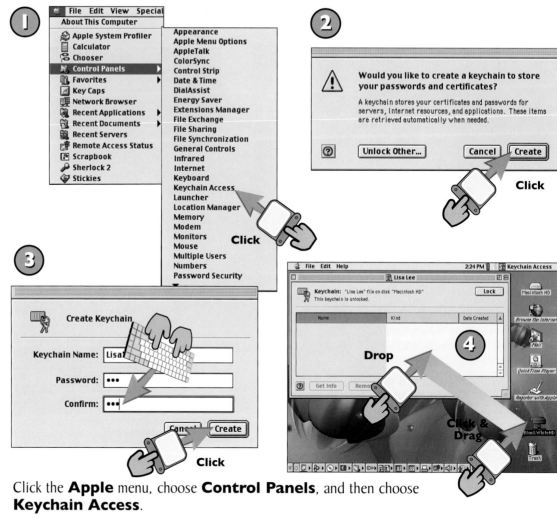

1 Click the **Apple** menu, choose **Control Panels**, and then choose **Keychain Access**.

2 Click on the **Create** button.

3 Type in a name and password for your keychain. Then click on the **Create** button.

4 Mount a file server on your desktop. Use **Chooser** or **Network Browser** to log in to a file server. Click on the file server's icon and drag it to the Keychain window.

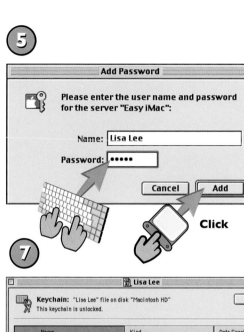

Click

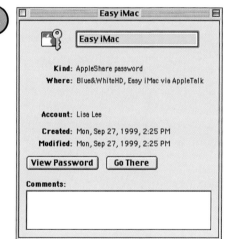

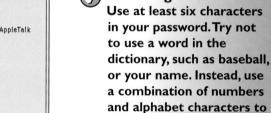

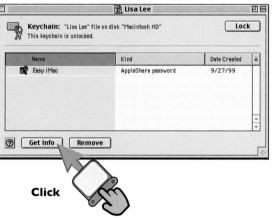

Click

✔ **Learn How to Log In**
For more information about how to log in to a file server, see the previous two tasks.

✔ **Choosing a Password**
Use at least six characters in your password. Try not to use a word in the dictionary, such as baseball, or your name. Instead, use a combination of numbers and alphabet characters to create your password.

✔ **Remembering Your Password**
If you forget a password to a file server, contact the administrator for that server to reset your password. If you forget your password for your keychain, create a new keychain by following the steps in this task.

Type your login name and password for the file server, and then click on the **Add** button.

Click on the file server. Double-click the server icon to mount in on your desktop.

Click on the **Get Info** button.

View information about the selected server.

PART 10

Maintaining Your iBook

This part introduces three general concepts that are useful for maintaining your iBook: identifying your iBook's System information, regular maintenance, and troubleshooting.

Tasks involved in identifying your system information include using Apple's System Profiler application, About This Computer, and the Get Info window. Backups, Disk First Aid, and Norton Utilities' Speed Disk are all tools you can use for regularly maintaining your iBook. Finally, troubleshooting tasks include using the Reset button, Extensions Manager, and how to perform a clean install of Mac OS.

To safeguard your data files, you should periodically make an extra copy, called a **backup**. Although your iBook includes two CD-ROMs with a backup of the original software installed on your iBook, be sure to create at least one copy of any important folders or files just in case a digital disaster strikes.

Tasks

Task #		Page #
1	Displaying Disk Information	208
2	Viewing a Battery's Life	209
3	Scanning Your Disk for Errors	210
4	Using the Reset Button	211
5	Defragmenting a Disk	212
6	Backing Up Files on Your iBook	213
7	Restoring Backup Files	214
8	Restoring Your iBook's Software	215
9	Using Apple System Profiler	216
10	Maintaining Your iBook Hardware	217
11	Rebuilding Your Desktop	218
12	Increasing Application Memory	219
13	Displaying System Information	220
14	Using Extensions Manager	222
15	Performing a Clean Install of Mac OS	224
16	Getting a Software Update	226

Task 1: Displaying Disk Information

You can display information about your hard drive, such as the size, the amount of space used, and the amount of free space. You can also choose a label for the hard drive icon; the label is used in the hard drive window's title bar to identify the disk by color.

Mac OS Extended File Format

Your iBook is formatted with the Mac OS Extended File format. Although you can reformat the disk with the Mac OS Standard File format, sticking with the Extended File format is recommended. The Extended File format fixes a limitation with the Standard File system format that limited the number and size of files you could create or store on a hard disk formatted with the Standard File system.

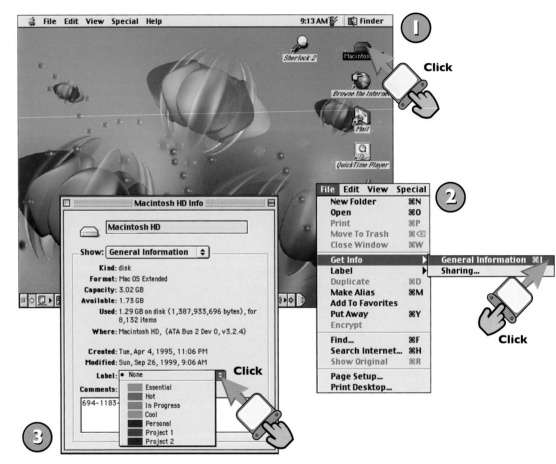

① Click the **Macintosh HD** icon.

② Open the **File** menu, choose the **Get Info** command, and select **General Information**.

③ View the disk information in the General Information window. Click the **Label** pop-up menu to choose a label for the Macintosh HD icon.

Task 2: Viewing a Battery's Life

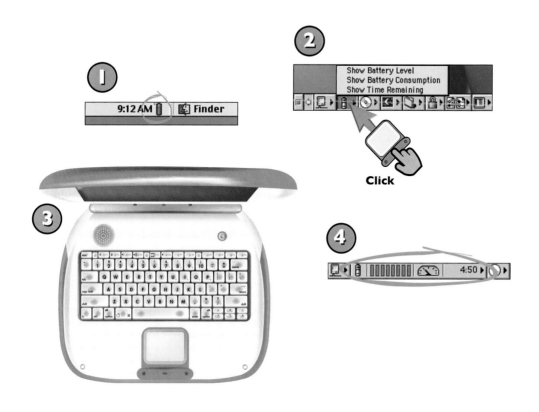

Click

Be sure you have four to six hours of battery power to spare on your iBook. Your battery life might vary depending on how you use your iBook. Sometimes you just want to know how much of that time you've used up and how much you have left. Apple provides three easy, speedy ways of monitoring your battery life on your iBook.

 Recharge Anytime
Your iBook uses a lithium ion battery. You can recharge your iBook whether you use it for one minute, one hour, or six hours. Lithium ion batteries don't have a memory. This means your battery won't have a shorter battery life if you recharge it before you've completely drained all the power from the battery.

① View the battery level in the battery icon in the menu bar.

② Click the **battery module** in the Control Strip and choose **Show Battery Level**. Full bars indicate how much battery power is available.

③ Click **Special** and choose **Sleep**. The green light below your iBook screen flashes.

④ View the battery level of your iBook in the Control Strip module.

Task 3: Scanning Your Disk for Errors

Sometimes parts of your hard disk get damaged, and you might see an error message when you try to open or save a file. Alternatively, you might notice lost or disarrayed data in some of your files. You can scan and repair the disk for damage using Apple's Disk First Aid application.

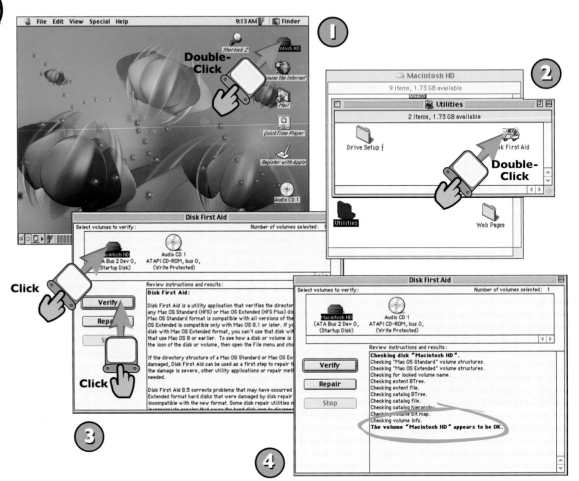

✓ **Disk First Aid to the Rescue**
If your iBook crashes, Mac OS will automatically run Disk First Aid when you start up your iBook. Any damage found will be repaired.

✓ **Check Out Norton Utilities, Too**
A better tool for scanning and repairing your hard disk is Symantec's Norton Utilities for Macintosh, version 4.0 or later.

1 Double-click the **Macintosh HD** icon.

2 In the Macintosh HD window, double-click the **Utilities** folder. Then, in the Utilities window, double-click the **Disk First Aid** icon.

3 Click the icon representing your hard drive in the Disk First Aid window (in this case, **Macintosh HD**), and then click the **Verify** button.

4 If Disk First Aid says your hard disk appears to be OK, as is the case here, you're in the clear. If a problem is found, click the **Repair** button.

Task 4: Using the Reset Button

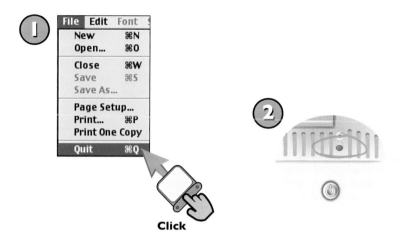

Click

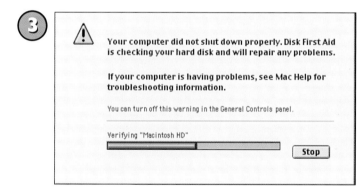

> As you use your iBook, you might encounter hardware or software incompatibilities that result in a crash. A *crash* is when your iBook restarts or unexpectedly stops working normally. It might freeze or show a blank error message. Alternatively, you might be able to move the mouse but not click anything onscreen.

✓ Where's the Reset Button?
The **Reset** button is above the power button on your iBook. Extend one end of a paper clip and insert it into the hole above the iBook's power button. Press the **Reset** button gently to restart your iBook.

Power Off with the Shut Down Command
Use the **Shut down** command in the **Special** menu whenever you can to power off your iBook. Use the **Reset** button only if there is no other way to turn off your iBook.

1. If you can, quit any applications and save any open documents.

2. Use the tip of a paper clip to press the **Reset** button located above your iBook's Power button. After you press the Reset button, you might also need to press the **Power** button.

3. When your iBook restarts, it will automatically run Apple's Disk First Aid software to verify there are no errors on the startup disk.

Task 5: Defragmenting a Disk

When a file is stored on your hard drive, it doesn't all end up in one place. Instead, Mac OS places as much of the file as possible in the first available space (called a *cluster*) on the hard drive, moves to the next cluster to store the next part of the file, and so on until the whole file is stored. Because this storage method fragments your disk files, you might find that, after a while, it takes a long time to open a file or start a program. To speed access to files and to help prevent potential problems with fragmented files, you can *defragment* your disk, putting files in clusters as close to each other as possible.

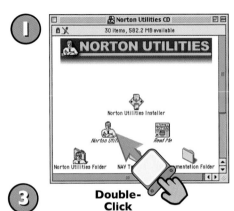

Double-Click

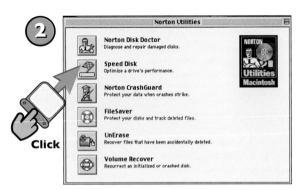

Click

Click

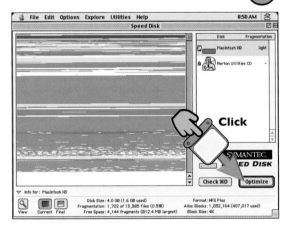

Click

Back Up Before Defragmenting

Be careful when defragmenting. You might want to back up first. See Task 6, "Backing Up Files on Your iBook," for information about backing up.

① Insert the Norton Utilities CD, and double-click its icon on your desktop. Then double-click the **Norton Utilities** icon.

② Click the **Speed Disk** icon in the Norton Utilities window.

③ After you click **OK** in the alert dialog box, click the **Check** button to determine how fragmented your drive is.

④ Information about your hard disk, including fragmentation, appears in the lower portion of the window. Click **Optimize** to defragment your hard drive.

End Task

Task 6: Backing Up Files on Your iBook

Start Here

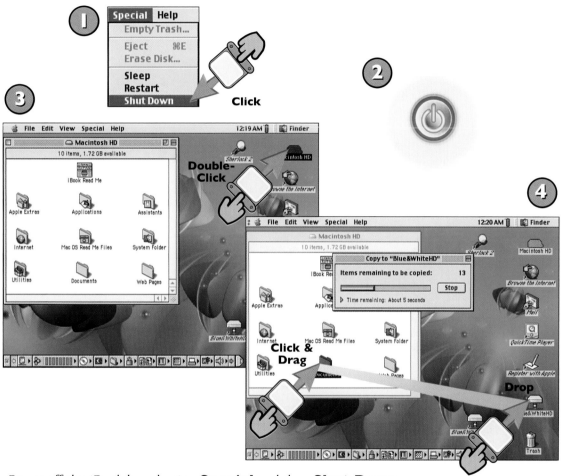

To safeguard your data, you should back up the files on your iBook. That way, if something happens to the original files, you can restore them with this extra copy. To store backups of your files and folders, it's a good idea to purchase an external USB drive, such as an Iomega zip drive. Zip disks store up to 100MB of files, almost 10 times more than a floppy disk. Alternatively, if you plan on frequently backing up tons of information, you might want to purchase a tape backup system. This method is faster and more convenient than backing up to floppy disks or to a disk file.

① Power off the iBook by selecting **Special** and then **Shut Down**.

② Log into a network server, or connect an external USB hard drive to your iBook. Power on the iBook. You can also connect a tape drive or removable disk drive, such as a zip drive.

③ Double-click the **Macintosh HD** icon and select any folders or files you want to back up.

④ Drag the folders or files to the external hard drive icon on your desktop. Mac OS copies the folders and files to the external disk drive.

✓ **Backing Up the First Time**
The first time you perform a backup, you might want to back up all the files on your system. After you have a complete backup, you can then back up only selected files.

End Task

Task 7: Restoring Backup Files

If you ever face some cataclysmic digital disaster with your iBook, you'll be glad you took the time to back up your important files. This task shows you how to restore those files from the external drive on which the backup has been stored to your iBook's hard drive. However, you can similarly restore your backup from a floppy disk, network server, or removable media.

Test-Restore a Backup
Even though you can access and work with the backed-up files on the second hard disk just as you would the internal disk on your iBook, it's still a good idea to go ahead and restore them to your system.

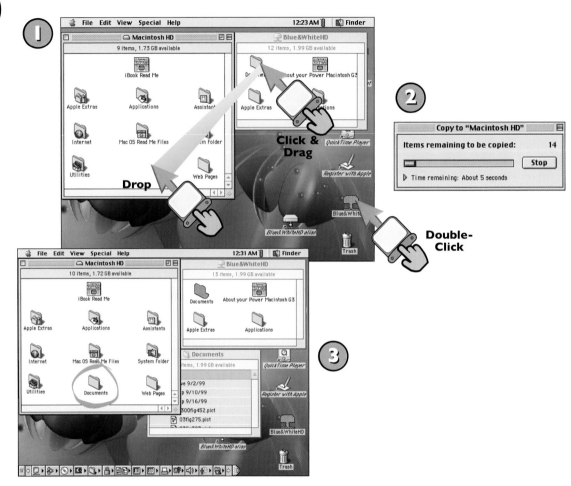

(1) Double-click your external or network server drive. Locate the files or folders you want to restore. Drag them from the external drive's window and drop them on the Macintosh HD window.

(2) Wait for the files to copy from the network server to your iBook.

(3) The backup files are restored to the Macintosh HD window.

Task 8: Restoring Your iBook's Software

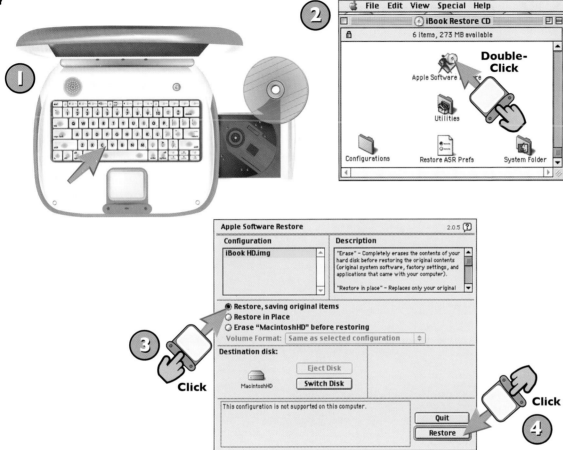

Along with your iBook comes a **CD-ROM,** called **iBook Restore,** that can restore the original software installed on your iBook in the event some disaster wipes your system clean (you'll find this **CD** in the book of **CD-ROMs** that came with your iBook).

✓ **Restore Selected Files**
You can restore selected files from the iBook Restore CD. Simply double-click the **iBook HD.img** file in the Configuration list in the Apple Software Restore window (see step 2). After the image mounts on your desktop, you can drag-copy any files or folders from the image file to your iBook's hard disk.

✓ **Startup with the Option Key**
Hold down the **Option** key at startup. Use the onscreen buttons to search for and select any available startup devices, such as a CD or hard disk connected to your iBook.

① Insert the iBook Restore CD-ROM, and then restart your iBook. Press and hold the **C** key during startup.

② Double-click the **iBook Restore CD** icon on the desktop, and then double-click the **Apple Software Restore** icon in the iBook Restore CD window.

③ Click the **OK** button in the Apple Software Restore welcome dialog box, and then review the settings in the Apple Software Restore main window.

④ Click the **Restore** button. Apple Software Restore will restore the files from the CD onto your hard drive.

End Task

Task 9: Using Apple System Profiler

When you are troubleshooting, you sometimes need to display information about your system. You can find this information in the Apple System Profiler.

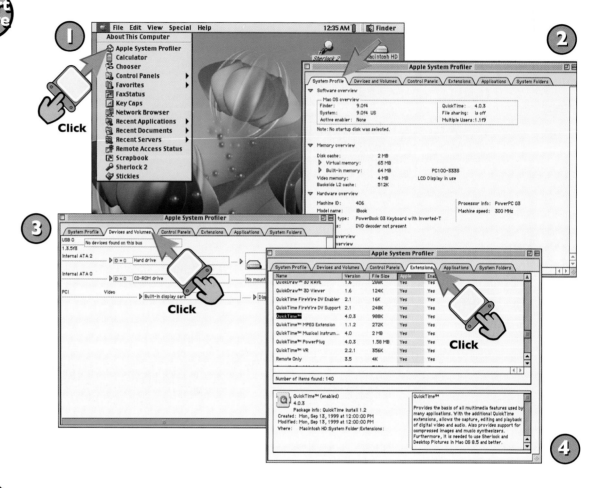

✓ **Memory Consumption**
You can view memory usage information for Mac OS and any running application by selecting the **About This Computer** command in the **Apple** menu.

✓ **Other System Information**
Some applications, such as Microsoft Word 98 and Internet Explorer 4.5, have a system information window built into the **About** box. Click the **System Info** or **Support** button in the **About** box for these applications.

1 Click the **Apple** menu and choose **Apple System Profiler**.

2 View the hardware, software, memory, network, and production information in the **System Profile** tab.

3 Click the **Devices and Volumes** tab to view the internal and external devices connected to your iBook.

4 Click the **Control Panels**, **Extensions**, and **Applications** tabs to view the software currently installed and running on your iBook.

Task 10: Maintaining Your iBook Hardware

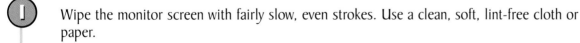

An iBook looks so great when you first take it out of the box, it's no wonder people can't keep their hands off it. As you use your iBook, you might notice fingerprints on your screen, or cheese puffs in-between the keys on your keyboard. You can keep using your iBook regardless of the earthly or unearthly elements that might cling to it. However, if you want to keep it looking as cool as it did when you had your out-of-box experience, follow the steps in this task.

But Won't We Freeze If There's No Power?
Be sure to disconnect the wall-based power and remove your battery before you start to clean your iBook.

What About My Hands, Madge?
If you're not sure what to use to clean your iBook, try using a cotton swab or a dry cloth towel with a small dab of water.

1. Wipe the monitor screen with fairly slow, even strokes. Use a clean, soft, lint-free cloth or paper.

2. Press the plastic tabs at the top of your iBook keyboard and lift up the keyboard. Gently shake your keyboard to remove any dust or other particles from the keyboard's keys.

3. Wipe the trackpad area and mouse button. Be sure the button click is free of debris. Wipe the speaker and power button areas. Remove any particles stuck in a hinge, hole, or joint area.

4. Check your Ethernet, USB, and modem ports. Check to see whether any pins are blocking any of these ports.

Task 11: Rebuilding Your Desktop

Start Here

All the icons for your folders and files are stored in two invisible, secret database files on your hard drive called the *desktop database*. If you notice that your application or document icons lose their custom icon, try rebuilding your desktop. If you have a large collection of custom icons and add or remove them on a regular basis, you might want to rebuild your desktop after moving many icons on or off your hard disk to update the desktop database.

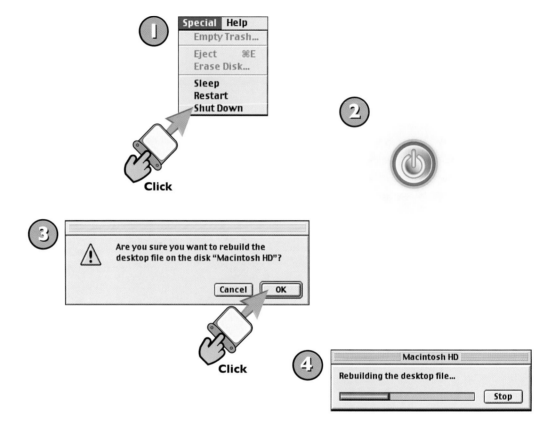

 **Zap Your Parameter Memory**
If you hold down the **Command+Option+P+R** keys right after powering on your iBook, you will clear (or zap) the **PRAM**. Several control panel settings, such as your monitor colors and printer settings, will be changed back to their default settings when **PRAM** is cleared.

1 Power off your iBook.

2 Power on the iBook, and hold down the **Command+Option** keys until the rebuild dialog box appears.

3 Click **OK** when Mac OS asks you whether you want to rebuild your desktop.

4 Wait for the progress bar to indicate that your iBook has finished rebuilding the desktop. When the desktop appears, you can use your iBook.

End Task

Task 12: Increasing Application Memory

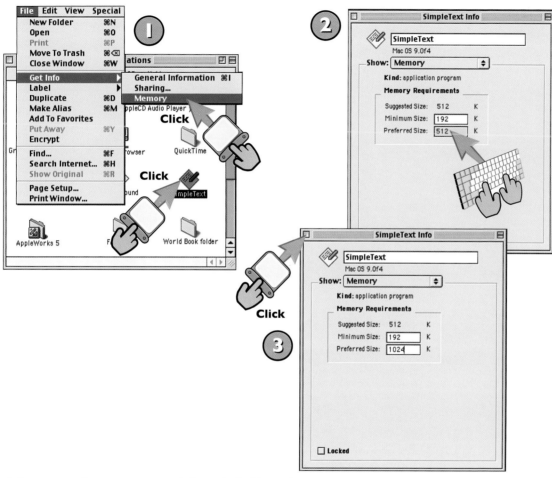

When you use an application, Mac OS sets aside a specific amount of memory for that application to consume. (The publisher of an application determines the minimal and suggested amount of memory the application uses as a default setting.) As you use an application, you might observe slower performance when you are working on a large document, or you might see an error message indicating that the application is running low on memory as you open more than one window. This task will show you how you can increase the amount of memory an application uses.

✓ Quit the Application First

You cannot adjust the memory settings for an application while it is open and running. You must quit the application first, and then change its memory settings.

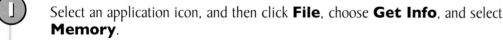

① Select an application icon, and then click **File**, choose **Get Info**, and select **Memory**.

② In the **Preferred Size** text field, type a larger number.

③ Click the **Close** box. The next time you start the application, it will use the preferred size.

Task 13: Displaying System Information

As you are using applications, you might want to know how much memory is being used and how much is available. This information is always available in Mac OS in the **About This Computer** window. For the most detailed information about what hardware and software settings are on your iBook, use the Apple System Profiler application.

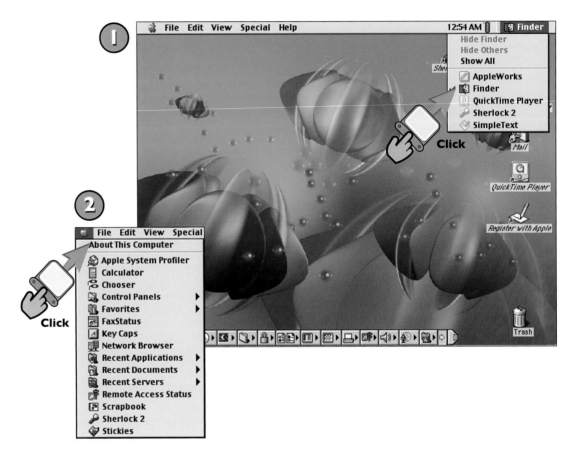

Monitor Application Memory Usage
You can use the About This Computer window to monitor the amount of memory in any open application running on your iBook.

  If an application other than Finder is active, click the **Applications** menu and choose **Finder**.

  Click the **Apple** menu, and then choose the **About This Computer** command.

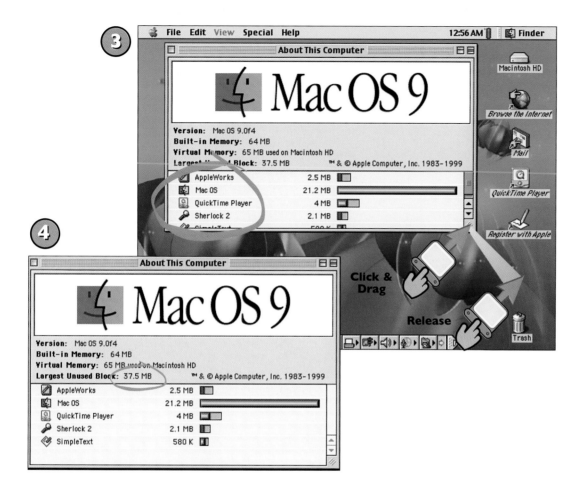

 Click & Drag

Release

 Each open application is listed, along with the amount of allocated memory and how much of it is being used. Click the **Grow** box and drag the mouse to view all items in the window.

 The Largest Unused Block is the amount of free memory available to your applications.

✅ **Spotting Memory Problems Early**
If you add up all memory allocated for open applications along with the largest unused block, it should approximately add up to the amount of virtual memory (if virtual memory is on in your Memory control panel) or built-in memory. If the numbers don't match, restart your Mac.

 End Task

Task 14: Using Extensions Manager

Mac OS contains a core set of *extensions*, which enable features such as networking and printing, and devices such as a **CD-ROM** drive. Extensions also enable technologies such as **AppleScript, QuickTime, QuickDraw 3D,** and the Appearance features in Mac OS. Many Macintosh products that use extensions are commercial products, which are largely compatible with Mac OS 9. You can use Extensions Manager to keep track of the different control panels and extensions you add to your system folder.

✓ **View Type and Creator Information**
You can view type and creator information in Extensions Manager. Click the **Edit** menu and choose **Preferences,** and then check the **Type and Creator** check box to add these columns to the Extensions Manager window.

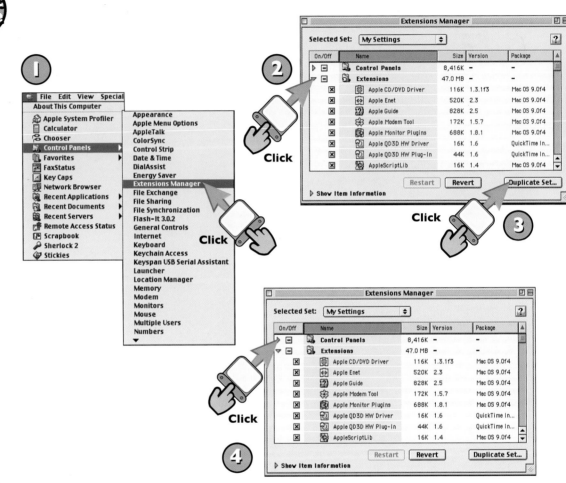

1. Click the **Apple** menu, choose **Control Panels**, and then choose **Extensions Manager**.

2. Click the arrow next to the **Control Panels** or **Extensions** folder to view the control panels and extensions installed in the system folder.

3. Click the **Duplicate Set** button and type some text to name the new set.

4. Click the arrow to the left of the **Control Panels** folder icon.

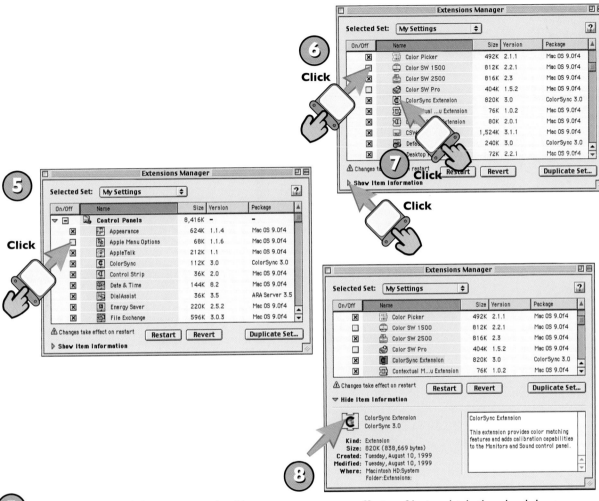

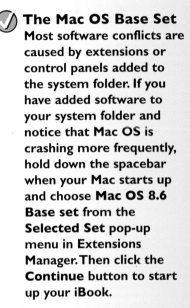

The Mac OS Base Set
Most software conflicts are caused by extensions or control panels added to the system folder. If you have added software to your system folder and notice that **Mac OS** is crashing more frequently, hold down the spacebar when your Mac starts up and choose **Mac OS 8.6 Base set** from the **Selected Set** pop-up menu in Extensions Manager. Then click the **Continue** button to start up your iBook.

Extensions Manager saves a group of extensions as an Extensions Manager set. The information stored in a set is saved to a file located in the Extensions Manager Preferences folder, which is located in the Preferences folder of your system folder.

View Files by Package
Click the **View** menu and choose **as Packages** to view items by the software package group they belong to.

(5) Click the check box next to the file you want to turn off. Any file in which the check box is empty will not load when your iBook starts up.

(6) If you know which printer you will use, you can turn off any extraneous printer extensions in the Extensions Manager set.

(7) To view more information about an item, click it, and then click the **Show Item Information** arrow.

(8) The item information is displayed.

Task 15: Performing a Clean Install of Mac OS

Start Here

There are two ways to install Mac OS software onto your hard drive. The default setting is to update an existing system folder. When a system folder is updated, the installer application tries to replace as many of the older system resources as possible with new ones, and it is usually successful. A clean install of Mac OS, however, creates a new system folder on your hard drive. This task uses the iBook Software Install CD to install Mac OS 9.

✓ **When to Do a Clean Install**
You should only need to perform a clean install if you must replace the system folder on your iBook.

✓ **Create a Backup**
After you complete the clean installation of Mac OS, create a backup copy of the system folder. Then you can restore the backup of the clean system folder instead of doing another clean installation from scratch.

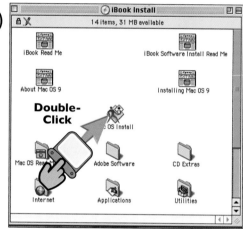
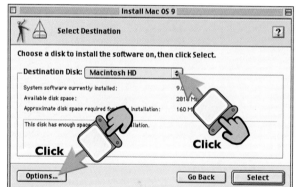
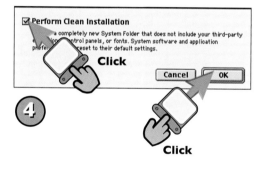

 Press the button on the iBook's CD-ROM drive, insert the iBook Software Install CD-ROM in the iBook, restart, and hold down the **C** key as the iBook starts up.

 Double-click the **iBook Install** icon on the desktop, and then double-click the **Mac OS Install** icon in the iBook Install window.

 Select the hard drive you want to use from the **Destination Disk** drop-down list, and then click the **Options** button.

 Click the **Perform Clean Installation** check box, and then click **OK**.

Next Step

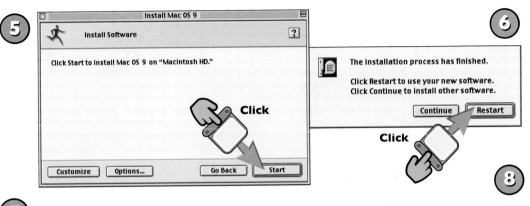

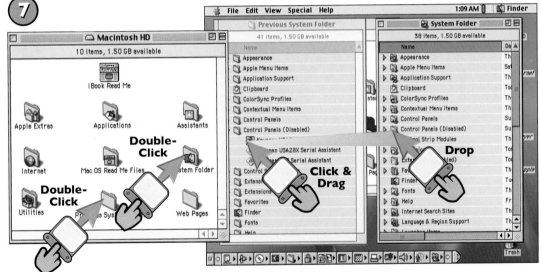

5 Continue through the Install Mac OS application windows. Finally, click the **Start** button to install Mac OS.

6 After the installation is complete, click the **Restart** button.

7 After your iBook restarts, double-click the **Macintosh HD** icon. Double-click the **Previous System Folder** and **System Folder** icons.

8 Move any files or folders you might need from the previous system folder to the new system folder.

⚠ Move Non-Apple Files
After you complete a clean install, the new system folder will have only Mac OS software. Any third-party control panel, extensions, or applications you had installed with your previous system folder might need to be moved or reinstalled into the new system folder.

Task 16: Getting a Software Update

Apple provides free software updates for your iBook's software. You can access Apple's software over the Internet using the Software Update control panel. Software Updates fix software problems. By updating your iBook with new software, it will run more efficiently, and might even get a little faster.

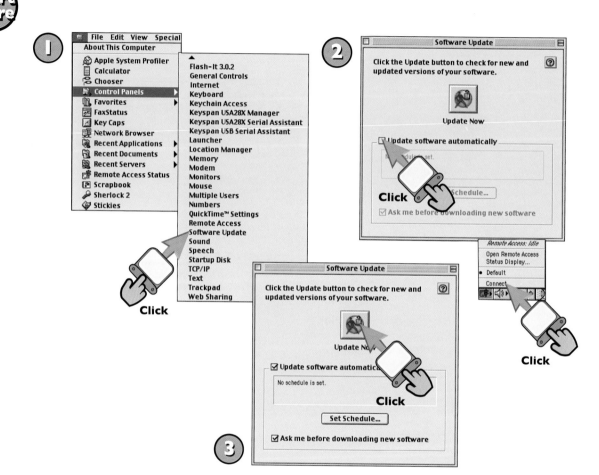

✓ **Apple Software Updates**
Apple's Web site provides the latest information about your iBook in addition to software updates for all Apple products. Go to www.apple.com/support for more information about the latest software updates for iBooks.

(1) Click the **Apple** menu, choose **Control Panels**, and select **Software Update**.

(2) Click **Connect** in the **Remote Access** Control Strip module. Click the **Update Software Automatically** check box to schedule your iBook to check for software updates.

(3) Click the **Update Now** button.

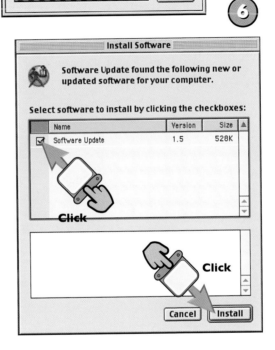

Click

Click

Click

4 Click the **OK** button if you want the Software Update control panel to start searching for updates on the Internet.

5 Wait for the list of software updates to download to your iBook.

6 Review the list of software in the Install Software window. Click on a software package, and then click the **Install** button to complete the upgrade.

 Additional Software Updates
Many software publishers also provide free software updates for their applications. Visit www.download.com or www.zdnet.com to look for the latest software updates from iBook software publishers.

iBook Software

Your iBook is bundled with several applications that are preinstalled onto your hard disk. A backup of these applications is available on the iBook Restore CD-ROM. The iBook bundle also contains software applications such as the World Book Encyclopedia, which is on a separate CD-ROM. Other applications included with the iBook software bundle include AppleWorks, Adobe Acrobat, Bugdom, and Nanosaur.

Tasks

Task #		Page #
1	Viewing Files with Adobe Acrobat	230
2	Starting AppleWorks's Word Processor	231
3	Formatting Your Word Processing Document	232
4	Creating a Spreadsheet with AppleWorks	234
5	Drawing and Painting with AppleWorks	236
6	Creating a Database with AppleWorks	238
7	Sending a Fax	240
8	Synchronizing Data with Your Palm Device	242
9	Managing Data with Your Palm Device	244
10	Finding Facts in the World Book Encyclopedia	246
11	Playing Nanosaur	248
12	Playing Bugdom	250

Task 1: Viewing Files with Adobe Acrobat

Start Here

Some of the instruction manuals included with the software on your iBook, such as the manual for Bugdom, can be viewed with Adobe Acrobat. Adobe Acrobat can open files, but the files themselves cannot be modified or edited. You cannot create any files with Adobe Acrobat Viewer.

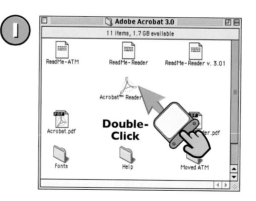

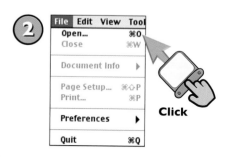

✓ **Spotting Acrobat File Icons**
Any Adobe Acrobat file will have an icon similar to the Adobe Acrobat symbol. Acrobat filenames usually end in .pdf.

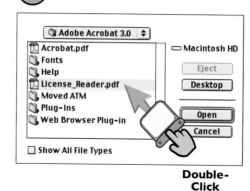

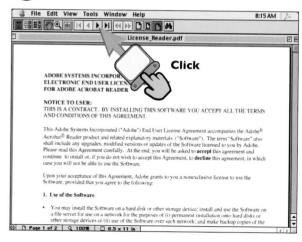

✓ **When to Print a File**
If an Acrobat document is more than a few pages long, you might want to print it.

✓ **Go Directly to Any Page**
Click the page number information at the bottom left of the document window to open a dialog box window. Type the page number you want to go to, and press **Enter** to go to the page you want.

1 Double-click the **Macintosh HD** icon, open the **Applications** window, and then open the **Adobe Acrobat** window. Finally, double-click the **Acrobat Reader** icon.

2 Click **File** and choose **Open**.

3 Select a file to view (in this case, **License_Reader.pdf**).

4 Use the **Function Up Arrow** and **Function Down Arrow** keys to view the pages of the document; use the toolbar buttons to turn pages in the document.

End Task

Task 2: Starting AppleWorks's Word Processor

Start Here

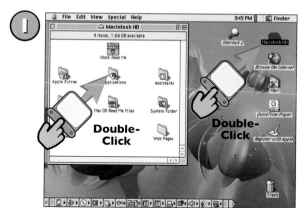
Double-Click   **Double-Click**

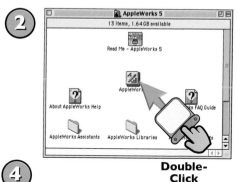
Double-Click

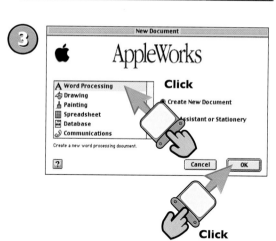
Click

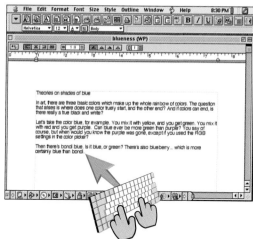

Click

AppleWorks 5 is a multifeatured application that contains a word processor, spreadsheet, and database application. The word processor in AppleWorks can open large documents, which is one of the main limitations of SimpleText and other text document viewers. Plus, you can use AppleWorks to create and edit your own documents. This task shows you how to start the AppleWorks word processor.

1. Open the **Macintosh HD** window, double-click **Applications**, and then double-click the **AppleWorks 5** folder icon.

2. Double-click the **AppleWorks** icon.

3. Click **Word Processing**, and then click **OK**.

4. The AppleWorks word processor opens; simply click in the window and type to start working on your new document.

 Learn More About Formatting Text
For more information about working with text, see Task 3, "Typing Text in Stickies," and Task 7, "Formatting Text in SimpleText ," in Part 9, "Using iBook Accessories."

After you've typed a bit of text in your AppleWorks word-processed document, you might want to pep it up a bit. Formatting text makes it easier for you and others to read. It can also help emphasize key elements of your message.

✅ **What You See Is What You Get**

The default view for the word processor is to show the margin settings in addition to the text area of the file. The layout of the window matches the way it will print. The term *WYSIWYG*, which stands for *what you see is what you get*, is used to describe this kind of feature in an application.

✅ **Share Text**

You can use the Copy and Paste commands in the Edit menu to move text or graphics from the word processor or painting programs in AppleWorks and add them to an AppleWorks spreadsheet or database file.

Task 3: Formatting Your Word Processing Document

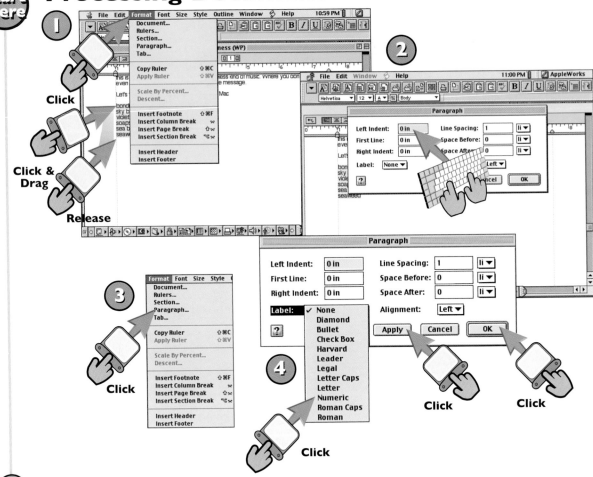

1 Select some text in the document window. Click **Format** to view the formatting options available to you.

2 To set the indents and spacing in your document, specify them in the Paragraph window. Open it by selecting **Paragraph** from the **Format** menu.

3 To convert a set of paragraphs into a numbered list, select the paragraphs and choose **Paragraph** from the **Format** menu.

4 Select **Numeric** from the **Label** drop-down menu. Click **Apply**. Click **OK**.

Next Step

Click

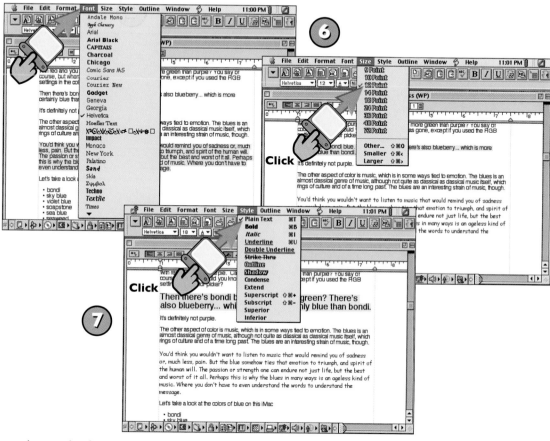

5 To change the font in your document, select some text, and then click the **Font** menu and choose the font you want to change.

6 Select some text, and then click the **Size** menu to change the font size of the selected text.

7 Select some text. Click the **Style** menu to assign one or several font styles to the selected text.

Task 4: Creating a Spreadsheet with AppleWorks

Another kind of document used on your iBook is a spreadsheet. Spreadsheets are commonly used to track both scheduling- and accounting-related tasks. You can create long lists with an expandable way to track information, or you can automate AppleWorks to update information in another document, such as a database, whenever the spreadsheet changes.

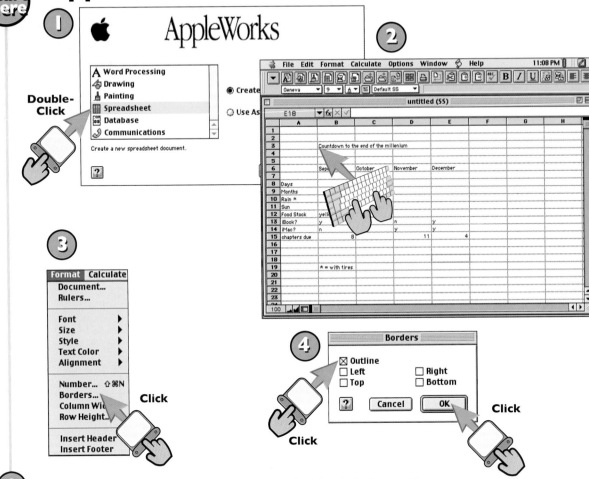

Start Here

Double-Click

Click

Click

Click

Click

✓ **Cell Behavior**
When you click a cell, the border around the cell becomes highlighted.

✓ **Tab Key**
Click a cell to select it, and then press the **Tab** key to move to the next cell.

✓ **Format Text**
You can format text in a spreadsheet in the same way you format text in a word processor.

1. In AppleWorks's New Document window, double-click **Spreadsheet**.

2. Type some information into several cells of the spreadsheet. Each square on the spreadsheet is a cell. You can type text, numbers, or an equation into a cell.

3. Add a border to a series of selected cells by choosing **Borders** from the **Format** menu.

4. Click a check box to choose the type of border you want. Click **OK** to save your changes.

Next Step

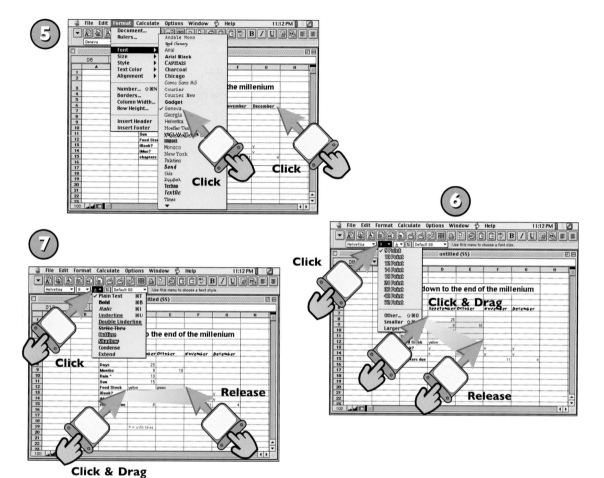

⑤ Select the cells you want to modify. Click the **Format** menu and choose a font from the submenu.

⑥ Select one or more cells, and then click the **font size** pop-up menu in the toolbar to change the size of the font in the selected cells.

⑦ Select one or several cells, and then click the **style** pop-up menu in the toolbar to give your text a different font style.

✅ **Spreadsheet or Database?**
Sometimes it's difficult to decide whether to store information in a spreadsheet or in a database file. If you do not need to view the information in a spreadsheet with different layouts of information, you can probably use a spreadsheet to track information.

✅ **Equations**
You can use equations in a spreadsheet to automate calculations. For example, type 1 in cell A1, and 3 in cell B1. Then type sum=(A1+B1) into cell C1 and press **Enter**. Cell C1 shows 4, which is the sum of 1+3.

The drawing and painting tools in AppleWorks are great for creating charts for presentations, or diagrams that you can add to documents or Web sites. A diagram could show the process flow of a work task, such as how a chapter is edited for a book or how to create a Web page. With AppleWorks's painting tools, you can draw freehand in a paint document. This task shows you how to use both drawing and painting tools. Double-click the **AppleWorks** icon before performing the steps in this task.

✓ **Combine Data**

You can add your drawing to a word-processing document or spreadsheet within AppleWorks by clicking the **Edit** menu and choosing **Copy**, clicking in the document where you want to add the drawing, and choosing **Paste** from the **Edit** menu.

Task 5: Drawing and Painting with AppleWorks

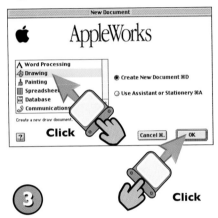

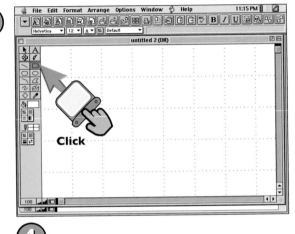

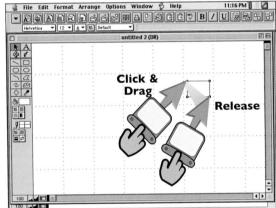

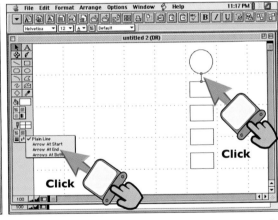

Click the **File** menu and choose **New**. Click **Drawing** in the New Document window, and then click **OK**. (Refer to step 1 of Task 2 if you need help opening this window.)

Click a shape in the toolbox that you want to add to your diagram or chart.

Click in the document window and drag the mouse to draw the shape you selected in step 2. Add other shapes and lines as needed.

To create an arrow, click a line, and then choose the type of arrow from the arrow toolbox.

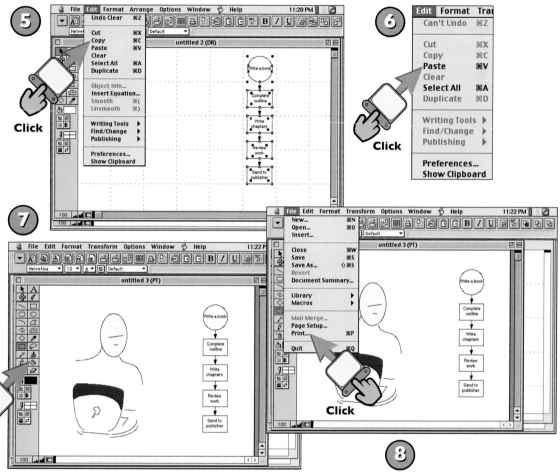

Clear a Painting
Double-click the **Eraser** tool to clear a paint document window in AppleWorks.

Different Toolboxes
The drawing tools in AppleWorks consist primarily of shapes. The Paint toolbox contains a superset of tools, including the drawing tools.

Make a Mistake?
If you draw a crooked line, or border the wrong item in your painting, press **Command+Z** or click the **Edit** menu and choose **Undo**. AppleWorks removes the previous shape or stroke added to a paint or drawing document.

⑤ Complete your drawing. Select it, click the **Edit** menu, and choose **Copy**.

⑥ Click **File** and choose **New**. Double-click **Painting** to create a new paint document. Click **Edit** and choose **Paste** to add the drawing to the new paint window.

⑦ Click the toolbox tools, and draw in the document window to create your painting. For example, click the **Paint Bucket** tool, and then click an area in your painting to add color.

⑧ Click **File** and choose **Print** to print your paint document.

Documents and spreadsheets are great tools for creating and viewing information. The best thing about putting information into a database is that you can store a good amount of information in one file, but view it almost any way you like, dynamically. For example, you can create a database of all your documents and spreadsheets to keep track of them. A more common use of a database is for storing name, address, and phone number information.

✓ **When to Use a Database**
Most businesses use a database to track inventory and product sales. Database files are also used on many Web sites, including e-commerce Web sites.

Task 6: Creating a Database with AppleWorks

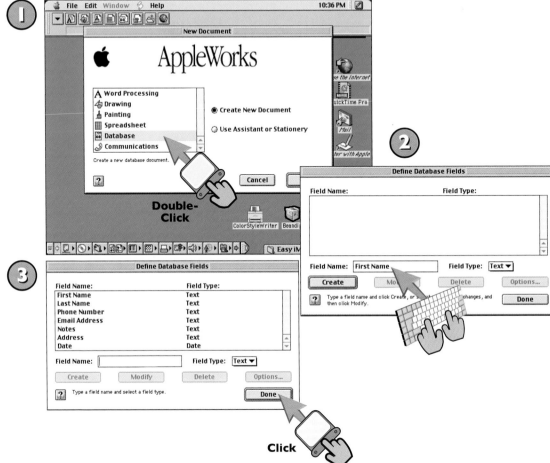

Double-Click

Click

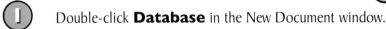

① Double-click **Database** in the New Document window.

② Type the name of a field you want to use in your database (in this case, **First Name**).

③ Create any other fields you want to use, and then click **Done**.

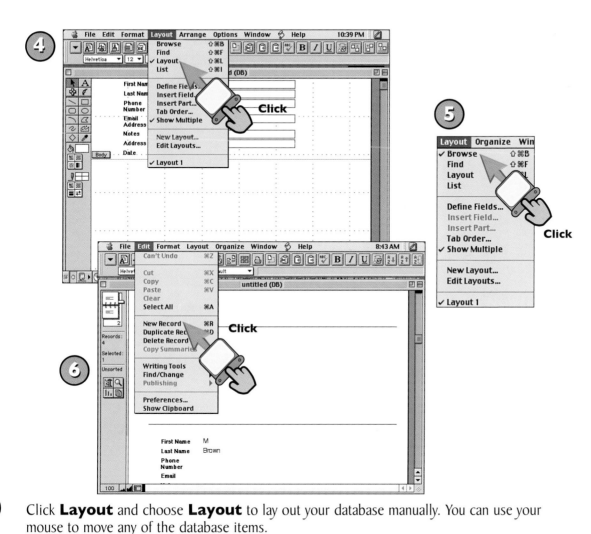

Tired of Data Entry?
You can use AppleScript to automate information that is placed in a database from the word processor or spreadsheet areas of AppleWorks.

AppleScript is the name of the scripting language built into Mac OS. You can use AppleScript to automate any applications that have AppleScript support. See Part 8, Task 11, "Using AppleScript," for more information about automating software on your iBook.

④ Click **Layout** and choose **Layout** to lay out your database manually. You can use your mouse to move any of the database items.

⑤ Click **Layout** and choose **Browse** to browse database records or to enter or view information in the database.

⑥ Click **Edit** and choose **New Record** to add new files to your database; click the **Notepad** icon in the toolbox to move to the previous or next database record.

Databases and the Internet
Many Web sites use databases to link a wide range of information, such as for shopping on the Internet or for storing phone numbers.

Task 7: Sending a Fax

Besides connecting to the Internet, you can use the modem on your iBook to turn it into a fax-sending machine. Your iBook has **Fax STF** software preinstalled. Your iBook can send or receive a fax in those rare instances when you've got to transfer information while you are on the go.

✓ **Fax Versus Email**
In most situations, it's much easier to communicate via email instead of waiting for a facsimile to arrive. However, if you need a hard copy of a file—for example, requiring a signature—you'll need to use your iBook to send a file to a fax machine.

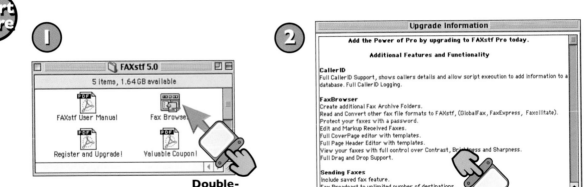

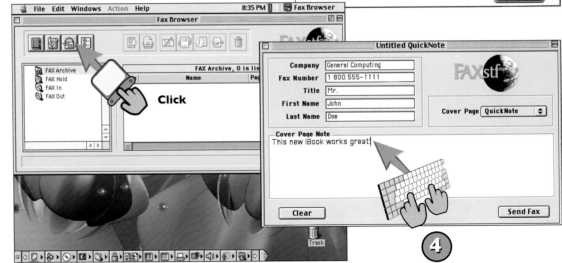

1. Double-click the **Macintosh HD** icon, and then double-click the **Applications** folder icon. Double-click the **FAXstf** folder icon, and then double-click the **Fax Browser** icon.

2. Click the **Done** button in the Upgrade Information window.

3. To fax a brief message, click the **QuickFax** button.

4. Type the name, fax number, and a message in the QuickNote window, or press **Command+K** to open a new fax window.

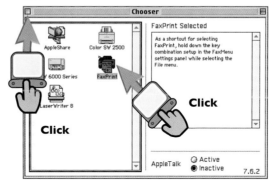

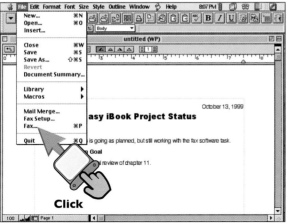

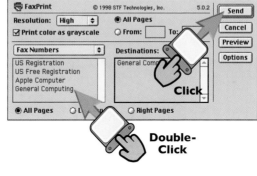

5 Click the **Send Fax** button and wait for your iBook to connect to the fax machine.

6 To fax a document, click the **Apple** menu and select **Chooser**. Click the **FaxPrint** icon. Click the **Close** box to save your changes.

7 Double-click the document you want to fax. For example, I've selected an AppleWorks document. Click **File** and choose **Fax**.

8 Double-click a contact in your fax address book, and then click the **Send** button.

If You Have to Reinstall
Be sure to restore both the System folder as well as the FAXstf folder if you ever reinstall the fax software onto your iBook.

If you use a calendar, address book, to-do list, or keep notes handy, you might have a **Palm device**. There are many kinds of Palm devices, such as the Palm III, Palm IIIe, Palm V and Palm VII. Fortunately, your iBook can exchange data with all these Palm devices, although you might need to purchase a **USB-to-PDA** adapter, too. This task shows you how to synchronize information between your iBook and your Palm device.

Install Palm Software
You must install the Palm Desktop software onto your iBook before you can perform any of the steps in this task, as well as the following task. Double-click the **Macintosh HD** icon, and **Applications** and **Palm Desktop** folder icons. Then double-click the **Palm Desktop Installer** icon and follow the onscreen instructions to install the Palm software onto your iBook.

Task 8: Synchronizing Data with Your Palm Device

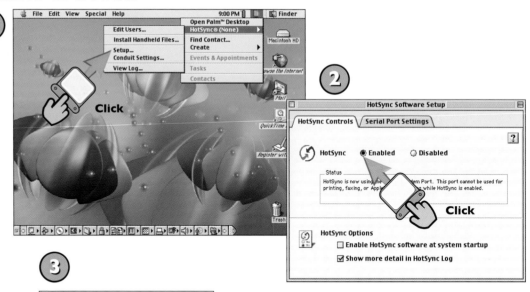

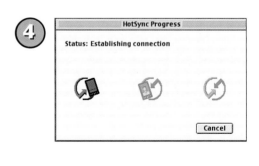

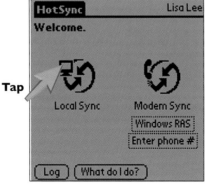

Click the **Palm Desktop** icon, choose **HotSync**, and then select **Setup**.

Click the **Enabled** option button.

On your Palm device, tap on the **Local Sync** button.

Wait for the synchronization to complete. Your Palm information is now on your iBook.

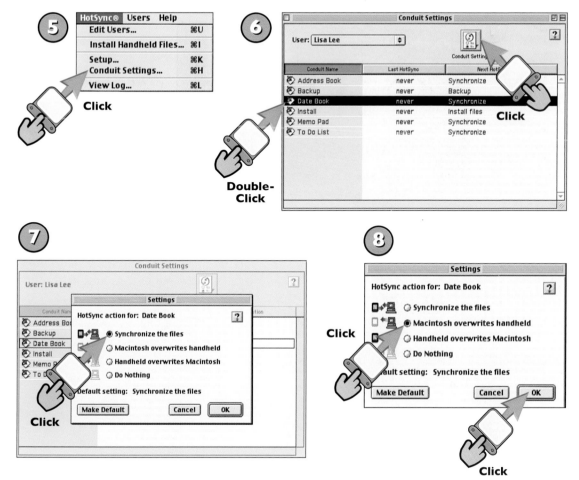

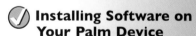

Installing Software on Your Palm Device

You can use your iBook to upload new applications to your Palm device. Double-click the **Internet Explorer** icon and go to http://www.palm.com and click any links that interest you. You can also find Palm software on http://www.download.com. Download the files you want to install on your Palm device, and then use HotSync to install them onto your Palm device.

⑤ Click the **HotSync** menu and choose **Conduit Settings** to customize how your data is synchronized.

⑥ Double-click a conduit you want to modify. Then click the **Conduit Settings** button.

⑦ Click the **Synchronize the files** option button if you want to make your iBook match the data on your Palm device.

⑧ Click **Macintosh overwrites handheld** for your iBook data to overwrite data on your Palm device. Click **OK**. Tap **Local Sync** on your Palm device to resynchronize your data.

Task 9: Managing Data with Your Palm Device

Sometimes you might use your iBook to schedule an appointment or add a name to your address book. Other times, you might use your Palm device to do the same. The previous task shows you how the Palm Desktop software enables you to configure your iBook to overwrite the data from your Palm device or let its data be modified by the Palm device. This task shows you how to view your Memos, Address Book, To-Do Lists, and Calendar information on your iBook.

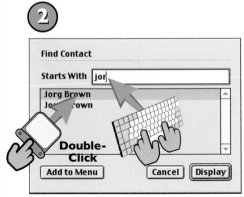

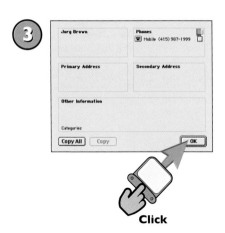

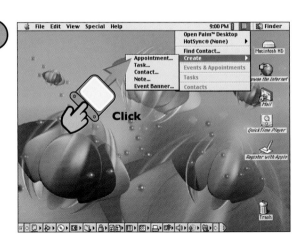

✅ **Import Lists**
Save a list of addresses in tab-delimited format. Open the Palm Desktop software and import the address list into your calendar's address book, and then synchronize the list to your Palm device.

1 Click the **Palm Desktop** icon in the menu bar and choose **Find Contact**.

2 Type a few characters of the contact you want to find. Then double-click the contact name or click the **Display** button.

3 View the contact information. Click the **OK** button to exit the window.

4 Click the **Palm Desktop** menu, choose **Create**, and then choose **Appointment**.

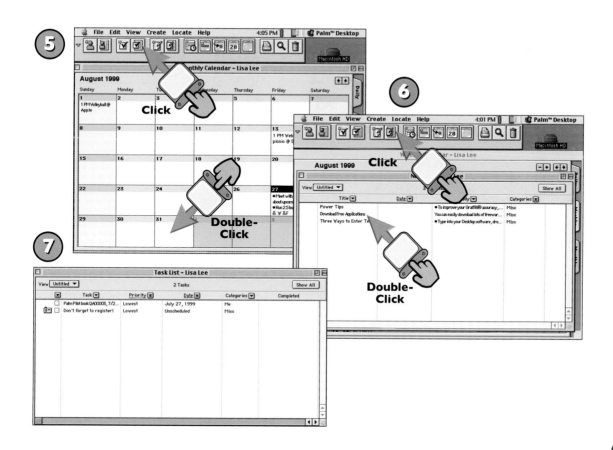

5 View the calendar info. Double-click any day on the calendar to add an appointment. Click the **Task List** button.

6 View your To-Do list. Double-click any item to view more details or modify an item. Click the **Note List** button.

7 View a list of your memos from your Palm device. Double-click any item to view the full memo or to modify any item.

✓ **Default Settings for Synchronization**
The more time-consuming way to manage your information is to not delete any data from your iBook or your Palm device. Instead, you can manually remove any duplicate items from either computing device at your leisure.

One way to keep information at your fingertips is to use an encyclopedia. Of course, there's more information on the Internet. The good news is the World Book Encyclopedia brings you the best of both worlds. You must run the World Book Encyclopedia installer application before you can perform the steps in this task.

✓ **Which CD to Use**
Insert the Disc 1 World Book Encyclopedia CD-ROM. If you want to access any information on disk 2, the software will prompt you to swap CD-ROM discs.

✓ **Access More Information on the Internet**
Click the **What's Online** button and World Book will connect to the Internet and let you search for information on the information superhighway.

Task 10: Finding Facts in the World Book Encyclopedia

Double-Click

Click

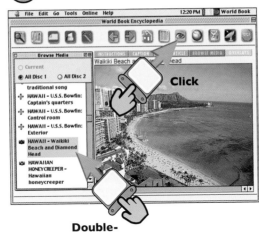

Double-Click

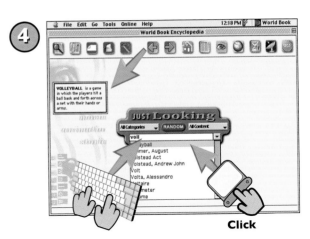

Click

① Double-click the **Macintosh HD** icon and then the **Applications** folder icon. Double-click the **World Book folder** icon and then the **World Book** application icon.

② Click the **Media** button.

③ Double-click a media item to view it. Click the **Just Looking** button.

④ Type a few characters into the text field to view a list of topics in the encyclopedia.

Next Step

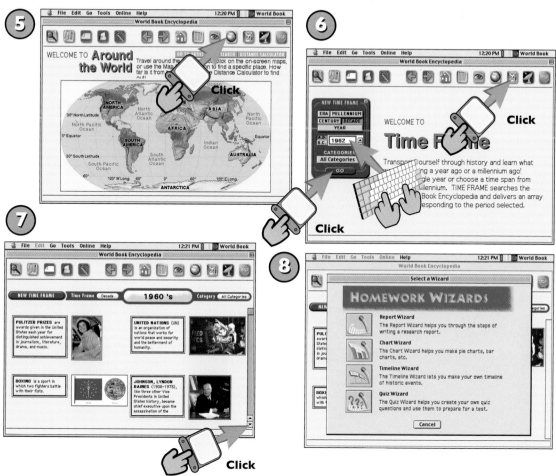

5. Click the **Around the World** button to view a map of the world.

6. Click the **Time Frame** icon. Type a year and press **Go**.

7. World Book displays a list of events from the time frame.

8. Click **Tools** and choose the **Wizards** menu command to access a window full of Homework Wizards.

 View Your Usage History
Click the **Go** menu and choose **History** to view a history of the World Book areas you've used since starting the World Book application.

Task 11: Playing Nanosaur

Your iBook comes with a dinosaur game, Nanosaur, which is a full-color, interactive, 3D game. In it, you are a dinosaur who must collect different dinosaur eggs and avoid being killed by other dinosaurs in order to move to higher levels of adventure.

Start Here

Double-Click

Double-Click

✅ Goal of the Game
There are several different kinds of eggs on each level of Nanosaur. You must collect one of each kind of egg on each level and then find the teleporter to move to the next level.

✅ Customize Your Keyboard Controls
If you want to view the key controls, press the **left-** or **right-arrow** key and choose the **question mark** before you start a game. Press the **spacebar** to exit the help screen.

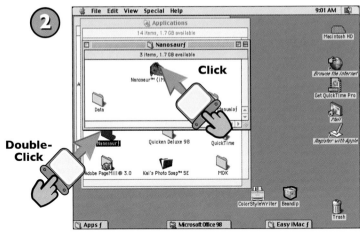

Click

Double-Click

 Double-click the **Macintosh HD** icon, and then double-click the **Applications** folder icon.

 Double-click the **Nanosaur***f* folder icon, and then click the dinosaur image to begin a game.

Next Step

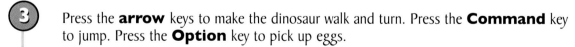

③ Press the **arrow** keys to make the dinosaur walk and turn. Press the **Command** key to jump. Press the **Option** key to pick up eggs.

④ Press the **spacebar** to fire the gun. Watch out for the Tyrannosaurus Rex!

End Task

Task 12: Playing Bugdom

If you like 3D effects in games, you might enjoy playing **Bugdom.** Open floating walnuts to gather green clovers, special powers, and keys that open doors. Use the arrow keys to walk around the flora and fauna in a beautiful 3D world. But watch out for slugs and red ants!

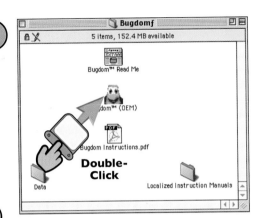

Game Options
You can change the keyboard commands used to control your bug in Bugdom. Click **Settings** in the Main Menu window to access these game options.

✓ **Game Tips**
To move around with a little more control, try using the Shift key to walk forward and use the trackpad for turning.

Double-click the **Macintosh HD** icon, then double-click the **Applications** icon. Double-click the **Bugdom*f* folder** icon, then double-click the **Bugdom** application icon.

Click the **Start** button in the Main Menu screen.

Move your finger along the trackpad to move your bug. Your bug's statistics, such as number of lives, are viewable at the top of the screen.

Click the trackpad's mouse button to open floating walnuts. Move over the floating walnut to pick up its contents.

Stay away from the red ants. They have spears!

Click the trackpad's button to free the ladybug.

When you're ready to go to the next level, enter the cave.

⚠ **Add Memory**
The publisher of Bugdom, **Pangea Software,** recommends your iBook have at least 48MB of memory installed in order to experience the highest resolution and fastest interactive performance with **Bugdom.**

accessory   One of the applications that comes free with iBook. Examples include Notepad, Scrapbook, and Apple Audio CD Player.

active window   The window you're currently using. You can tell a window is active by looking at its title bar: If the bar shows dark letters on a gray background, the window is active. Inactive windows show gray letters on a light gray background.

address book   A common feature in email applications that enables you to store email addresses in an address book format. In Outlook Express, you can type in a partial email address that is already entered in your address, and the address book, also known as a *contact list*, autocompletes the address in your email's To, CC, or BCC fields in the email.

AirPort   The name of Apple's radio-wave-based wireless network technology for your iBook. AirPort supports up to nine network devices per AirPort hub.

AppleScript   The name of Apple's scripting language, which is built into Mac OS. You can automate applications and tasks in Mac OS by using AppleScript scripts.

application   Software that accomplishes a specific set of tasks or functions. This term is used interchangeably with the term *program*.

application window   A window that contains a running application, such as Internet Explorer or SimpleText.

ASCII text file   A file that uses only the American Standard Code for Information Interchange character set (techno-lingo for the characters you see on your keyboard).

back up   The process of making a copy of your files. The backup copy can be restored to replace the original.

battery   The power source for your iBook when it's not plugged into a wall-based power outlet. iBooks use a lithium ion battery, which provides up to six hours of battery power.

blueberry   The shade of blue of an iBook.

boot   To start your computer. The term *booting* comes from the phrase "pulling oneself up by one's bootstraps," which refers to the fact that your computer can load everything it needs to operate properly without any help from you.

bps   Bits per second. The rate at which a modem or other communications device spits data through a phone line or cable.

browser   An application you use to surf sites on the World Wide Web. The browsers that come with your iBook are called Internet Explorer and Netscape Navigator.

byte   A single character of information.

CD-ROM drive   A special computer disk drive that's designed to handle CD-ROM discs, which resemble audio CDs. CD-ROMS have enormous capacity (about 500 times that of a typical floppy disk), so they're most often used to hold large applications, graphics libraries, huge collections of shareware, or your local backup if you have a CD recorder.

channel   A special World Wide Web site that features changing content that is sent automatically to your computer at predefined intervals. See also *subscription*.

character formatting   Changing the look of text characters by altering their font, size, style, color, and more.

check box   A square-shaped switch that toggles a dialog box option on or off. The option is toggled on when a check mark or x appears in the box.

click   To quickly press and release the mouse button.

Clipboard   An area of memory that holds data temporarily during cut-and-paste operations.

Collapse box   Hides all window content except for the window title bar. This box is located in the upper-right corner of any Finder window, and most document windows. See also *Uncollapse box*.

commands   The options you see in a pull-down menu. You use these commands to tell the application what you want it to do next.

data files   The files used by applications to bring features to your iBook. See also *program files*.

deinstall   A synonym for uninstall. To remove software from your iBook.

delay   The amount of time it takes for a second character to appear when you press and hold down a key.

desktop   A metaphor for the iBook screen. Starting a Mac OS application is similar to putting a folder full of papers (the application window) on your desk. To do some work, you pull some papers out of the folder (the document windows) and place them on the desktop.

device driver A small program that controls the way a device (such as a mouse) works with your iBook.

dialog box A window that pops up on the screen to ask you for information or to seek confirmation of an action you requested.

digital camera A special camera that saves pictures using digital storage (such as a memory card) instead of film.

directory See *folder*.

disk cache A specific amount of hard drive space used to store a small of amount of frequently used data in order to increase the overall performance of software on your iBook.

document window A window opened in an application. Document windows hold whatever you're working on in the application.

double-click To quickly press and release the trackpad's mouse button twice in succession.

double-click speed The maximum amount of time Mac OS allows between the mouse clicks of a double-click.

double-tap Same as double-click, except instead of clicking, tap twice on the trackpad. Go to the Trackpad control panel to activate this feature.

drag To press and hold down the mouse button and then move the mouse.

drag-and-drop A technique you can use to run commands or move things around. You use your mouse to drag files or folders to a document window or to the desktop and drop them there to add or convert them to a format compatible with the application.

DRAM Stands for *Dynamic Random Access Memory*. See *memory*.

DVD drive DVD stands for *Digital Versatile Disk*. A DVD drive is similar to a CD-ROM drive, but is capable of storing up to 15GB of data. See also *CD-ROM drive*.

email Short for *electronic mail*. Email is a tool for communicating across networks as well as on the Internet. Email applications enable their users to exchange messages with each other.

Erase Disk A command in the Special menu that formats floppies or hard drives to work with your iBook. See also *formatting*.

Ethernet A network protocol commonly used to transfer data between two or more computers. Your iBook has a 10/100BASE-T Ethernet connector.

favorite A Web site you add to your Favorites menu in a browser, such as Internet Explorer, or in the Apple menu on your iBook.

file An organized unit of information stored on your hard disk.

file sharing A feature in Mac OS software that enables you to share the files on your iBook with other Macintoshes or AppleTalk computers.

file system The technology used to create, track, and modify files and folders stored on your hard disk. Your iBook uses the Mac OS File System, which comes in two flavors: the Hierarchical File System (HFS), also known as the Mac OS standard format; and HFS Plus, also known as the Mac OS extended format. Your iBook hard disk is formatted with the extended format.

floppy disk A portable storage medium that consists of a flexible disk protected by a plastic case. Your iBook does not have a floppy disk drive.

folder A storage location on your hard disk in which you keep related files together.

font A character set of a specific typeface, type style, and type size.

Format bar A series of text boxes and buttons that enable you to format the characters in your document. The Format bar typically appears under the toolbar.

formatting The process of setting up a disk so that a drive can read its information and write information to it (not to be confused with character formatting).

fragmented When a single file is chopped up and stored in separate chunks scattered around a hard disk. You can fix this by running Norton Utilities' Speed Disk application.

full backup Backs up all the files in a current backup job. See also *incremental backup*.

gigabyte 1,024 megabytes. Also referred to as a *gig* when spoken, or abbreviated as *GB* when written. Your iBook has a 3GB hard drive or hard disk. Also see *byte*, *kilobyte*, and *megabyte*.

Grow box Enlarge or shrink any Finder window and most document windows by clicking and dragging the lower-right corner of a window.

hard disk The main storage area inside your iBook.

home page   The first page that loads when you start a browser, or the first page of a Web site.

hover   To place the mouse pointer over an object for a few seconds. If you have Balloon Help on, for example, a help balloon appears over most Finder items, such as icons and window controls.

HTML   Stands for *Hypertext Markup Language*. This is the language used to create Web pages.

hub   A network device that contains jacks (such as Ethernet or USB jacks). A hub enables you to connect to network computers or USB devices.

hyperlink   Highlighted text or graphic on a Web page that points to another location on the document or to a different document.

icons   The little pictures that Mac OS uses to represent applications, folders, and files.

incremental backup   Backs up files only in the current backup job that have changed since the last full backup.

infrared port   A communications port, usually found on notebook computers and some printers. Infrared ports enable two devices to communicate by using infrared waves instead of cables. This port is not available on iBooks.

insertion point cursor   The blinking vertical bar you see inside a text box or in a word processing application, such as SimpleText. It indicates where the next character you type will appear.

Internet   A network of networks that extends around the world. By setting up an account with an Internet service provider, you can access this network.

intranet   The implementation of Internet technologies for use within a corporate organization rather than for connection to the Internet as a whole.

IR   Short for *infrared*. See also *infrared port*.

Java   An Internet technology that enables one application to be created for a variety of computer platforms.

Kbps   One thousand bits per second (bps). Today's modern modems transmit data at either 28.8Kbps or 56Kbps.

keyboard   iBooks have a full-size, built-in keyboard. You can use the Keyboard control panel to assign keyboard shortcuts to the function keys on your iBook's keyboard.

kilobyte   1,024 bytes. This is often abbreviated to *K* or *KB*. See also *megabyte* and *gigabyte*.

LAN   See *local area network*.

link   See *hyperlink*.

list box   A small window that displays a list of items, such as filenames or directives.

local area network   A network in which all the computers occupy a relatively small geographical area, such as a department, an office, a home, or a building. All the connections between computers are made via network cables as opposed to a modem or other hardware device.

log off   To disconnect from the Internet or network.

log on   To connect to the Internet or a network by entering a valid username and password.

Macintosh HD   The name of the hard disk icon on your iBook.

maximize   To increase the size of a window to its largest form. A maximized application window fills the entire screen (except for the taskbar). A maximized document window fills the entire application window.

Mbps   One million bits per second (bps).

megabyte   1,024 kilobytes, or 1,048,576 bytes. This is often abbreviated in writing as *M* or *MB* and is often referred to as a *meg* in speech. See also *gigabyte*.

memory   Also known as RAM or SDRAM. Mac OS, applications, and software in general run in available memory on your iBook. The more memory you can add to your computer, the better your computing experience will be. iBooks have a standard 32MB of memory installed.

menu bar   The bar at the top of your iBook screen. The menu bar contains pull-down menus that enable you to execute commands.

minimize   To reduce the size of a window.

modem   An electronic device that enables two computers to exchange data over phone lines.

mouse   The mouse on your iBook is replaced with a trackpad. To move the mouse, drag your finger along the surface of the trackpad. To select an item, press the mouse button, also referred to as the *trackpad button*, located below the trackpad.

multitasking   The capability to run several programs at the same time.

network   A collection of computers connected via special cables or other network hardware (such as modems or infrared parts) to share files, folders, disks, peripherals, and applications. See also *local area network*.

newsgroup   An Internet discussion group devoted to a single topic. These discussions progress by messages being posted to the group.

Open Transport   Apple's networking technology. Open Transport is used to connect to an Internet service provider as well as to connect with other computers on a network.

Page Holder   A window in Internet Explorer 4.5 used to store a Web page for quick access.

plug-in   A software component commonly used with software applications. Specifically used with Internet browsers to add functionality, such as the capability to play back QuickTime movies on a Web page, or to play sound over the Internet on your iBook.

point   To place the mouse pointer so that it rests on a specific screen location.

pop-up window   A Finder window located at the bottom of your desktop.

port   The connection into which you plug the cable from a device such as a mouse or printer.

printer   An external, peripheral device that can connect to your iBook's USB port or over a network. A printer uses paper to display text and/or graphics from documents you create on your iBook.

program files   The files that run your applications. See also *data files*.

pull-down menus   Hidden menus that you open from an application's menu bar to access the commands and features of the application.

QuickDraw 3D   Apple's 3D technology. Enables applications, such as games, to show three-dimensional objects and fonts.

QuickTime   Apple's multimedia technology. Enables applications that use QuickTime to play animation, movies, and sounds. Your iBook is bundled with QuickTime 4.0.

radio button   A dialog box option that appears as a small circle, often in groups of two or more.

RAM   Stands for *random access memory*. The memory in your iBook that Mac OS uses to run your applications.

RAM disk   A specific amount of memory used as a hard disk on your desktop. You can run applications or store files on a RAM disk.

repeat rate   After the initial delay, the rate at which characters appear when you press and hold down a key.

Reset switch   A hardware switch that restarts your iBook. It is located above your iBook's keyboard.

resolution   The number of dots per inch of your desktop (example: 800×600).

scalable font   A font in which each character exists as an outline that can be scaled to different sizes. Mac OS includes such scalable fonts as Arial, Courier New, and Times New Roman. To use scalable fonts, you must have a software program called a type manager to do the scaling. Mac OS comes with its own type manager, TrueType.

scrollbar   A bar that appears at the bottom or on the right side of a window when the window is too small to display all its contents.

SDRAM   The type of memory your iBook uses to run Mac OS and its applications.

serial port   A type of hardware port not found on an iBook. Hardware peripherals with serial ports can use a USB-to-serial port adapter to connect to an iBook.

Sherlock 2   Apple's speedy search engine built into Mac OS 9. Sherlock can search your hard disk, file contents, or the Internet.

spring-loaded folders   The behavior of Finder folders when you drag and hover an item over a folder icon.

subscription   A method of checking for new or changed data on a World Wide Web site or channel. The subscription sets up a schedule for checking a particular site to see whether it has changed in any way since the last time it was checked.

surf   To travel from site to site on the World Wide Web.

tangerine   The shade of orange of iBooks.

tap   Same as click, but applies only to the trackpad. Instead of clicking on the trackpad button, tap once on the trackpad. Go to the Trackpad control panel to activate this feature.

text box   A screen area in which you type text information, such as a description or a filename.

text editor   An application that lets you edit files that contain only text. AppleWorks, SimpleText, Note Pad, and Stickies are all text editors included with your iBook.

title bar   The area on the top line of a window that displays the window's title.

toolbar   A series of application-specific buttons that typically appears beneath the menu bar.

tracking speed   The speed at which the mouse pointer moves across the screen when you move the mouse on its pad.

trackpad   Replaces the mouse on an iMac, although you can also attach a USB mouse to your iBook. Move your finger along the trackpad surface to control the onscreen cursor. You can also set the trackpad to recognize a single- and/or double-click.

Trash   A special folder on your desktop that enables your iBook to remove files and folders from its hard disk. Don't forget to empty the Trash every now and then.

TrueType   A font-management technology that comes with Mac OS.

type size   A measure of the height of a font. Type size is measured in *points*; there are 72 points in an inch.

type style   Character attributes, such as normal, bold, and italic. Other type styles are underline, shadow, and outline.

typeface   A distinctive graphic design of letters, numbers, and other symbols.

Uncollapse box   If the window area is collapsed, clicking this box displays the previous hidden window area below the window title bar. This box is located in the upper-right corner of any Finder window. See also *Collapse box*.

URL   Stands for *universal resource locator*, or the Internet address you type into a Web browser's Address text field to go from one Web site to another.

USB   Stands for *Universal Serial Bus*. The port iBooks use to enable peripheral devices such as mice, keyboards, cameras, printers, scanners, joysticks, hard drives, and hubs to connect to your iBook.

virtual memory   A method for managing memory on your iBook, using the hard drive to swap data to available memory (RAM) in order to run software applications and Mac OS.

window   A rectangular screen area in which Mac OS displays applications and documents.

World Wide Web   Part of the Internet, or Information Superhighway. A global network of computers that provides information, entertainment, and services for just about anything you can think of.

word wrap   A word-processor feature that automatically starts a new line when your typing reaches the end of the current line.

write protection   A hardware or software setting that prevents Mac OS from writing data to a hard drive or removable media, such as a zip or floppy disk.

zip drive   A special disk drive that uses portable disks (slightly larger than a floppy disk), which hold 100MB of data.

Zoom box   Located next to the Collapse box in a Finder window title bar. Clicking the Zoom box once resizes a window to its maximum size. Clicking it again resizes it to the previous size selected.

Symbols-A

3D graphing window, 198
3D grid, moving, 199
10BASE-T cables, 67

About This Computer command (Apple
  menu), 73, 216, 220
accessories
    AppleCD Audio Player, 191-192
    calculator, 198-199
    Chooser, selecting network devices, 200-201
    graphing calculator, 198-199
    Key Caps, 185
    Keychain Access, 204-205
    Network Browser, 202-203
    QuickTime Player. See QuickTime Player
    Scrapbook, 188-189
    Sherlock 2, 190
    SimpleText, 184-187
    Stickies, 182-183
account names (EarthLink), 33
accounts, 180-181
Acrobat, 230
activating AppleTalk, 201
active windows, 17, 83
Add Page to Favorites command,
  Favorites menu (Internet Explorer), 40
adding
    aliases, 164, 167
    attachments (Outlook Express), 53
    Favorites (Internet Explorer), 40
    folders (Apple menu), 169
    information (palm devices), 244-245
    memory, 72
    patterns (Patterns list), 142
    printer icons (desktops), 134
    text (Stickies), 183
    USB devices, 62-63
addresses
    importing (palm devices), 244
    URLs, 37
Adobe Acrobat, 230
AirPort, 68-69
alerts
    flashing menu bars, 151
    sound, 152-154

aliases. See also icons
    adding, 164
    Apple menu, 167-170
    deleting, 118, 166
    deletion warnings, 164
    files, 118
    fixing, 164
    folders, 118
    italics, 165
    names, 118
    Recent Applications folder, 167
    renaming, 165
    servers, 200
    Show Original command (context menu), 118
    starting applications, 80
    undeleting, 166
AOL (America Online), 34, 53
Appearance control panel, 140-144
Apple menu, 15, 167-170
Apple menu commands. See commands
Apple picture guide, 4
Apple System Profiler (Apple menu),
  216
Apple Web site, 36
    Sherlock 2 plug-ins, 22
    updating software, 74, 226
AppleCD Audio Player, 191-192
AppleScript, 174-175
AppleTalk control panel, 67, 201
AppleWorks
    databases, 235, 238-239
    drawing/painting tools, 236-237
    sharing text, 232
    spreadsheets, 234-235
    word processor, 231-233
applications. See also software
    Adobe Acrobat, 230
    AppleWorks
        databases, 238-239
        drawing/painting tools, 236-237
        sharing text, 232
        spreadsheets, 234
        word processor, 231-233
    Chooser, selecting network devices, 200-201
    Finder, 138
    installing, 172
    Internet Applications folder, 32

Internet Setup Assistant, 28-31
    Key Caps, 185
    Mac OS Setup Assistant, 6-9
    memory, increasing, 219
    menu bars, 15
    open
        battery issues, 97
        memory issues, 82, 97
        switching, 82
        viewing, 82, 138
    opening, 171
    QuickTime Player. See QuickTime Player
    quitting, 96-97
    Scrapbook, 188-189
    Script Editor (AppleScript), 174-175
    Sherlock 2, 190
    SimpleText, 184-187
    sleep, 97
    starting, 78-81
    switching, 138
    TotalAccess (EarthLink), 32-33
    uninstalling, 173
    viewing system information, 216, 220-221
Applications menu, 82, 138-139
Arrange command (View menu), 104
ascending sorts (windows), 104
assigning function keys, 160-161
assistants
    Internet Setup Assistant, 28-31
    Mac OS Setup Assistant, 6-9
attachments (Outlook Express), 53
audio. See sound
Automated Tasks folder, 174-175
automating
    calculations (spreadsheets), 235
    tasks, 174-175

B

Back button (Internet Explorer), 38
background printing, 129
backgrounds (desktops), 140-143
backups
    defragmenting hard drives, 212
    files, 213-214

Mac OS clean installs, 224
tape drives, 213
uninstalling applications, 173
zip drives, 213
balloons (help), 24
Base set extensions, loading, 223
base stations (AirPort), 68
batteries, 4
charging, 25, 66, 209
duration, 65
open applications, 97
replacing, 65
spares, 65
viewing power status, 209
blind carbon copies (Outlook Express), 53
bookmarks. *See* **Favorites**
Borders command, Format menu (AppleWorks spreadsheets), 234
browsers. *See* **Internet Explorer**
browsing, Internet, 38-39, 202-203
Bugdom game, 250-251
buses (USB), 62-63
buttons
Back (Internet Explorer), 38
Forward (Internet Explorer), 39
Home (Internet Explorer), 39
Power (startup), 5
Recents (Network Browser), 203
Reset, 211
Shortcuts (Network Browser), 202
Zoom, sizing windows, 13
Buttons view (windows), 102-105

C

cables
10BASE-T, 67
changing, 75
crossover, 67
power, 65
calculations (spreadsheets), automating, 235
Calculator, 198-199

Calculator command (Apple menu), 198
canceling print jobs, 131
carbon copies (Outlook Express), 53
cards (AirPort), 68
CD Control Strip, 152-153, 191
CD-ROMs
Software Install CD-ROM, 141-142
audio, 152-153, 191
cells (spreadsheets), 234
Change Setup command (Printing menu), 132
changing
cables, 75
default printer, 127
file labels, 119
folder labels, 119
printer setups, 132-133
views, 102-103
charging batteries, 25, 66, 209
checking memory, 73
Chooser
adding desktop printer icons, 134
network devices, 200-201
selecting printers, 64, 126, 133
clean installs (Mac OS), 224-225
cleaning hardware, 217
clearing system settings, 218
click-and-a-half (mouse), 100
Clipboard, 90-94
clock, 156-157
closing. *See also* **quitting**
dialog boxes, 19
documents, 96
folders, 101
menus, 78
windows, 10, 101
clusters (hard drives), 212
collapsing windows, 11
color
file/folder labels, 119
highlight colors, 144
monitors, 148
Stickies, 182
synchronizing, 145
ColorSync control panel, 145
columns (lists), 104

commands
Apple menu
About This Computer, 73, 216, 220
Apple System Profiler, 216
Calculator, 198
Chooser, 126, 133-134, 200
Control Panels, Appearance, 140-144
Control Panels, ColorSync, 145
Control Panels, Control Strip, 149
Control Panels, Date & Time, 156
Control Panels, Energy Saver, 146
Control Panels, Extensions Manager, 75, 222
Control Panels, File Sharing, 176
Control Panels, File Synchronization, 120
Control Panels, Keyboard, 160
Control Panels, Location Manager, 158
Control Panels, Monitors, 148
Control Panels, Mouse, 155
Control Panels, Multiple Users, 180
Control Panels, Software Update, 226
Control Panels, Sound, 150-154
Control Panels, Trackpad, 155
Key Caps, 185
Network Browser, 202
Recent Applications, 78
Scrapbook, 188
Sherlock 2, 106, 190
Stickies, 182
context menus, 16
Empty Trash, 122
Move to Trash, 121
Select All, 112
Show Original, 118
Edit menu
Copy, 90, 94
Cut, 92
Paste, 90-95
Preferences, 8, 119, 159
Select All, 112
Undo Paste, 92
Favorites menu (Internet Explorer), 40-42
File menu
Duplicate, 88
Get Info, 177
Get Info, General Information, 208
Get Info, Memory, 219
Make Alias, 118, 167
Move to Trash, 121, 168
New, 88
New Folder, 113, 169

commands

New Location, 158
Open, 83, 86
Open Dictionary, 175
Open Script, 174
Print, 20, 128
Print Desktop, 126
Put Away, 115
Quit, 96-97, 108
Save, 84
Save As, 84-85
File menu (Internet Explorer), Quit, 49
File menu (Outlook Express)
New, Mail Message, 53
Print, 51
Quit, 59
Save As, 51
Format menu (AppleWorks), 232-234
Go menu (World Book Encyclopedia),
History, 247
Help menu
Mac Help, 20
Show Balloons, 24
menu bars, 15
Message menu (Outlook Express), Reply to
Sender, 52
Printing menu
Change Setup, 132
Set Default Printer, 127
Start Print Queue command, 130
Stop Print Queue command, 130
Special menu
Empty Trash, 122
Restart, 25
Shut Down, 25, 62, 211
Sleep, 25, 63
Tools menu (World Book Encyclopedia),
Wizards, 247
View menu, 104-105
consumption, memory, 216, 220-221
configuration
AirPort, 68-69
control panels, 18
Internet connections, 28-29
AOL, 34
automatic disconnection, 31, 35, 50
EarthLink's TotalAccess, 32-33
keyboards, 160-161, 248-250
Location Manager, 158-159
Mac OS Setup Assistant, 6-9

modems (Internet Setup Assistant), 29
shutdowns, 171
startup, 171
connecting
Palm devices, 70-71
printers, 64
connections
AirPort, 69
Internet
AOL, 34
automatic disconnection, 31, 35, 50
automatic reconnections, 35, 50
configuring, 28-31
EarthLink's TotalAccess, 32-33
manual reconnections, 35
troubleshooting, 35
networks, 67, 201
PPP protocol, 31
connectors, 10BASE-T, 67
context menus
cursors, 16
deleting folders, 169
displaying, 16
Empty Trash command, 122
Move to Trash command, 121
navigating, 16
Select All command, 112
Show Original command (aliases), 118
contextual help (balloons), 24
control panels
Appearance, 140-143
AppleTalk, 67, 201
ColorSync, 145
Control Strip, 149
Date & Time, 156-157
dialog boxes comparison, 18
Energy Saver, 146-147
Extensions Manager, 75, 222-223
File Sharing, 176-177
File Synchronization, 120
Keyboard, 160-161
Location Manager, 158-159
Monitors, 148
Mouse, 155
Multiple Users, 180-181
open, 138
Software Update, 226-227

Sound, 150-154
Trackpad, 155
**Control Panels, Appearance command
(Apple menu), 140-144**
**Control Panels, ColorSync command
(Apple menu), 145**
**Control Panels, Control Strip command
(Apple menu), 149**
**Control Panels, Date & Time command
(Apple menu), 156**
**Control Panels, Energy Saver command
(Apple menu), 146**
**Control Panels, Extensions Manager
command (Apple menu), 75, 222**
**Control Panels, File Sharing command
(Apple menu), 176**
**Control Panels, File Synchronization
command (Apple menu), 120**
**Control Panels, Keyboard command
(Apple menu), 160**
**Control Panels, Location Manager
command (Apple menu), 158**
**Control Panels, Monitors command
(Apple menu), 148**
**Control Panels, Mouse command (Apple
menu), 155**
**Control Panels, Multiple Users
command (Apple menu), 180**
**Control Panels, Software Update
command (Apple menu), 226**
**Control Panels, Sound command (Apple
menu), 150-154**
**Control Panels, Trackpad command
(Apple menu), 155**
Control Strip, 149, 191-192
controls (document windows), 96
Copy command (Edit menu), 90, 94
copying. *See also* **dragging; moving**
data between documents, 94-95
documents, 88
files, 114
folders, 114
keyboard shortcuts, 94
text, 90-91
crashes, 211
crossover cables, 67

cursors
context menus, 16
hand (windows), 101
magnifying glass, 100
customizing. *See also* **setting**
keyboards (games), 248-250
Stickies, 182
volume, 192
Cut command (Edit menu), 92

D

data, copying between documents, 94-95
databases (AppleWorks), 235, 238-239
date, 156-157
Date & Time control panel, 156-157
defragmenting hard drives, 212
deleting
aliases, 118, 164-168
Favorites (Internet Explorer), 40, 43
files, 121
folders, 113, 121, 168-169
messages (newsgroups), 57
network servers (desktops), 203
Page Holder (Internet Explorer), 45
patterns (Patterns list), 142
printer icons (desktops), 135
Scrapbook items, 189
text (Stickies), 183
descending sorts (windows), 104
deselecting
files/folders, 110
text, 89
desktops
desktop database, 218
patterns, 142
pictures, 140-141
printer icons, 129, 134-135
rebuilding, 218
sorting, 104
themes, 143
views, 102
windows, managing, 17
details (hard drives), viewing, 208

devices
network, selecting, 200-201
palm
adding/viewing information, 244-245
connecting, 70-71
importing address lists, 244
installing Palm Desktop software, 242
synchronizing, 71, 242-245
USB, 62-63
dialing options, configuring Internet connections, 30
dialog boxes, 18-19, 128
dictionaries (AppleScript), 175
disabling
extensions, 75
Location Manager, 158
disconnections, Internet, 31, 35, 50
Disk First Aid, starting, 210
displaying context menus, 16
displays, 148
documentation (Apple picture guide), 4
documents. *See also* **files**
closing, 96
copying, 88
copying data, 94-95
dragging, selecting printers, 127
formatting, 232-233
new, 88
open, switching, 83
opening, 81-83, 86-87
printing, 128
saving, 84-85, 97
window controls, 96
Dogpile Web site, 46
domain names (URLs), 37
double-clicks, 10, 103
download.com Web site
Palm device software, 243
updating software, 227
downloading
alert sounds, 154
Sherlock 2 plug-ins, 22
TotalAccess, 32
dragging. *See also* **copying; moving**
Applications menu, 139
deleting files/folders, 121
documents, selecting printers, 127

files, 114-115
folders, 114-115
search results, 109
text, 93
DRAM (dynamic random-access memory), 72
drawing tools (AppleWorks), 236-237
drivers, printer, 126, 132-133
drives. *See* **specific drive types**
Duplicate command (File menu), 88
duplicating files/folders, 114
dust, 4

E

EarthLink, 28, 32-33
Edit menu commands
Copy, 90, 94
Cut, 92
Paste, 90-95
Preferences, 8, 119, 159
Select All, 112
Undo Paste, 92
editing
audio (QuickTime Player), 194-195
configurations (Location Manager), 159
keyboard configuration, 160-161
media files (QuickTime Player), 197
QuickTime movies, 196-197
scripts, 174-175
setup configuration (Mac OS Setup Assistant), 6-7
video (QuickTime Player), 194-195
email
fax comparison, 240
Outlook Express, 26, 51-53, 59
Empty Trash command (Special menu), 122
emptying trash, 122-123. *See also* **deleting**
Energy Saver control panel, 146-147
engines. *See* **search engines**
errors
crashes, 211
links, 38

Ethernet

Ethernet, 67
expanding windows, 11
Extended File format, 208
extensions
  disabling, 75
  information, viewing, 222-223
  Mac OS Base set extensions, 223
  URLs, 37
Extensions Manager, 75, 222-223

F

Favorites (Internet Explorer)
  adding, 40
  deleting, 40, 43
  folders, 41-43
  naming, 42-43
  navigating, 41
Favorites menu commands (Internet Explorer)
  Add Page to Favorites, 40
  New Folder, 42
  Organize Favorites, 42
faxes, 240-241
FaxSTF software, 240-241
File menu commands
  Duplicate, 88
  Get Info, 177
    General Information, 208
    Memory, 219
  Make Alias, 118, 167
  Move to Trash, 121, 168
  New, 88
  New Folder, 113, 169
  New Location, 158
  Open, 83, 86
  Open Dictionary, 175
  Open Script, 174
  Print, 20, 128
  Print Desktop, 126
  Put Away, 115
  Quit, 96-97, 108
  Save, 84
  Save As, 84-85

File menu commands (Internet Explorer), Quit, 49
File menu commands (Outlook Express)
  New, Mail Message, 53
  Print, 51
  Quit, 59
  Save As, 51
File Sharing control panel, 176-177
File Synchronization control panel, 120
file systems, 208
files. See also documents
  aliases, 118
  Apple menu, organizing, 170
  backups, 213-214
  copying, 114
  deleting, 121
  deselecting, 110
  dragging, 114-115
  labels, changing colors, 119
  media, 193, 197
  moving, 115
  names, 116
  opening, 184
  recovering (Norton FileSaver), 122
  searching, 106-109, 190
  selecting, 110-112
  sharing, 146, 176-177
  sound, 195
  synchronizing, 120
  system, 112, 115
  text, 184
  viewing (Adobe Acrobat), 230
Finder, 8, 138
finding files/folders (Sherlock 2), 190
fixing aliases, 164
flashing menu bars, 151
floating menus, 139
folders. See also windows
  aliases, 118
  Apple menu, 168-170
  Assistant, 28
  Automated Tasks, 174-175
  closing, 101
  copying, 114
  creating, 113

  deleting, 113, 121, 169
  deselecting, 110
  dragging, 114-115
  Favorites (Internet Explorer), 41-43
  Internet Applications, 32
  labels, changing, 119
  More Automated Tasks, 174
  moving, 115
  names, 113, 116
  opening, 101
  pop-up, 117
  Recent Applications, 167
  searching, 106-109, 190
  selecting, 110-112
  sharing, 176-177
  Shut Down Items, 171
  Startup Items, 171
  synchronizing, 120
  System, 112, 115
fonts
  selecting, 233-235
  sizing, 233-235
  Stickies, 182
  viewing, 185
foreground printing, 129
Format menu commands (AppleWorks), 232-234
formatting
  cells, 234
  documents, 232-233
  spreadsheets, 234-235
  text, 187
Forward button (Internet Explorer), 39
forwarding messages (Outlook Express), 52
fragmentation (hard drives), 212
function keys, assigning, 160-161

G-H

games
  Bugdom, 250-251
  Nanosaur, 248-249
Get Info command (File menu), 177

Index

Page
262

Get Info, General Information command (File menu), 208
Get Info, Memory command (File menu), 219
Go menu commands (World Book Encyclopedia), History, 247
graphic links, 39
Graphing Calculator, 198-199
grouping Favorites (Internet Explorer), 41-43

hand cursors, navigating windows, 101
hard drives
 clusters, 212
 defragmenting, 212
 desktop database, 218
 details, viewing, 208
 Extended File format, 208
 navigating, 100
 repairing, 210
 scanning, 210
 spinning down, 146-147
 Standard File system, 208
hardware
 cleaning, 217
 troubleshooting, 74-75
help. *See also* troubleshooting
 Apple documentation, 4
 Apple Web site, 36
 balloons, 24
 batteries, 4
 Help menu, 74
 iBook Software Restore, 215
 Internet help (Sherlock 2 search engine), 22
 Mac Help, 20-21
 setup, 4
Help menu commands
 Mac Help, 20
 Show Balloons, 24
hiding
 Control Strip, 149
 Page Holder (Internet Explorer), 45
highlight colors, 144
History command, Go menu (World Book Encyclopedia), 247
History list (Internet Explorer), 48

Home button (Internet Explorer), 39
hubs (Ethernet), 67
hyperlinks. *See* links

I

iBook Restore, 215
iBook Software Install, 224-225
icons. *See also* aliases
 Adobe Acrobat, 230
 desktop printers, 134-135
 desktops, sorting, 104
 Printer, viewing print queue, 129
 Trash, 123, 131
 windows, 10, 104
Icons view (windows), 104
images, viewing (SimpleText), 186
importing address lists (Palm devices), 244
Inbox (Outlook Express), 51
increasing application memory, 219
installation
 applications, 172
 clean installs (Mac OS), 224-225
 Palm Desktop software, 242
 Palm device software, 243
 printer software, 64
 reinstalling FaxSTF software, 241
 USB software, 62-63
 World Book Encyclopedia, 246
Internet. *See also* ISPs
 alert sounds, downloading, 154
 connections
  AOL, 34
  automatic disconnection, 31, 35, 50
  automatic reconnections, 35, 50
  configuring, 28-31
  EarthLink's TotalAccess, 32-33
  manual reconnections, 35
  troubleshooting, 35
 Internet Applications folder, 32
 navigating
  History list (Internet Explorer), 48
  links, 38-39
  Page Holder (Internet Explorer), 44-45

search engines
 Dogpile Web site, 46
 Sherlock 2, 22, 46-47
setting time, 157
surfing (Network Browser), 202-203
World Book Encyclopedia, 246
Internet Explorer, 26. *See also* Outlook Express
 Favorites, 40-43
 History list, 48
 navigating, 36-39
 Page Holder, 44-45
 quitting, 49
 sites, subscribing, 40
 starting, 35
Internet service providers. *See* ISPs
Internet Setup Assistant, 31
 modem configuration, 29
 quitting, 30
 starting, 28
ISPs (Internet service providers), 26. *See also* Internet
 AOL, 34, 53
 configuring Internet connections, 30
 EarthLink, 28, 32-33
 selecting, 28-29
italics (alias names), 165

J-L

jobs, print
 canceling, 131
 pausing, 130
 restarting, 130
 selecting printers, 127-128
 short, 130-131
 viewing print queue, 129

Key Caps, 185
Keyboard control panel, 160-161
keyboards
 configuration
  Bugdom game, 250
  editing, 160-161
  Nanosaur game, 248

selecting text, 89
shortcuts
copying, 94
deleting folders, 113
pasting, 94
quitting applications, 96-97
selecting all files/folders, 112
Sherlock 2 search engine, 106-108
Keychain Access, 204-205
keys
Control, 16
Option, 101

labels (files/folders), 119
limited accounts, 180
links
errors, 38
Favorites (Internet Explorer), 40-43
graphics, 39
Mac Help, 20
navigating, 38
Page Holder (Internet Explorer), 44-45
List view (windows), 102-104
lists
address, importing (Palm devices), 244
columns, moving, 104
History (Internet Explorer), 48
newsgroups
Patterns, 142
updating, 55
windows, 104
**loading extensions (Mac OS Base set
extensions), 223**
Location Manager, 158-159
login names, 204-205

M

Mac Help, 20-21
Mac OS (Mac Operating System), 15
Base set extensions, loading, 223
clean installs, 224-225
Mac Help, 20-21
menu bars, 15
printer support, 126

Mac OS Setup Assistant, 6-9
magnifying glass cursors, 100
maintenance, cleaning hardware, 217
**Make Alias command (File menu), 118,
167**
making backups, 213
managing windows, 17
media files, 193, 197
memory
adding, 72
applications, increasing, 219
Bugdom, 251
checking, 73
consumption, viewing, 216, 220-221
DRAM, 72
open applications, 82, 97
physical, 73
PRAM, resetting default settings, 218
Scrapbook, 189
SDRAM, 72
SO-DIMMs, 72
virtual, 73
menu bars
Apple menu, 15, 78-79
Applications menu, 82
commands, 15
date/time, 156
flashing, 151
navigating, 15
menus. See also commands
Apple, 168-170
Applications, 138-139
closing, 78
context
cursors, 16
deleting folders, 169
displaying, 16
Empty Trash command, 122
Move to Trash command, 121
Select All command, 112
Show Original command (aliases), 118
**Message menu commands (Outlook
Express), Reply to Sender, 52**
messages
newsgroups, 56-58
Outlook Express, 51-53
microphones, 152, 194

**Microsoft Internet Explorer. See Internet
Explorer**
modems, 29
moisture, 4
monitors, 148
Monitors control panel, 148
More Automated Tasks folder, 174
mouse. See also trackpads
click-and-a-half, 100
double-clicks, 103
options, setting, 155
selecting text, 89
trackpads comparison, 155
Mouse control panel, 155
**Move to Trash command (File menu),
121, 168**
movies (QuickTime), editing, 196-197
moving. See also copying; dragging
3D grid, 199
Applications menu, 139
columns (lists), 104
files, 112, 115
folders, 115
search results, 109
text, 92-93
windows, 12, 17
MSNBC Web site, 38
multiple user accounts, 180-181
Multiple Users control panel, 180-181
muting sound, 151

N

names
account (EarthLink), 33
aliases, 118, 165
domain (URLs), 37
Favorites (Internet Explorer), 42-43
files, 116
folders, 113, 116, 177
labels, 119
selecting files/folders, 110
Nanosaur game, 248-249

navigating
context menus, 16
Favorites (Internet Explorer), 41
hard disks, 100
Internet
History list (Internet Explorer), 48
links, 38-39
Page Holder (Internet Explorer), 44-45
Internet Explorer, 36-39
Mac Help, 21
menu bars, 15
windows, 14, 101
Network Browser, 202-203
Network Browser command (Apple menu), 202
networks
10BASE-T cables, 67
AirPort, 68-69
connections, 67
crossover cables, 67
devices, selecting, 200-201
files, sharing, 176-177
folders, sharing, 176-177
servers, 204-205
New command (File menu), 88
new documents, creating, 88
New Folder command, Favorites menu (Internet Explorer), 42
New Folder command (File menu), 113, 169
New Location command (File menu), 158
New, Mail Message command, File menu (Outlook Express), 53
newsgroups (Outlook Express)
deleting messages, 57
posting messages, 57
quitting, 59
reading messages, 56
replying, 58
searching, 54-55
subscribing, 54-55
threads, 56-57
unsubscribing, 55-56
updating, 55
normal accounts, 180
Norton FileSaver, 122

Norton Utilities
defragmenting hard drives, 212
Norton FileSaver, 122
scanning/repairing hard drives, 210

O

Open command (File menu), 83, 86
Open Dictionary command (File menu), 175
Open Script command (File menu), 174
opening. See also **starting**
applications, 171
documents, 81-83, 86-87
files, 184, 230
folders, 101
windows, 10
operating systems (OSs). See **Mac OS**
Option key, 101
Organize Favorites command, Favorites menu (Internet Explorer), 42
organizing
Apple menu, 170
Favorites (Internet Explorer), 41-43
OSs (operating systems). See **Mac OS**
Outlook Express, 26. See also **Internet Explorer**
AOL conflict, 53
attachments, 53
Inbox, 51
messages, 51-53
newsgroups
deleting messages, 57
posting messages, 57
reading messages, 56
replying, 58
searching, 54-55
subscribing, 54-55
unsubscribing, 55-56
updating, 55
quitting, 59
starting, 50

P

Page Holder (Internet Explorer), 44-45
painting tools (AppleWorks), 236-237
Palm Computer Web site, 243
Palm Desktop software, installing, 242
Palm devices
adding/viewing information, 244-245
connecting, 70-71
importing address lists, 244
installing device software, 243
installing Palm Desktop software, 242
synchronizing, 71, 242-245
Panels account, 180-181
Pangea Software, 251
paper clips (Reset button), 211
Paragraph command, Format menu (AppleWorks word processor), 232
passwords
forgotten, 205
Mac OS Setup Assistant, 8
selecting, 205
storing (network servers), 204-205
Paste command (Edit menu), 90-95
pasting. See **copying; moving**
paths (pop-up folders), 117
patterns, 142
pausing print jobs, 130
performance
balloon help, 24
file sharing issues, 177
phone numbers, configuring Internet connections, 30
physical memory, 73
pictures, desktop backgrounds, 140-141
playing
Bugdom, 250-251
CDs, 152-153, 191
media files, 193
Nanosaur, 248-249
plug-ins (Sherlock 2), 22, 190
Point-to-Point Protocol (PPP), 31
pop-up folders, 117
pop-up menus. See **context menus**
posting messages (newsgroups), 57

power
  batteries
    charging, 25, 66, 209
    duration, 65
    open applications, 97
    replacing, 65
    spares, 65
    viewing status, 209
  cables, 65
  Energy Saver control panel, 146-147
Power button (startup), 5
powering down, 25, 97
PPP (Point-to-Point Protocol), 31
PRAM, resetting default system settings,
  218
Preferences command (Edit menu), 8,
  119, 159
previewing desktop background
  pictures, 141
Print command (File menu), 20, 51, 128
Print Desktop command (File menu),
  126
Print dialog box, 128
print jobs
  canceling, 131
  pausing, 130
  restarting, 130
  selecting printers, 127-128
  short, 130-131
  viewing print queue, 129
Printer icon, viewing print queue, 129
printers. See also printing
  connecting, 64
  desktop icons, 134-135
  drivers, selecting, 126, 132-133
  Mac OS Setup Assistant, 8-9
  nondefault printers, 127
  removing, 64
  selecting, 127-128, 133
  serial ports, 64
  setup, 126-127, 132-133
  software, installing, 64
  software compatibility, 126
printing. See also printers
  AirPort, 69
  background/foreground comparison, 129
  documents, 128

Mac Help topics, 20
messages (Outlook Express), 51
print queue, 129-131
Printing menu commands
  Change Setup, 132
  Set Default Printer, 127
  Start Print Queue, 130
  Stop Print Queue, 130
programs. See applications; software
protection, 4
protocols (URLs), 37
Put Away command (File menu), 115

Q-R

queue, print, 129-131
quick menus. See context menus
QuickTime Player
  audio/video editing, 194-195
  media files, 193
  QuickTime movie editing, 196-197
  registration, 194-196
Quit command (File menu), 96-97, 108
  Internet Explorer, 49
  Outlook Express, 59
quitting. See also closing
  applications, 96-97
  Internet Explorer, 49
  Internet Setup Assistant, 30
  Mac OS Assistant, 7
  Mac OS Setup Assistant, 9
  Outlook Express, 59
  Sherlock 2 search engine, 47, 108

RAM (Random Access Memory), 82. See
  also memory
reading messages (Outlook Express), 51,
  56
rebuilding desktops, 218
Recent Applications command (Apple
  menu), 78
Recent Applications folder, 167
Recents button (Network Browser), 203
recharging batteries, 4, 66, 209

reconnecting Internet connections, 35,
  50
recording sounds, 152-153
recovering files, 122
registering QuickTime Player, 194-196
reinstalling FaxSTF software, 241
Remote Access, reconnecting Internet
  connections, 35
removing
  printers, 64
  USB devices, 63
renaming
  aliases, 165
  files/folders, 116
repairing hard drives, 210
replacing batteries, 65
Reply to Sender command, Message
  menu (Outlook Express), 52
replying
  newsgroups, 58
  Outlook Express, 52
Reset button, 211
resetting default system settings,
  zapping PRAM, 218
resizing windows, 13
resolution (monitors), 148
Restart command (Special menu), 25
restarting
  iBook, 25
  print jobs, 130
restoring
  backups, 214
  system software, 215
running Disk First Aid, 210

S

Save As command (File menu), 51, 84-85
Save command (File menu), 84
saving
  configurations (Location Manager), 158
  desktop themes, 143
  documents, 84-85, 97
  messages (Outlook Express), 51

search criteria (Sherlock 2), 190
scanning hard drives, 210
Scrapbook, 188-189
Scrapbook command (Apple menu), 188
screens, 148
screenshots, creating, 186
Script Editor (AppleScript), 174-175
scripts (AppleScript), 174-175
scrollbars (windows), 101
scrolling windows, 14
SDRAM (synchronous dynamic RAM), 72
search criteria (Sherlock 2), 190
search engines. *See also* **searching**
 Dogpile Web site, 46
 Sherlock 2
  downloading plug-ins, 22
  Internet help, 22
  keyboard shortcuts, 106-108
  moving search results, 109
  quitting, 47, 108
  searching, 47
  searching files, 106-109
  searching folders, 106-109
  setting search options, 107
  sorting search results, 109
  starting, 46-47, 106
searching. *See also* **search engines**
 files, 106-109
 folders, 106-109
 help (Sherlock 2), 22
 Mac Help, 20-21
 newsgroups (Outlook Express), 54-55
 World Book Encyclopedia, 246-247
security
 Panels account, 181
 passwords
  forgotten, 205
  Mac OS Setup Assistant, 8
  selecting, 205
  storing (network servers), 204-205
Select All command (Edit menu), 112
selecting
 account names (EarthLink), 33
 alert sounds, 154
 dialog box options, 18-19
 files, 110-112

folders, 110-112
fonts, 233-235
ISPs, 28-29
network devices (Chooser), 200-201
passwords, 205
printers
 Chooser (Apple menu), 133
 drivers, 126, 132-133
 print jobs, 127-128
 startup device options, 215
 text, 89
sending
 faxes, 240-241
 messages (Outlook Express), 53
serial ports, 64
servers
 aliases, 200
 network, 203-205
 sharing files/folders, 176
Set Default Printer command (Printing menu), 127
setting. *See also* **customizing**
 Apple menu options, 79
 date, 156-157
 default printer, 127
 desktop appearance, 140-143
 dialog box options, 18-19
 Energy Saver control panel, 146-147
 Finder options, 8
 highlight colors, 144
 History list (Internet Explorer), 48
 Location Manager, 158-159
 monitors, 148
 mouse options, 155
 Page Holder (Internet Explorer), 44-45
 passwords (Mac OS Assistant), 8
 search options (Sherlock 2), 107
 startup configuration, 171
 time, 156-157
 time zones, 156
 trackpad options, 155
 view options (windows), 105
setup, 4
 editing settings (Mac OS Setup Assistant), 6-7
 printers, 126-127, 132-133
sharing
 drawings, 236
 files, 146, 176

folders, 176-177
iBook, 180-181
text, 232
Sherlock 2 command (Apple menu), 106, 190
Sherlock 2 search engine, 190
 downloading plug-ins, 22
 Internet help, 22
 keyboard shortcuts, 106, 108
 moving search results, 109
 quitting, 47, 108
 searching, 47, 106-109
 setting search options, 107
 sorting search results, 109
 starting, 46-47, 106
shortcut menus. *See* **context menus**
shortcuts
 keyboard
  deleting folders, 113
  pasting, 94
  quitting applications, 96-97
  selecting all files/folders, 112
  Sherlock 2, 106-108
 renaming files/folders, 116
Shortcuts button (Network Browser), 202
Show Balloons command (Help menu), 24
Show Details feature (Mac OS Setup Assistant), 9
Shut Down command (Special menu), 25, 62, 211
Shut Down Items folder, 171
shutdowns, 25
 applications, opening, 171
 installing USB software, 62-63
 Reset button, 211
 Shut Down command (Special menu), 211
Simple Finder, 8
SimpleText
 documents, opening, 81
 images, viewing, 186
 text
  files, creating, 184
  formatting, 187

sites (Web)

sites (Web), 32
- Apple Web site, 36
  - Sherlock 2 plug-ins, 22
  - updating software, 74, 226
- Dogpile Web site, 46
- download.com Web site
  - Palm device software, 243
  - updating software, 227
- EarthLink, 32
- Favorites (Internet Explorer),40-43
- History list (Internet Explorer), 48
- MSNBC Web site, 38
- Page Holder (Internet Explorer), 44-45
- Palm Computing Web site, 243
- subscribing (Internet Explorer), 40
- ZDNet Web site, 227

sizing
- Applications menu, 139
- Control Strip, 149
- desktop background pictures, 140
- fonts, 233-235
- Key Caps window, 185
- windows, 13

sleep, 25
- adding USB devices, 63
- Energy Saver control panel, 146-147
- file sharing, 146
- indicator light, 147
- open applications, 97
- options, 147

Sleep command (Special menu), 25, 63
SO-DIMMs (small outline dual inline memory modules), 72
software. See also applications
- AirPort, 68
- Bugdom, 250-251
- FaxSTF, 240-241
- Mac OS, clean installs, 224-225
- Nanosaur, 248-249
- Palm Desktop, 242
- Palm devices, 243
- printer support, 64, 126
- system, restoring, 215
- troubleshooting, 74-75
- updates, 74, 226-227
- USB, 62-63
- World Book Encyclopedia, 246-247

Software Install CD-ROM, 142
Software Update control panel, 226-227
Sort List command (View menu), 104
sorting
- desktops, 104
- search results (Sherlock 2), 109
- windows, 104

sound
- alerts, 152-154
- editing (QuickTime Player), 194-195
- files, 195
- microphones, 152, 194
- playing CDs, 152-153, 191
- setting options, 150-151
- volume, adjusting, 192

Sound control panel
- recording alert sounds, 152-153
- selecting alert sounds, 154
- setting sound options, 150-151

spare batteries, 65
speakers (Sound control panel), 150-151
Special menu commands
- Empty Trash, 122
- Restart, 25
- Shut Down, 25, 62, 211
- Sleep, 25, 63

speed
- balloon help, 24
- file sharing issues, 177
- mouse/trackpad settings, 155

spinning down hard drives, 146-147
spreadsheets (AppleWorks), 234-235
Standard File system, 208
Start Print Queue command (Printing menu), 130
starting. See also opening
- Apple System Profiler, 216
- AppleWorks word processor, 231
- applications, 78-81
- Bugdom, 250
- Disk First Aid, 210
- Extensions Manager, 222
- Internet Explorer, 35
- Internet Setup Assistant, 28
- Mac Help, 20
- Mac OS Assistant, 6

- Nanosaur, 248
- Outlook Express, 50
- Power button, 5
- restarts, 25
- Sherlock 2 search engine, 46-47, 106
- TotalAccess (EarthLink), 32

startup
- applications, opening, 171
- device options, selecting, 215
- Reset button, 211
- troubleshooting, 5

Startup Items folder, 171
Stickies, 182-183
Stickies command (Apple menu), 182
Stop Print Queue command (Printing menu), 130
stopping. See quitting
storing login name/password (network servers), 204-205
subscribing
- newsgroups (Outlook Express), 54-55
- sites (Internet Explorer), 40

sunlight, 4
surfing the Internet (Network Browser), 202-203. See also Internet Explorer
swapping cables, 75
switching
- applications, 138
- open applications, 82
- open documents, 83

synchronizing
- colors, 145
- files, 120
- folders, 120
- Palm devices, 71, 242-245

synchronous dynamic RAM (SDRAM), 72
system files, moving, 112, 115
System folder, 112, 115
system information, viewing, 216, 220-221
system software, restoring, 215
system volume, adjusting, 192

T

tape drives, 213
tasks, automating, 174-175
text
    copying, 90-91
    deselecting, 89
    dragging, 93
    formatting (SimpleText), 187
    moving, 92-93
    selecting, 89
    sharing (AppleWorks), 232
    Stickies, 182-183
text files, creating, 184
themes (desktops), 143
threads, 56-57
time, 156-157
time zones, 156
tools, drawing/painting (AppleWorks),
    236-237
Tools menu commands (World Book
    Encyclopedia), Wizards, 247
TotalAccess (EarthLink), 32-33
Trackpad control panel, 155
trackpads. See also mouse
    double-clicks, 10
    mouse comparison, 155
    navigating hard disks, 100
    options, setting, 155
trash. See also deleting
    canceling print jobs, 131
    deleting aliases, 166
    desktop printer icons, 135
    emptying, 121-123
    icons, 123
    uninstalling applications, 173
troubleshooting. See also help
    AirPort connections, 69
    Apple System Profiler, 216
    Disk First Aid, 210
    forgotten passwords, 205
    hardware, 74-75
    Internet connections, 35
    Norton Utilities, 210
    software, 74-75
    startup, 5

U-V

undeleting aliases, 166
Undo Paste command (Edit menu), 92
uninstalling
    applications, 173
    printer software, 64
    USB software, 63
Universal Serial Bus (USB), 62-63
unsubscribing from newsgroups
    (Outlook Express), 55-56
updating
    newsgroups (Outlook Express), 55
    software, 74, 226-227
URLs (Uniform Resource Locators), 37
USB (Universal Serial Bus), 62-63
user accounts, 180
utilities
    Disk First Aid, 210
    Norton Utilities
        defragmenting hard drives, 212
        Norton FileSaver, 122
        scanning/repairing hard drives, 210

video, editing (QuickTime Player),
    194-195
video memory (SDRAM), 72
View menu commands, 104-105
View Options command (View menu),
    105
viewing
    battery power status, 209
    Control Strip, 149
    extensions information, 222-223
    Favorites (Internet Explorer), 41
    files (Adobe Acrobat), 230
    fonts (Key Caps), 185
    hard drive details, 208
    highlight colors, 144
    History list (Internet Explorer), 48
    images (SimpleText), 186
    memory consumption, 216, 220-221
    open applications, 82, 138
    Palm device information, 244-245
    print queue, 129
    system information, 216, 220-221

views
    desktops, 102
    windows, 102-105
virtual memory, 73
volume, adjusting, 192

W-Z

Web sites. See sites
what you see is what you get
    (WYSIWYG), 232
windows. See also folders
    3D graphing, 198
    active, 17, 83
    closing, 10, 101
    collapsing, 11
    document, 96
    expanding, 11
    icons, 10
    Key Caps, 185
    managing, 17
    moving, 12, 17
    navigating, 101
    opening, 10
    scrolling, 14
    sizing, 13
    sorting, 104
    views, 102-105
Wizards command, Tools menu (World
    Book Encyclopedia), 247
word processor (AppleWorks), 231-233
World Book Encyclopedia, 246-247

ZDNet Web site, 227
zip drives, 213
zones, time, 156
Zoom button, 13